TECHNICAL HANDBOOK

BRIDGESTONE 350 GTR

BS

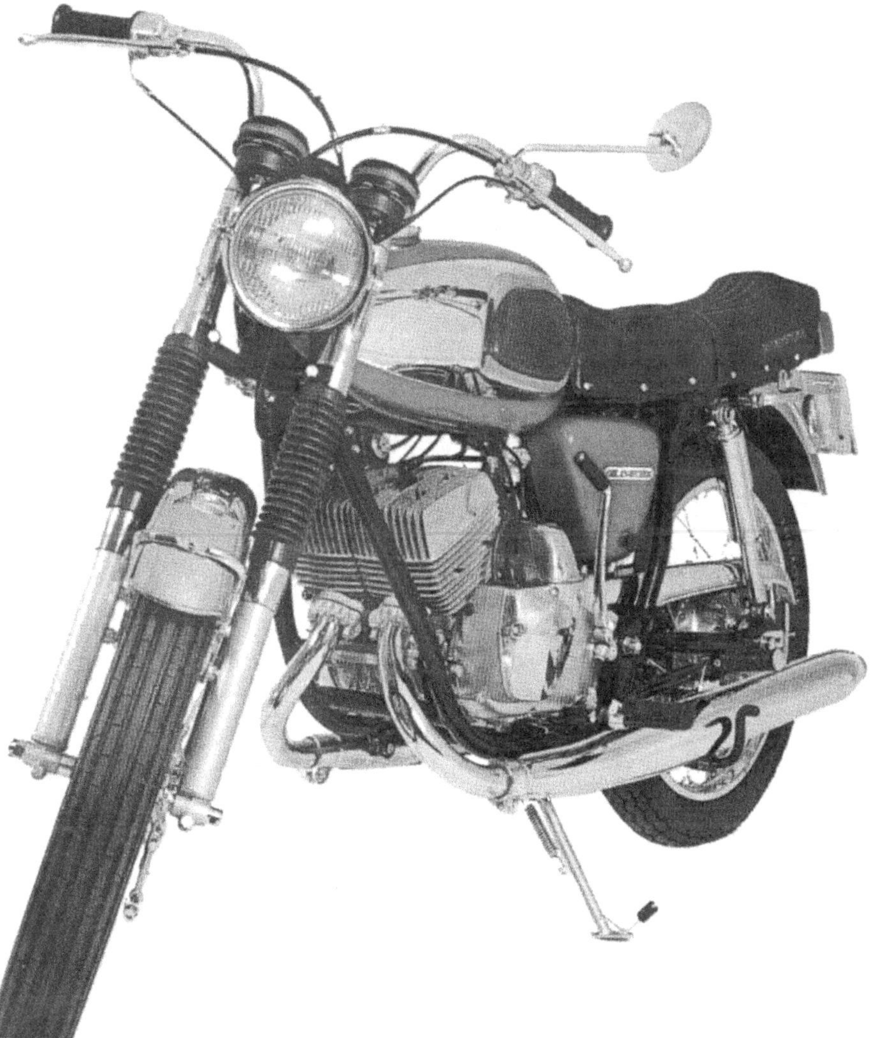

T7350E

INTRODUCTION

Welcome to the world of digital publishing ~ the book you now hold in your hand, was printed using the latest state of the art digital technology. The advent of print-on-demand has forever changed the publishing process, never has information been so accessible and it is our hope that this book serves your informational needs for years to come. If this is your first exposure to digital publishing, we hope that you are pleased with the results. Many more titles of interest to the classic automobile and motorcycle enthusiast, collector and restorer are available via our website at www.VelocePress.com. We hope that you find this title as interesting as we do.

NOTE FROM THE PUBLISHER

The information presented is true and complete to the best of our knowledge. All recommendations are made without any guarantees on the part of the author or the publisher, who also disclaim all liability incurred with the use of this information.

TRADEMARKS

We recognize that some words, model names and designations, for example, mentioned herein are the property of the trademark holder. We use them for identification purposes only. This is not an official publication.

INFORMATION ON THE USE OF THIS PUBLICATION

This manual is an invaluable resource for those interested in performing their own maintenance. However, in today's information age we are constantly subject to changes in common practice, new technology, availability of improved materials and increased awareness of chemical toxicity. As such, it is advised that the user consult with an experienced professional prior to undertaking any procedure described herein. While every care has been taken to ensure correctness of information, it is obviously not possible to guarantee complete freedom from errors or omissions or to accept liability arising from such errors or omissions. Therefore, any individual that uses the information contained within, or elects to perform or participate in do-it-yourself repairs or modifications acknowledges that there is a risk factor involved and that the publisher or its associates cannot be held responsible for personal injury or property damage resulting from the use of the information or the outcome of such procedures.

WARNING!

One final word of advice, this publication is intended to be used as a reference guide, and when in doubt the reader should consult with a qualified technician.

FOREWORD

The increasing use of motorcycles more than ever calls for efficient after service, not only to give the customer satisfaction with his motorcycle, but also to maintain his confidence in the dealer.

It is, therefore, essential to effect correct overhaul and repairs in a clean, well organized repair shop equipped with all the necessary special tools and instruments.

With this purpose in view this workshop manual has been prepared to indicate the methods of repair. The manual should be always available in the workshop, handy for every mechanic working on Bridgestone motorcycles.

BRIDGESTONE TIRE CO., LTD.
MOTORCYCLE SECTION

CONTENTS

Each of the individual 'Parts Catalogues' in this manual have their own index, the page numbers corresponding to that index are printed to the top corner of each page. The number printed to the center bottom of the page is the page number within the book. The contents list below refers to the book page number.

Workshop Manual (Technical Handbook)....................page 2

Tuning up for Competition.............................page 87

350GTR Parts Catalogue................................page 93

350GTO Parts Catalogue................................page 161

INDEX

		Page
1.	**TECHNICAL DATA**	6
2.	**FRONT AND SIDE VIEWS**	8
3.	**PERFORMANCE**	9
4.	**ENGINE**	11
	4-1. **Dismounting Engine**	
	A. Care to be observed	11
	B. Tools necessary	11
	C. Dismounting Engine	11
	4-2. **Mounting Engine on Frame**	13
	4-3. **Disassembling and Assembling Engine**	15
	A. Matters that require special attention	15
	B. Dismounting Engine	15
	C. Component parts of crank case	20
	D. Assembling Engine	21
5.	**CRANKSHAFT · PISTONS · CYLINDERS · ROTARY DISC VALVES**	24
	5-1. **Crankshaft and Rotary Disc Valves**	25
	A. Construction	25
	B. Inspection	25
	C. Lubrication of crankshaft	26
	D. Lubrication of transmission gears	26
	5-2 **Cylinders and Pistons**	27
	A. Construction	27
	B. Matters that require special attention	27
	C. Inspection	27
	D. Disassembling	27
6.	**CLUTCH**	28
	A. Construction	29
	B. Operation	29
	C. Clutch adjustment	30
	D. Disassembling clutch	30
	E. Inspection	31

7. **TRANSMISSION** ·· 32
   A. Construction ··· 33
   B. Operation ··· 33
   C. Component parts of gear change pedal and shift drum ································ 34
   D. Gear shift mechanism ··· 35
   E. Gear operation and gear ratios ··· 37
   F. Inspection ·· 39

8. **KICK STARTER** ·· 40
   A. Construction ··· 41
   B. Operation ··· 41
   C. Inspection ·· 41

9. **CARBURETORS** ·· 42
   A. Synchronizing carburetors ··· 43
   B. Indications of trouble at various engine speeds ·· 43
   C. Idling adjustment ·· 43
   D. Medium engine speeds adjustment ·· 44
   E. High engine speeds adjustment ··· 44
   F. Adjustment of carburetor float level ·· 45
   G. Trouble shootings of gasoline leakage from carburetor ································ 45

10. **OIL INJETION SYSTEM** ··· 46
    A. Operation ··· 47
    B. Oil intake ·· 48
    C. Oil outlet ·· 48
    D. Distribution of oil to both cylinders ·· 48
    E. Operation of worm wheel plunger in relation to the throttle grip ················ 49
    F. Adjustment of oil pump control wire ··· 50
    G. Special attention ··· 50
    H. How to mesh the plunger gear with the distributor gear ···························· 51

11. **FRAME** ·· 52
    11-1. Handlebar ·· 53
    A. Removing handlebar ··· 53
    B. Assembling ·· 53
    C. Inspection ·· 53

- 11-2. **Front fork** ··· 54
  - A. Operation ··· 55
  - B. Disassembling ··· 56
  - C. Assembling and inspection ··· 56
  - D. Removing the steering damper ··· 56
- 11-3. **Rear suspension** ··· 57
  - A. Construction ··· 57
  - B. Operation ··· 57
  - C. Adjustment of rear suspension ··· 58
- 11-4. **Wheels** ··· 59
  - A. Construction ··· 59
  - B. Checking of tire pressure and balance ··· 59

12. ELECTRICAL EQUIPMENT ··· 62

- 12-1. **A.C. Generator** ··· 63
  - A. Decription ··· 63
  - B. Charging current ··· 63
- 12-2. **Voltage regulator** ··· 63
- 12-3. **Ignition system** ··· 64
  - A. Contact breakers ··· 64
  - B. Adjusting the gap ··· 64
  - C. Checking and Adjusting ignition timing ··· 64
- 12-4. **Selenium rectifier** ··· 65
  - A. Special attention ··· 66
  - B. Inspection ··· 66
- 12-5. **Condenser** ··· 66
  - A. Inspection ··· 66
- 12-6. **Ignition coil** ··· 66
  - A. Inspection ··· 66
- 12-7. **Spark plug** ··· 67
  - A. Description ··· 67
  - B. Inspection and Adjustment ··· 67
- 12-8. **Battery** ··· 68
  - A. Inspection of specific gravity ··· 68
  - B. Storage of dry charged battery ··· 69
  - C. Initial charging rate ··· 69

- 12-9. **Lights** 70
  - A. Head lamp · Tail lamp 70
  - B. Speedometer · Ignition coil · Main switch 71
  - C. Bulbs 72
  - D. Adjustment of headlight beam 72
- 12-10. **Main switch** 73
- 12-11. **Horn** 73

13. TROUBLE SHOOTING 74
- 13-1. **Engine is hard to start** 74
- 13-2. **High engine revolution cannot be obtained** 75
- 13-3. **Unsatisfactory R.P.M.** 76
- 13-4. **Iregular revolutions** 77
- 13-5. **Unsatisfactory gear shifting** 77
- 13-6. **Common failures (One cylider goes dead)** 78
  - A. Electrical failure 78
  - B. Failures in fuel system 79
  - C. Mechanical failures 79

14. TOLERANCE AND FITS 80
- A. Engine 80
- B. Cylinder 80
- C. Piston 80
- D. Crankshaft and Rotary disc valve 81
- E. Clutch 81
- F. Number of teeth 82
- G. Fork guide 82
- H. A.C. generator and ignition coil 82
- I. Carburetor 82
- J. Oil pump 83
- K. Frame 83
- L. Suspension 83
- M. Lighting equipment 83
- N. Adjusting Torque 84

15. WIRING DIAGRAM 85

1. TECHNICAL DATA

∗Engine

(1)	Type:	2-stroke, Dual Cylinders
(2)	Piston Displacement:	344.9cc (21.5 cu-inches)
(3)	Bore & Stroke:	61 mm × 59 mm (2.40 × 2.32 inches)
(4)	Compression Ratio:	9.31 : 1
(5)	Max. Brake Horse Power:	40 HP/7500 rpm
(6)	Max. Torque:	4.0 kg-m/7000 rpm
(7)	Air Intake System:	Rotary disc valve
(8)	Starting System:	Kick Starter
(9)	Charging System:	A. C. Generator
		Contact breaker gap: 0.3–0.4 mm (0.012–0.016 inches)
(10)	Ignition System:	Battery
(11)	Ignition Timing:	$\left(25° \begin{smallmatrix}+1\\-2\end{smallmatrix}\right)$ degree before T.D.C.
(12)	Spark Plug:	N.G.K. B-8H, Electrode gap: 0.6 mm (0.024 inches)
(13)	Carbureter:	Type AMAL VM 26 SC
		Venturi: 26 mm
		Main Jet No.: 140 Throttle Valve Cut Away: 2.0
		Air Jet: 2.0 Adjustment of Needle Jet: 0.6
		Pilot Air Screw Positon: 2 turn back
		Needle Position: 3
(14)	Engine Lubrication:	2 cycle oil
(15)	Fuel:	Regular Gasoline
(16)	Transmission Oil:	1.5 liter (2/5 US gal.) in transmission case
		SAE No. 10 W/30 in all seasons or
		SAE No. 30 in summer and SAE No. 20 in winter

Transmission

(1)	Clutch:	Manual, Multiple discs, Dry type
(2)	Transmission:	Constant mesh 6-speeds
(3)	Gear Ratio:	Primary (Helical Gear) 1 : 3.095
		Gear Box: 1 st 1 : 2.46
		2 nd 1 : 1.647
		3 rd 1 : 1.25
		4 th 1 : 1.00
		5 th 1 : 0.852
		6 th 1 : 0.759
		Secondary (Chain) : 1 : 2.40
		Total Gear Ratio : 1 st 1 : 18.27
		2 nd 1 : 12.23
		3 rd 1 : 9.29
		4 th 1 : 7.43
		5 th 1 : 6.33
		6 th 1 : 5.64

Electrical Equipment

(1) Head Light: 12V–35/30W
(2) Tail Light: 12V–7W
(3) Stop Light: 12V–23W
(4) Speedometer Lamp: 12V–3W
(5) Tachometer Lamp: 12V–3W
(6) Neutral Indicator Lamp: 12V–3W
(7) 5th Gear Indicator Lamp: 12V–3W
(8) Headlight High Beam Lamp: 12V–3W
(9) Battery: 12V–6AH

Dimensions and Weight

(1) Overall Length: 2,110 mm (83.1 inches)
(2) Overall Width: 825 mm (32.5 inches)
(3) Overall Height: 1,115 mm (43.9 inches)
(4) Saddle Height: 810 mm (31.9 inches)
(5) Wheelbase: 1,375 mm (54.1 inches)
(6) Road Clearance: 145 mm (5.7 inches)
(7) Tire Size (Front): 3.25–19.4 ply
              (Rear): 3.25–19.4 ply
(8) Tire Pressure (Front): 2.0 kg/cm^2 (28.4 lbs/in^2)
              (Rear): 2.2 kg/cm^2 (31.3 lbs/in^2)
(9) Caster: 63°
(10) Trail: 105 mm (4.15 inches)
(11) Banking Angle: 46°
(12) Net Weight: 165 kg (363 lbs)
(13) Fuel Tank Capacity: 15 litre (3-4/5 US gal.)
      Including 3.2 litre (4/5 US gal.) reserve
(14) Oil Tank Capacity: 2.5 litre (3/5 US gal.)

Performance

(1) Max. Speed: 100–110 mph
(2) Climbing Ability: 1 in 2
(3) Fuel Consumption: 94 mpg/25 mph (40 km/litre at 40 km/h)
(4) Min. Turning Radius: 2.25 m (7.38 feet)
(5) Acceleration:
    (Standing Start 1/4 mile) 13.7 sec
    (Zero to 60 mph): 5.2 sec
(6) Braking Distance: (Less than 12 m at 50 km/h)
      39.4 feet, at 30 mph

FRONT AND SIDE VIEWS OF BRIDGESTONE 350 GTR

Dimensions in Millimeters (inches)

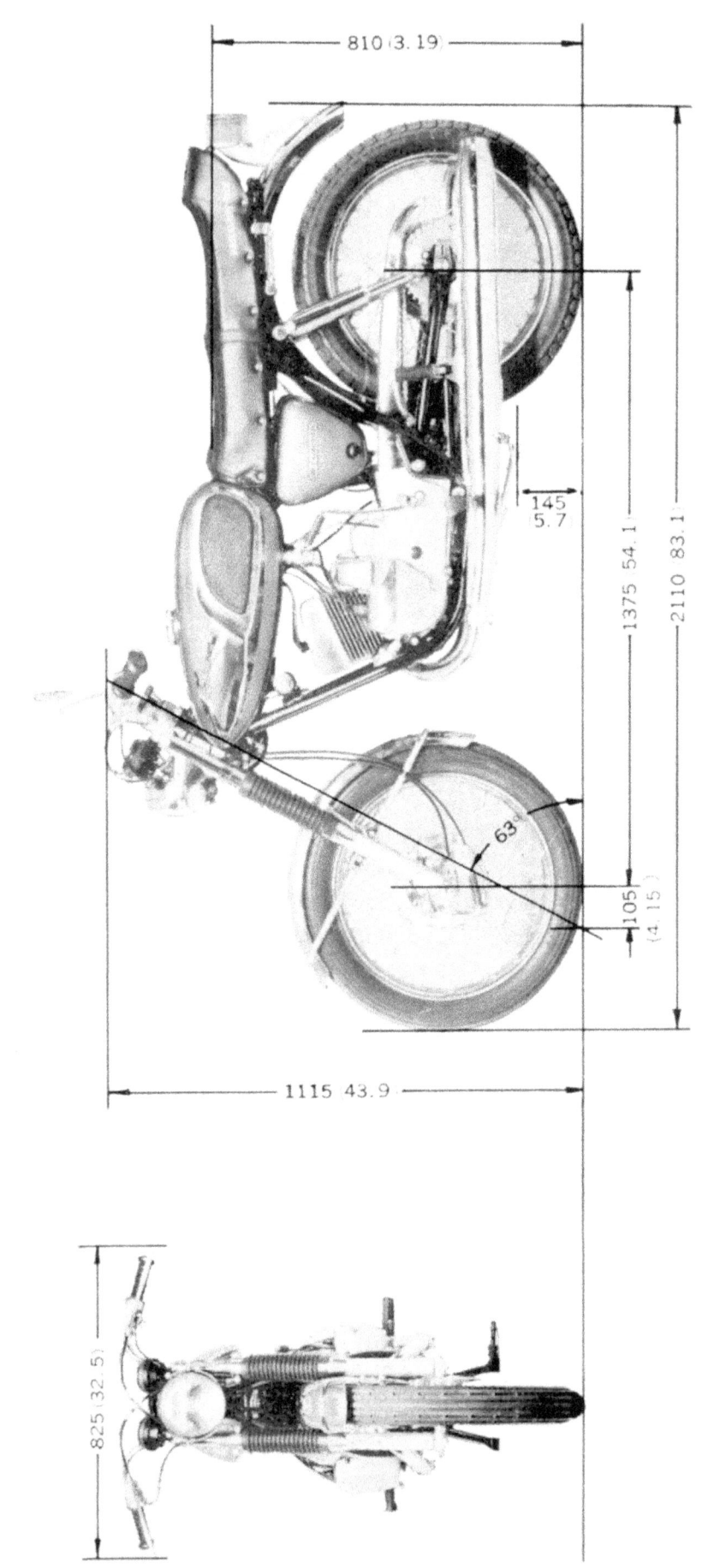

3. PERFORMANCE

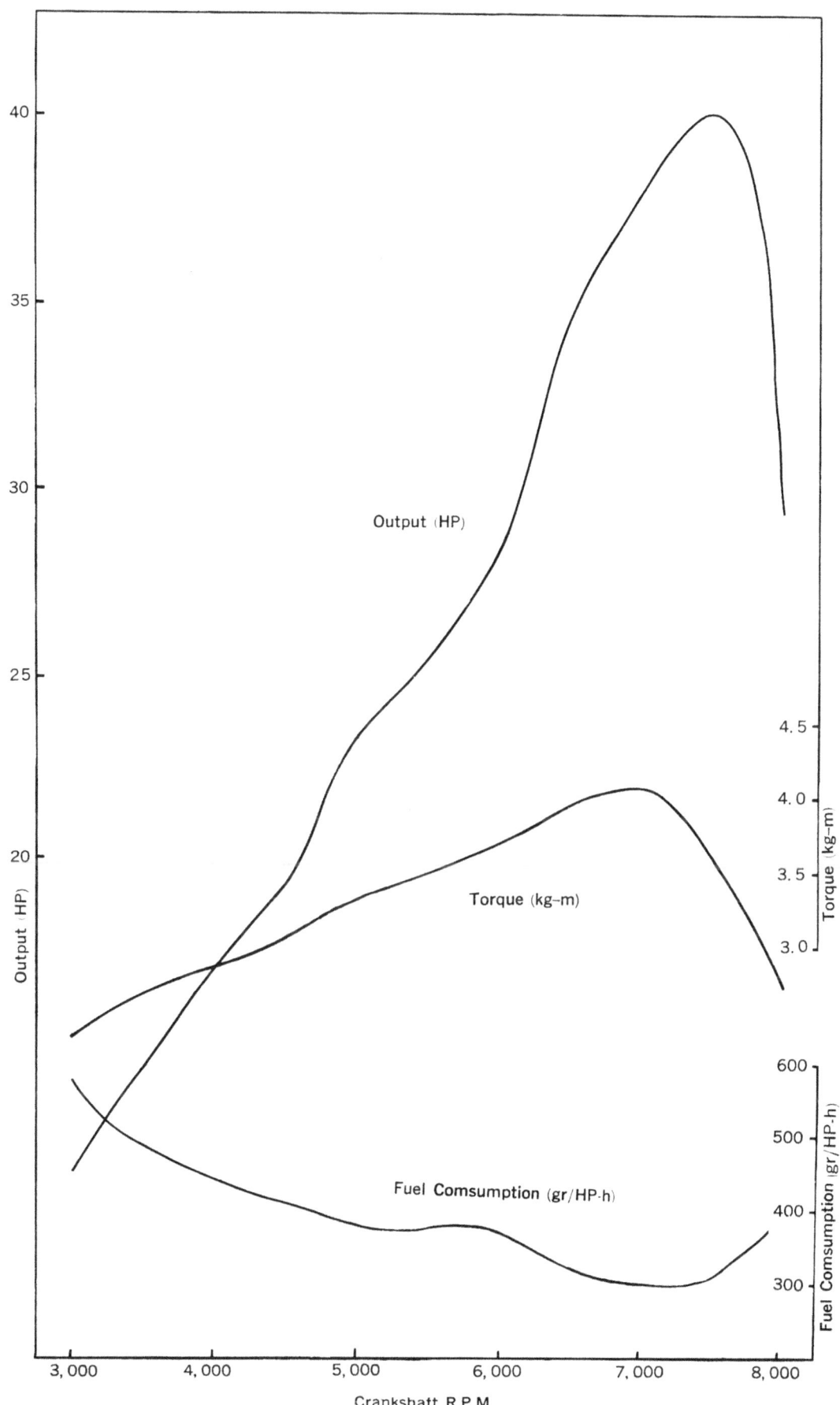

3. PERFORMANCE

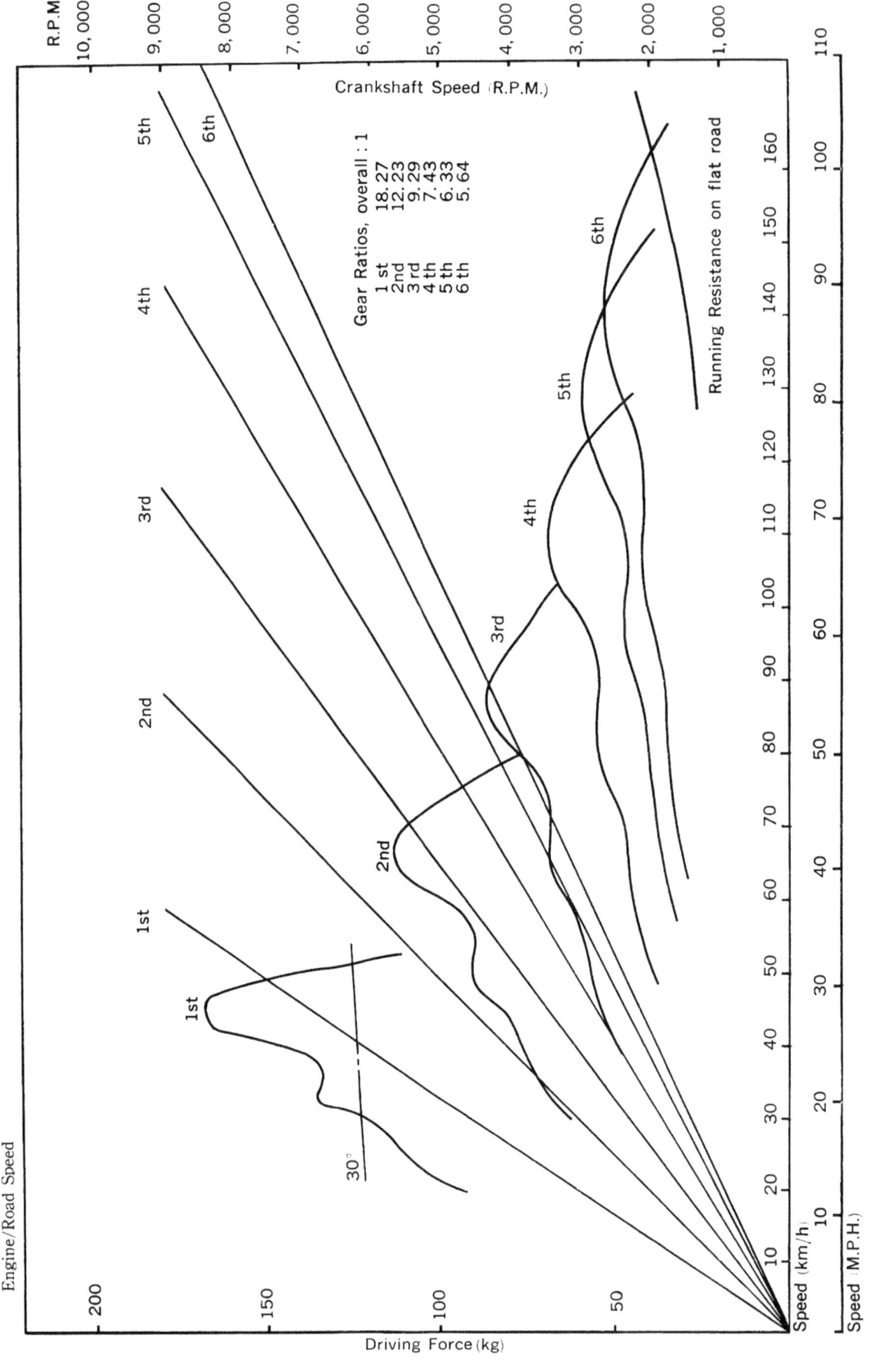

4. ENGINE

4-1 Dismounting Engine

A. Care to be observed:

1. Be careful not to damage the insulation of the various wires.
2. Be careful not oil the clutch parts as the dry type racing clutch is fitted to 350 GTR.

B. Tools necessary for dismounting and mounting the engine:

1. Standard Tools:
   1. Wrench   10×12mm
                             14×17
                             19×21
   2. Screw driver ⊕ No. 3, No. 2
   3. Screw driver ⊖
   4. Plier
   5. Combination plier
   6. T Type wrenches: 10, 12, 14, 23mm

2. Special Tools: (Fig. 1)
   1. Box wrench bar
   2. 20mm nut wrench
   3. 40mm ring nut wrench
   4. Driven gear stopper
   5. Clutch housing puller
   6. Clutch housing stopper
   7. Clutch hub stopper

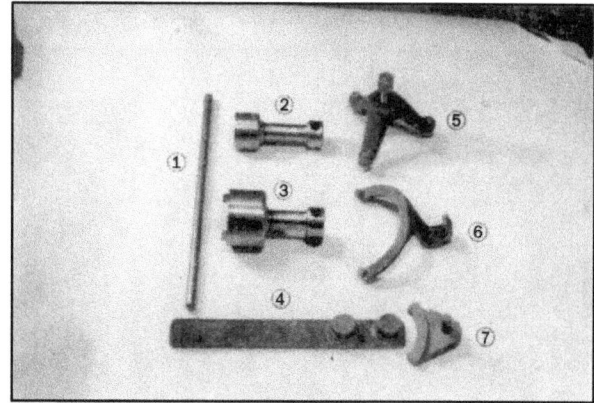

Fig. 1 Special tools

C. Dismounting Engine:

1. Remove dual seat after removing left side cover.
2. Disconnect main switch wires and A. C. Genetator wires from the terminals. (Fig. 2)

Fig. 2 Disconnecting wires

3. Remove both exhaust pipes by pulling out the four bolts. (Fig. 3)
4. Disconnect tachometer cable at the end of engine case, then remove high-tension terminal plug caps from spark plugs.

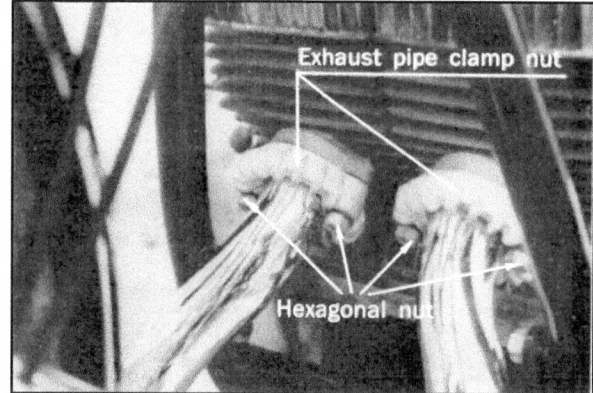

Fig. 3 Removing exhaust pipes

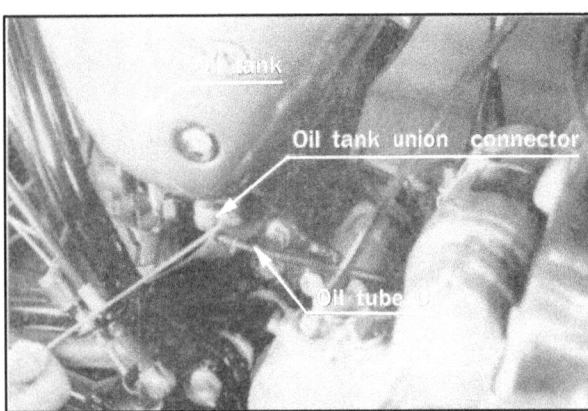

Fig. 4 Disconnecting oil tube c

5. Disconnect oil tube C from union connector on oil tank and plug the connector as shown in (Fig. 4)

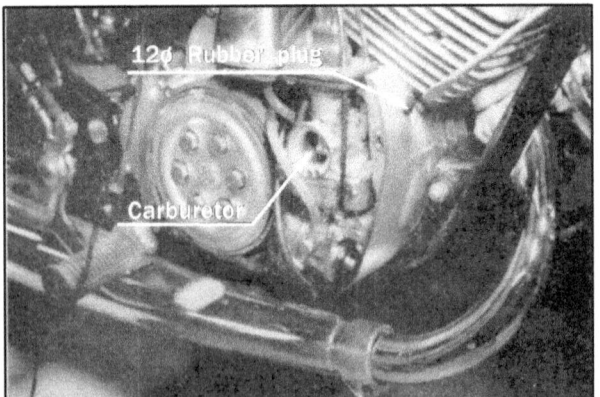

Fig. 5 Removing carburetor

6. Remove carburetor cover (R) by unscrewing the six screws [one (6×40), one 6×30), three (60×20), one (6×3)] and take off rubber plug, then pull out carburetor. (Fig. 5)
7. Remove left carburetor following the same procedure as for the right carburetor.
8. Remove change pedal and kick arm after taking off footrest (L).

Fig. 6 Removing dust cover & crankcase cover

9. Remove dust cover by unscrewing the two (6×40), (6×30) (6×25) (6×8) screws and one (6×20) screw of left crank case. (Fig. 6)

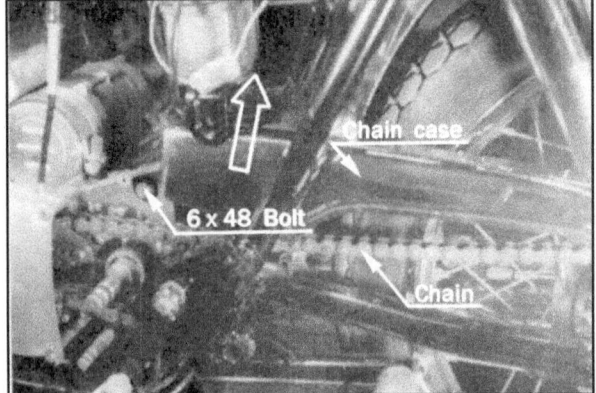

Fig. 7 Disconnecting chain

10. Disconnect chain and lift the front section of chain case by taking out the hexagonal bolt (6×48). (Fig. 7)

11. Take out four, engine mounting bolts: one (8×265), one (8×145), two (10×38) and then remove engine mounting bracket L. (Fig. 8)
12. Remove six screws (5×25) of air cleaner cover and dismount engine from left side.

Fig. 8 Unscrewing engine mounting bolts

Fig. 9 Fitting engine mounting bolts

4-2 Mounting Engine on Frame

The engine should be installed in the reverse order of its removal.
*Be careful of the following points:

1. Fit two (10×38) engine mounting bolts temporarily. (Fig. 9)

2. See that the wires work correctly and especially match the mark of the throttle valve and the projecting end of control lever of oil pump. (Fig. 10, 11)
3. Connect electric wires securely.

Fig. 10 Adjusting throttle valve

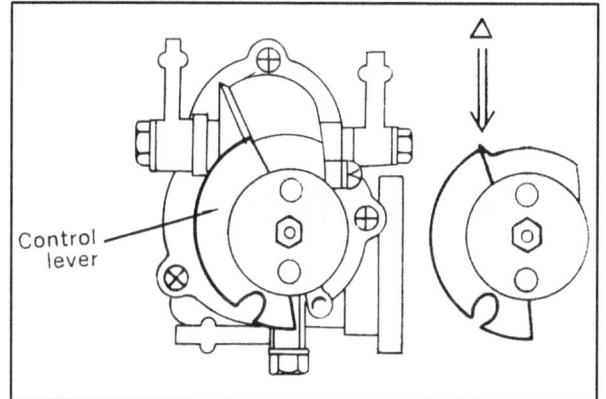

Fig. 11 Adjusting oil pump

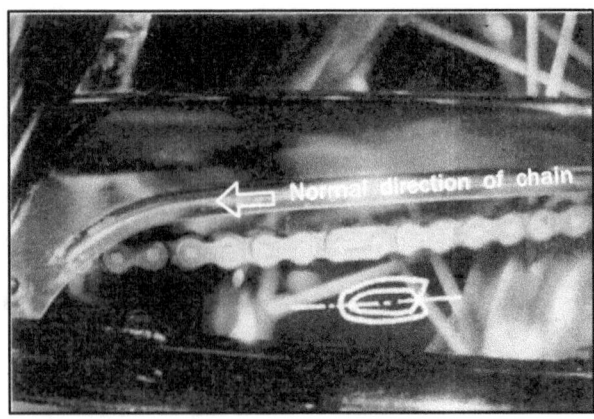

Fig. 12 Link of chain connector

4. The chain connector should be linked with the open end pointing in the reverse direction of the moving chain. (Fig. 12)
   Chain adjustment is correct when chain slack is approximately 10 mm (3/8") up or down when the rear wheel is on the ground.

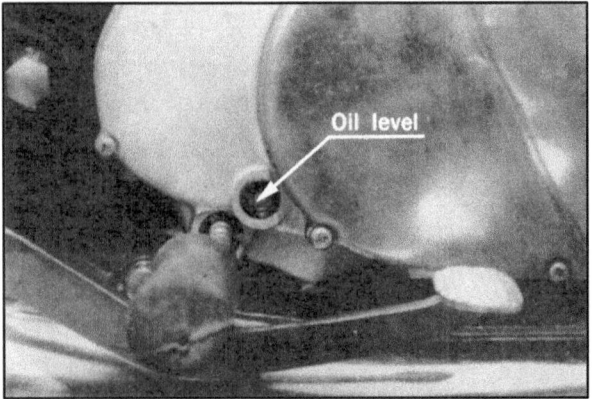

Fig. 13 Checking oil level

5. See that the transmission is filled with the proper amount of oil (1.5 litre = 2/5 US gal.) and check the oil level through the peephole only when the oil has settled in the transmission case. (Fig. 13)

Fig. 14 Exhausting oil bubbles

6. After starting the engine, exhaust air bubbles in the oil tube A, B & C by opening fully the control lever of oil pump at the engine idling speeds. (Fig. 14)

7. Fit carburetor cover (R) after checking the oil pump.

4-3 Disassembling and Assembling Engine:

A. Matters that require special attention.

1. When removing or installing the engine, use a wooden or plastic hammer and tap it lightly and uniformly so as not to strain any part.
2. When disassembling, take careful note of the position of the meshing gears and location of the many washers, and lay the parts out in an orderly manner, so that they may not get mislaid or confused when assembling.
3. The parts should be carefully cleaned except the clutch parts.
* This machine is equipped with dry racing type clutch which must be kept free from oil to ensure efficient action.
4. Bolt tightness of the clutch set bolt is 70—90kg/cm. (61—78 lbs–in)

B. Dismounting Engine

1. Disconnect oil tubes from the connector instead of disconnecting them from the check valves, to avoid air leakage. (Fig. 15)

Fig. 15 Position of check valves

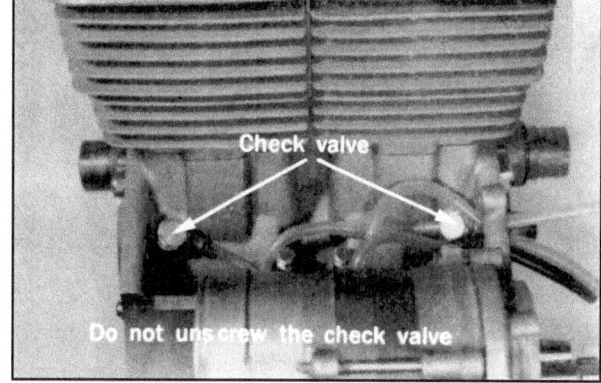

2. Pull out oil pump ass'y by removing two pump screws. (Fig. 16)
3. Remove clutch springs and clutch facings and all related parts by pulling out diagonally and evenly the six hexagonal bolts of the clutch set plate. (Fig. 16)

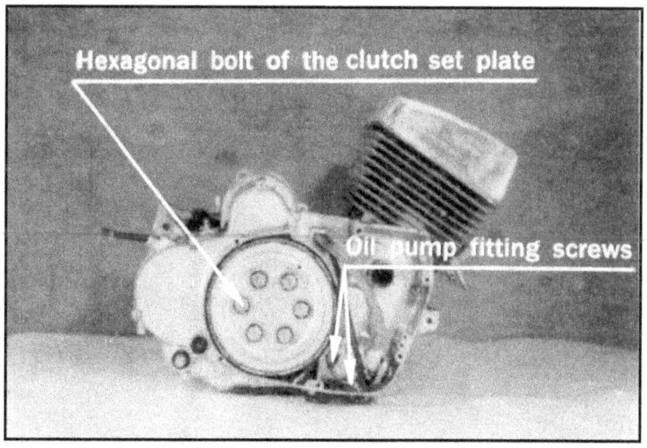

Fig. 16 Removing oil pump

4. Remove clutch hub nut (23mm) with clutch hub stopper (special tool). (Fig. 17)

Fig. 17 Removing clutch hub

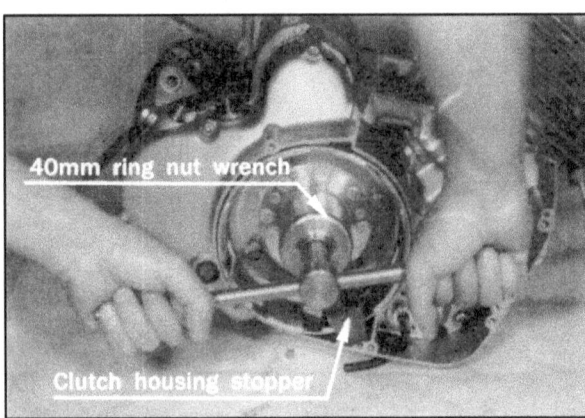

Fig. 18 Removing ring nut

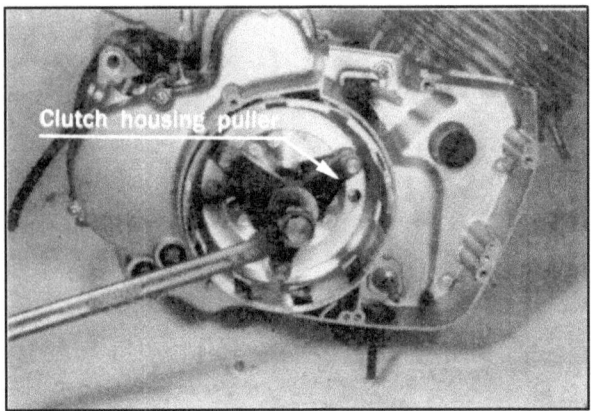

Fig. 19 Removing clutch housing

Fig. 20 Removing right crank case cover

Fig. 21 Removing pinion gear

5. Remove ring nut with the clutch housing stopper and the ring nut fitting tools (special tools) and then remove clutch housing. (Fig. 18, 19)

6. Remove right crank case cover by unscrewing ten screws of right crank cace cover. $(6 \times 55 \times 1)$ $(6 \times 40 \times 2)$ $(6 \times 30 \times 3)$ $(6 \times 25 \times 1)$ $(6 \times 45 \times 4)$. (Fig. 20)

7. Remove the left-hand threaded pinion gear nut with the driven gear stopper and 20mm nut wrench (special tool) and then remove the pinion gear. (Fig. 21)
Then, remove timing gear fitting bolt, timing gear, driven gear and kick idler gear.

8. Remove over-run stopper plate by unscrewing the screw (shown by the arrow A in Fig. 22). (Fig. 22)

   To do this, it is recommended to shift up the change shaft by fitting the change pedal. Then pull out change shaft.

9. Remove guide plate and ratchet comp. by unscrewing the two (6×12) screws (shown by the arrow B) of ratchet guide plate. (Fig. 22)

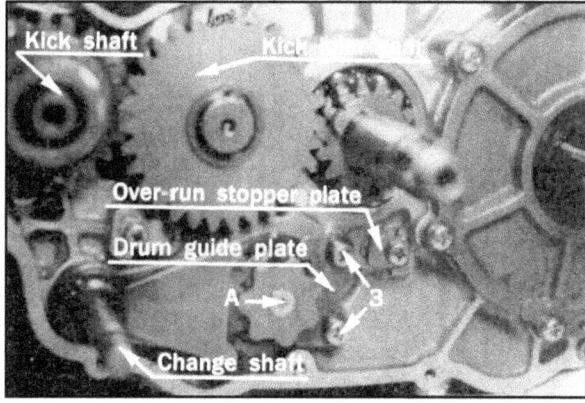

Fig. 22 Removing over-run stopper and guide plate

10. Remove rotary valve cover by unscrewing the six (6×16) screws of rotary valve cover. (Fig. 23)

Fig. 23 Removing rotary valve cover

11. Remove rotary valve cover, drive sprocket and neutral switch located on the left side of engine. (Fig. 24)

12. Take off eight cylinder head nuts and remove cylinder heads, gaskets and cylinders.

Fig. 24 Removing drive sprocket

13. Remove piston-pin circlips and then piston pins, pistons and needle bearings. (Fig. 25)

Fig. 25 Removing piston-pin circlips

Fig. 26 Removing AC generator

Fig. 27 Removing bolts of upper crank case

Fig. 28 Removing bolts of lower crankcase

Fig. 29 Gear Box

14. Remove screw (5×30) of AC Dynamo and hexagonal nut of set band and then, remove AC generator by pulling it out indirection A. (Fig. 26)

15. Remove rotary disc valves.

16. Remove four hexagonal bolts, one (8×80), one (8×90), and two (6×65) of upper crankcase. (Fig. 27)

17. Remove thirteen hexagonal bolts, one (8×114), three (8×90), two (8×62), five (6×62), one (8×100) and one (6×90) of lower crankcase. (Fig. 28)

18. Remove upper crank case cover. Fig. 29 shows the gear box after taking off the upper cover.

19. Remove crankshaft comp, counter shaft, drive shaft and kickshaft from lower case. Shift drum and forks need not be removed from the case.

It requires generally up to 19 steps to disassemble the engine, but when shift drum is to be removed, proceed as follows.

a) To remove shift drum, take off guide bolt, drum stopper, and guide stopper plate and then pull out two guide pin in the direction of right crank case cover. (Fig. 30. 31. 32)

b) Take off spilt pin of fork guide, remove fork guide and remove shift drum.

Fig. 30 Removing guide bolt & drum stopper

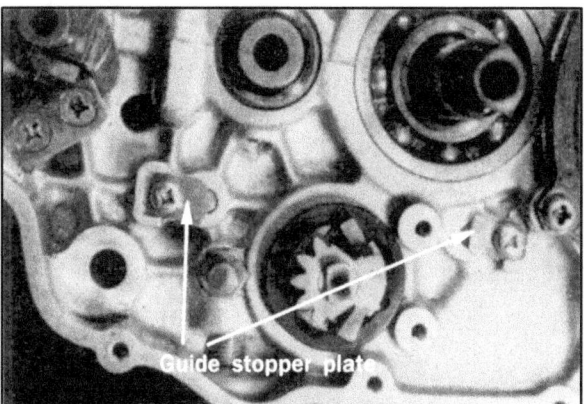

Fig. 31 Removing guide stopper plates

Fig. 32 Removing guide shafts

C. Component parts of crank case

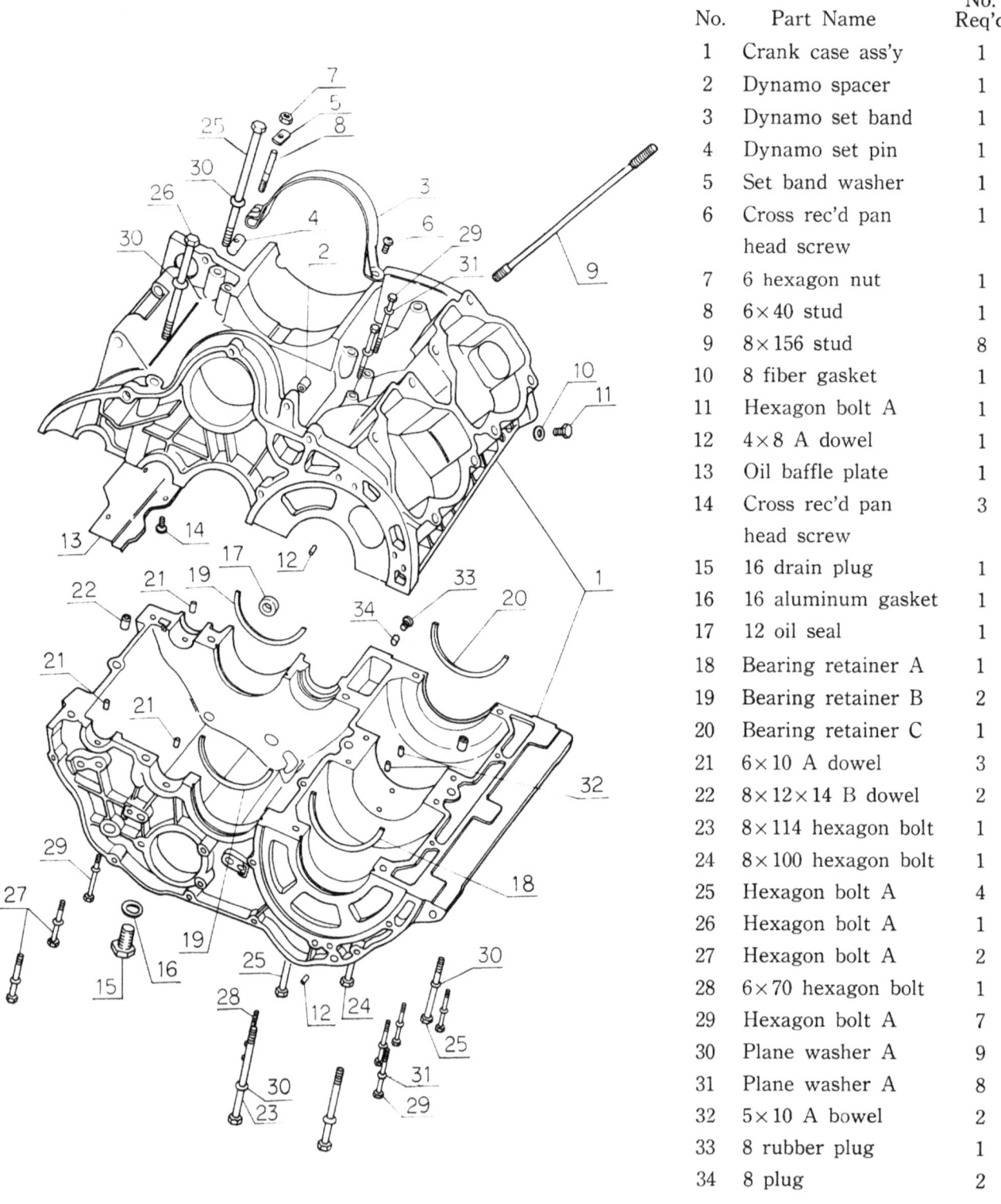

No.	Part Name	No. Req'd
1	Crank case ass'y	1
2	Dynamo spacer	1
3	Dynamo set band	1
4	Dynamo set pin	1
5	Set band washer	1
6	Cross rec'd pan head screw	1
7	6 hexagon nut	1
8	6×40 stud	1
9	8×156 stud	8
10	8 fiber gasket	1
11	Hexagon bolt A	1
12	4×8 A dowel	1
13	Oil baffle plate	1
14	Cross rec'd pan head screw	3
15	16 drain plug	1
16	16 aluminum gasket	1
17	12 oil seal	1
18	Bearing retainer A	1
19	Bearing retainer B	2
20	Bearing retainer C	1
21	6×10 A dowel	3
22	8×12×14 B dowel	2
23	8×114 hexagon bolt	1
24	8×100 hexagon bolt	1
25	Hexagon bolt A	4
26	Hexagon bolt A	1
27	Hexagon bolt A	2
28	6×70 hexagon bolt	1
29	Hexagon bolt A	7
30	Plane washer A	9
31	Plane washer A	8
32	5×10 A bowel	2
33	8 rubber plug	1
34	8 plug	2

D. Assembling Engine

The engine should be assembled in the reverse order of disassembling.

1. Be careful to set gears and thrust washers correctly.
2. Be careful to insert knock pin and knock ring of bearings correctly.
3. Grease shafts and gears with oil.
4. Apply liquid packing between upper and lower case covers.
5. When fitting hexagonal bolts the of cases, bolts should be fitted according to Fig. 33.
6. Set the over-run stopper as shown in Fig. 34, 35.

Fig. 33 Crankcase fitting

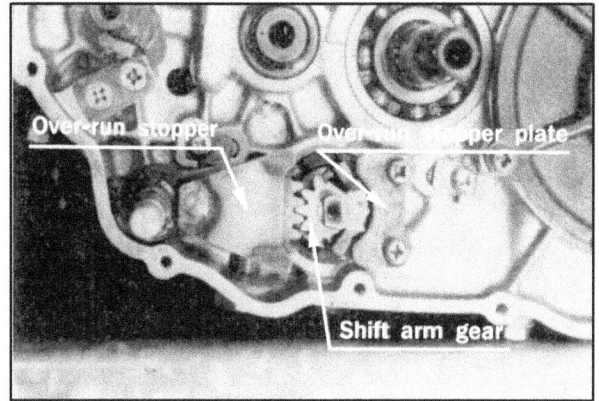

Fig. 34 Setting over-run stopper

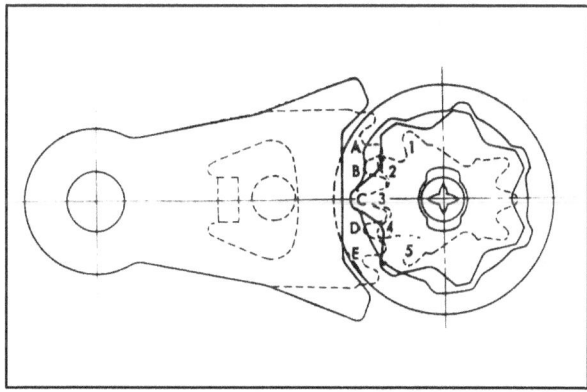

Fig. 35 Setting over-run stopper

7. To fit kick shaft stopper, assemble upper and lower crank case covers first and fit kick pedal temporarily to the kick shaft by cranking the engine. (Fig. 36–1, 2, 3)

Fig. 36-1 Fitting kick shaft stopper (1)

Fig. 36-2 Fitting kick shaft stopper (2)

Fig. 36-3 Fitting kick shaft stopper (3)

Fig. 37 Fitting kick rachet & change ratchets

8. Fit kick ratchet and change ratchets as shown in Fig. 37.
   Set the gears in neutral when fitting the ratchets.

Fig. 38 Fitting rotary valve

9. Match the key position of rotary valve collar with the mark on the rotary valve. (Fig. 38)

10. Set the timing marks on the timing gear, driven gear and pinion gear as shown in Fig. 39.

11. Be carefull in assembling clutch inner plates and clutch outer plate as they are of different thicknesses.

	Effective Serial No. Up to 21 S 01021	After Serial No. 21 S 01022
	thickness Q'ty	thickness Q'ty
Inner plate :	1.6 mm t 6	1.6 mm t 7
Outer plate :	3.0 mm t 1	— none

12. Grease the top of push rod when assembling push rod.

13. Match the mark on clutch hub with the 4 mmϕ hole on the pressure plate when assembling clutch pressure plate. (Fig. 40)

14. Mesh the oil pump gear with pinion gear by turning the worm shaft out side of right crankcase. (Fig. 41)

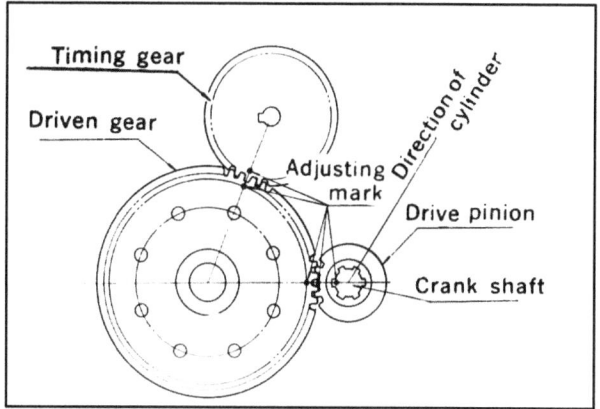

Fig. 39 Setting the timing marks

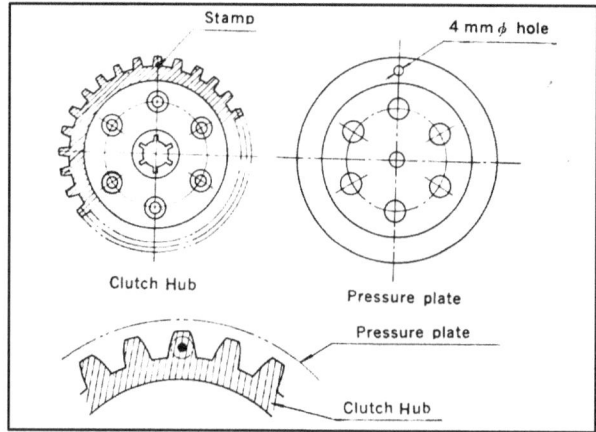

Fig. 40 Matching the 4 mm ϕ hole

Fig. 41 Meshing oil pump gear

15. Be careful when fitting the oil tubes

	Colour	Length	Remarks
Oil tube A	Transparent	340 mm (13.4 inches)	Left check valve
Oil tube B	Transparent	370 mm (14.6 inches)	Right check valve
Oil tube C	Black	530 mm (20.9 inches)	Oil tank

16. Adjust contact breaker point gap and ignition timing.

    Contact breaker gap   0.3–0.4 mm (0.012–0.016 inches)

    Ignition timing $25°^{+1}_{-2}$

    Ignition timing should be checked carefully.

17. Be careful of the location of washers.

5. CRANKSHAFT · PISTONS · CYLINDERS · ROTARY DISC VALVES

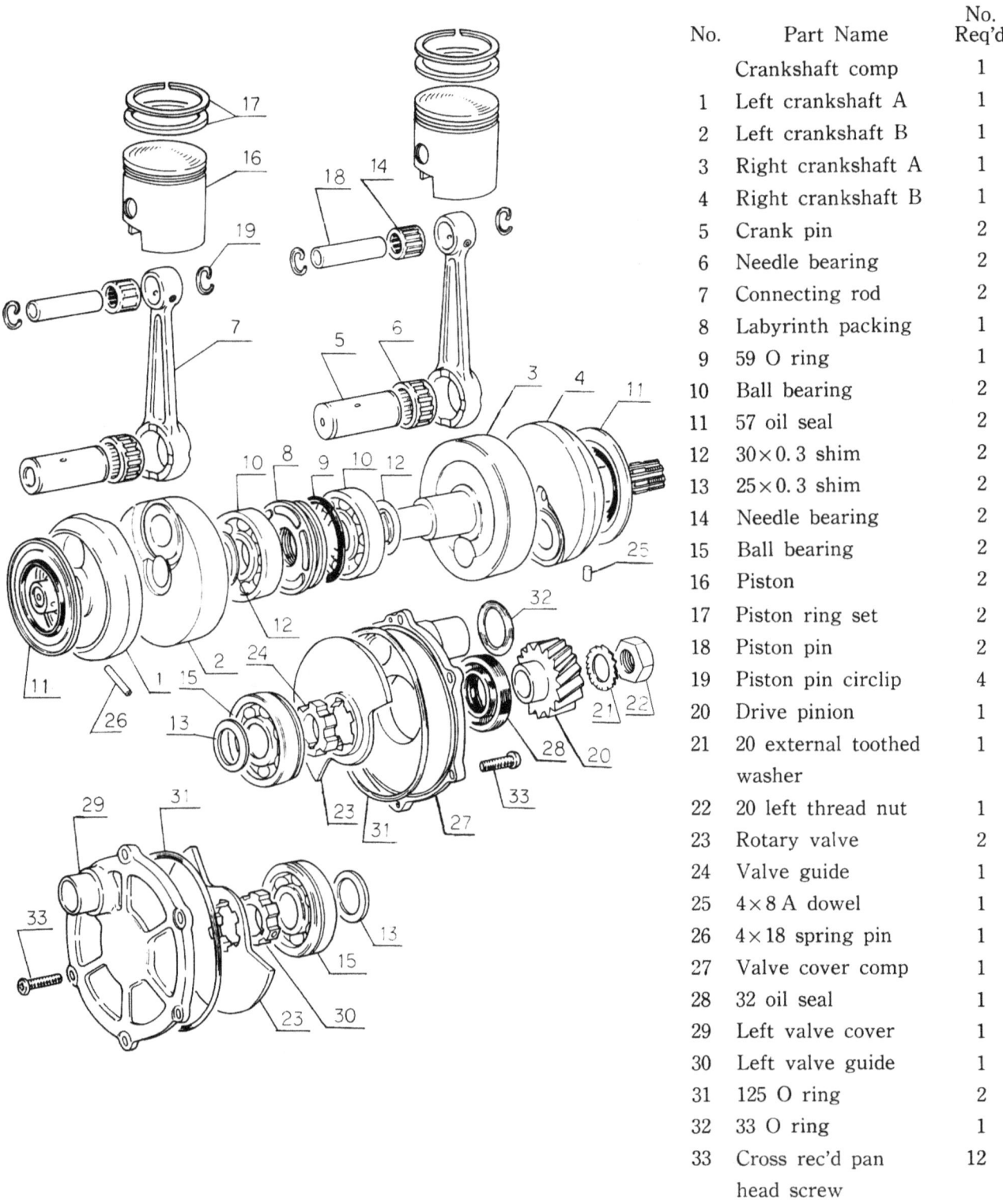

No.	Part Name	No. Req'd
	Crankshaft comp	1
1	Left crankshaft A	1
2	Left crankshaft B	1
3	Right crankshaft A	1
4	Right crankshaft B	1
5	Crank pin	2
6	Needle bearing	2
7	Connecting rod	2
8	Labyrinth packing	1
9	59 O ring	1
10	Ball bearing	2
11	57 oil seal	2
12	30×0.3 shim	2
13	25×0.3 shim	2
14	Needle bearing	2
15	Ball bearing	2
16	Piston	2
17	Piston ring set	2
18	Piston pin	2
19	Piston pin circlip	4
20	Drive pinion	1
21	20 external toothed washer	1
22	20 left thread nut	1
23	Rotary valve	2
24	Valve guide	1
25	4×8 A dowel	1
26	4×18 spring pin	1
27	Valve cover comp	1
28	32 oil seal	1
29	Left valve cover	1
30	Left valve guide	1
31	125 O ring	2
32	33 O ring	1
33	Cross rec'd pan head screw	12

Component parts of crankshaft · pistons · rotary disc valves

5-1. CRANKSHAFT AND ROTARY DISC VALVES

A. Construction

Dual cylinders, dual carburetors and dual rotary disc valves are incorporated in the Bridgestone 350 GTR engine.

Rotary disc valves are spline fitted at each end of the crankshaft of this parallel twin. (Fig. 42)

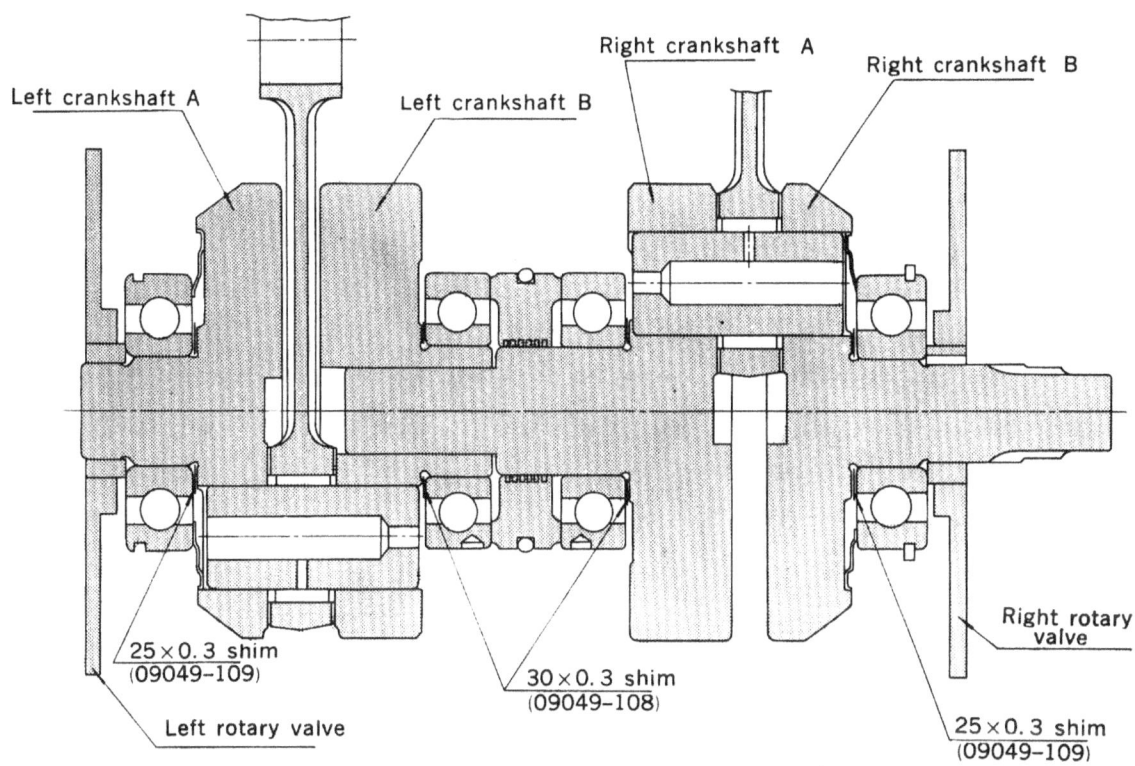

Fig. 42 Construction

B. Inspection

1. Measure crankshaft play with a dial gauge for tolerance and fit. (Fig. 43)
2. Inspect the part of the crankshaft where bearings are fitted for wear and excess play.
   If abnormal noise is produced or there is excessive play, replace the crankshaft with a new one.
3. If the connecting rod big end bearing is worn or damaged, replace the crankshaft ass'y with a new one.
4. If a disc valve is damaged, replace with a new one.
5. If an O ring is damaged or worn, replace with a new one.

Fig. 43 Measuring crankshaft play

C. Lubrication of crankshaft

Crankshaft bearings are lubricated automatically and correctly with oil fed from oil pump through oil tube B, C and union bolt.

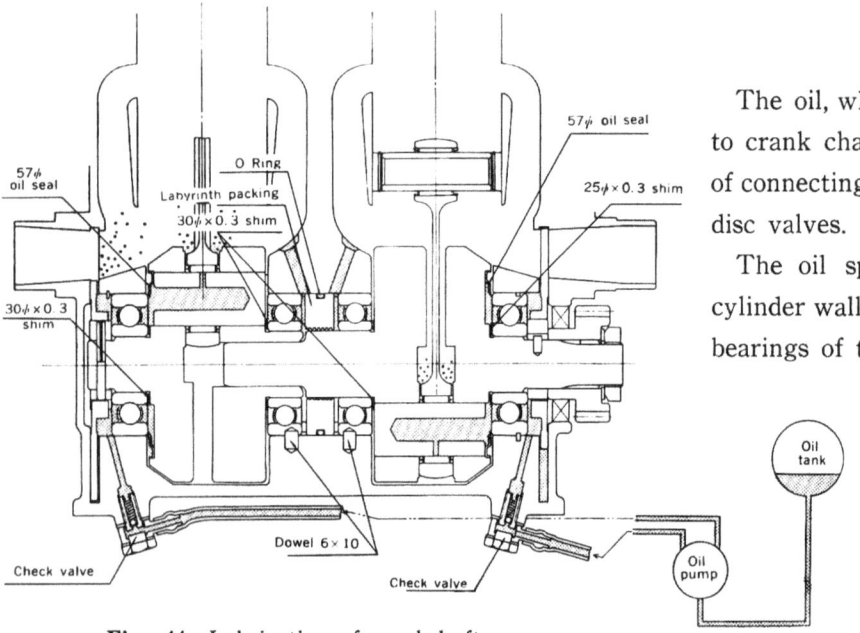

The oil, which lubricates bearings, is sprayed to crank chamber after lubricating the big end of connecting rod or passing the back of rotary disc valves.

The oil sprayed to crank shaft lubricates cylinder wall, small end of crankshaft and ball bearings of the crankshaft. (Fig. 44)

Fig. 44 Lubrication of crankshaft

D. Lubrication of transmission gears

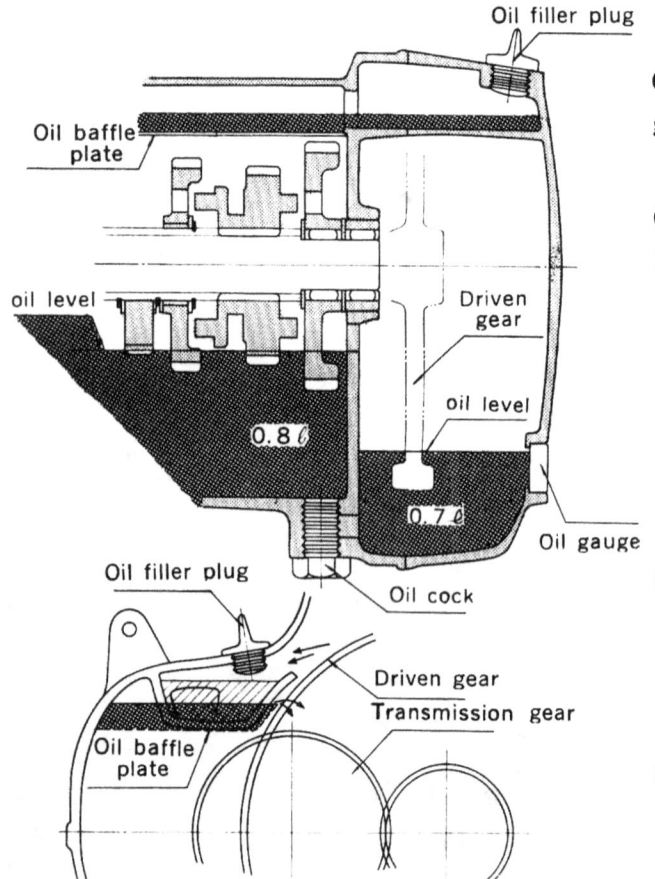

Oil stored in the gear box lubricates gears as shown.

Caution:

1. When refilling with new transmission oil, take off oil cock and fill in 1.5 litre (3/5 U.S. gal.) SAE No. 10W/30 in all seasons or SAE No. 20 in winter.

2. Check the oil level through the peephole, only when the oil has settled in the transmission case.

3. Change the oil periodically as follows.
      1 st oiling   after break-in
      2nd oiling   every 2,000 miles

Fig. 45 Lubrication of transmission gears

5-2. CYLINDERS AND PISTONS

A. Construction

The cylinders of the Bridgestone 350 GTR are made of aluminum alloy. Cylinder walls are honed after hard chrominum plating and then porous treated. Therefore, this engine has excellent cooling efficiency and as the heat expansion coefficient of the cylinder and piston is the same, the piston to cylinder clearance can be kept to a minimum and quiet engine operation is possible. Moreover the aluminum alloy cylinders reduce the weight of the engine.

B. Matters that require special attention.

1. Take care not to use chrominum plated piston rings.
   Always use the ferox treated piston rings.
2. Keep clean the air cleaner element.
3. Be careful to set the piston identification mark "EX" forward. (Fig. 46)

C. Inspection

1. Measure piston ring gaps as shown in Fig. 47. Replace it with a new one when gaps exceed 1mm (0.04 inches).
2. Check cylinder head gasket for damage, replace with a new one if necessary.
3. Remove carbon deposit on cylinder ports and cylinder head with cleaning solvent or gasoline.
4. Replace cylinder base packing with a new one.

D. Disassembling

1. Cylinder and piston can be taken off without dismounting engine from the frame by removing dual seat, fuel tank, horn and ignition coil (Fig. 48)

2. Before removing pistons, remove cylinder and cover the crankcase with cloth to prevent piston circlip from entering into the crankcase. (Fig. 49)

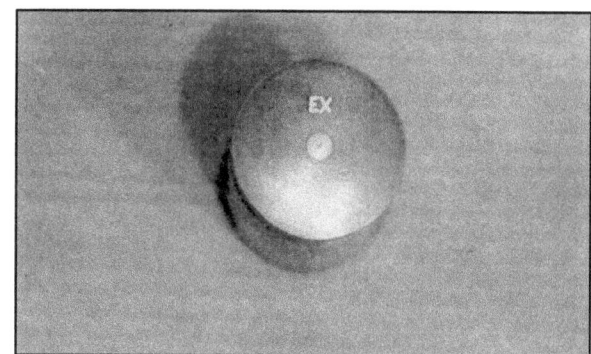
Fig. 46 Piston identification mark

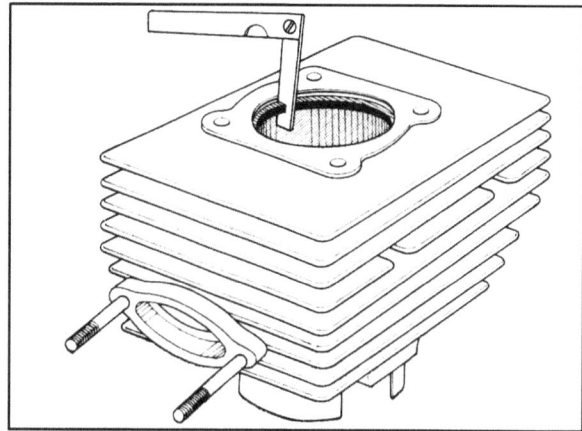
Fig. 47 Measuring piston ring gaps

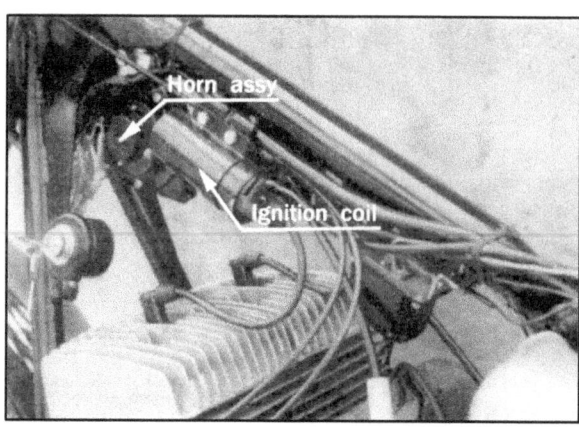
Fig. 48 Removing cylinder & piston

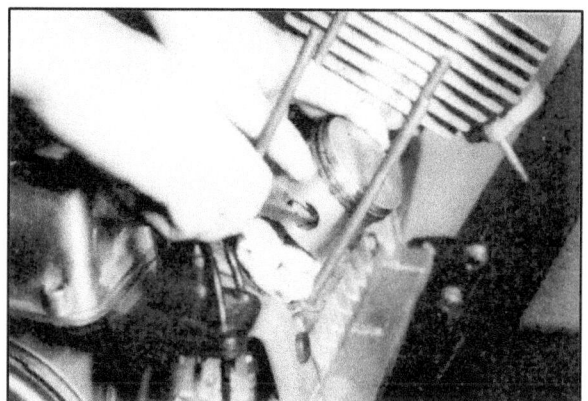
Fig. 49 Removing piston

6. CLUTCH

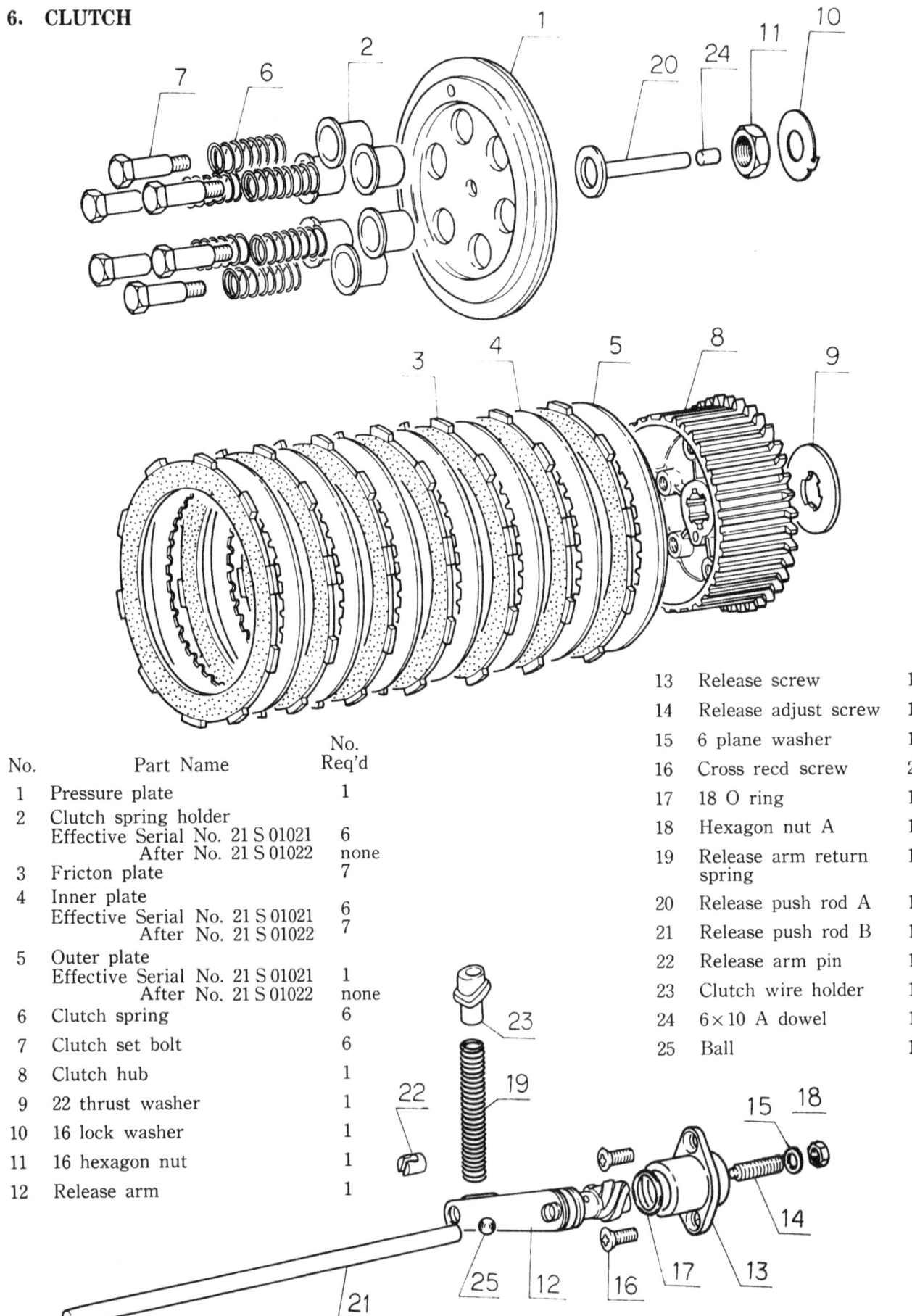

No.	Part Name	No. Req'd
1	Pressure plate	1
2	Clutch spring holder Effective Serial No. 21 S 01021 After No. 21 S 01022	6 none
3	Fricton plate	7
4	Inner plate Effective Serial No. 21 S 01021 After No. 21 S 01022	6 7
5	Outer plate Effective Serial No. 21 S 01021 After No. 21 S 01022	1 none
6	Clutch spring	6
7	Clutch set bolt	6
8	Clutch hub	1
9	22 thrust washer	1
10	16 lock washer	1
11	16 hexagon nut	1
12	Release arm	1
13	Release screw	1
14	Release adjust screw	1
15	6 plane washer	1
16	Cross recd screw	2
17	18 O ring	1
18	Hexagon nut A	1
19	Release arm return spring	1
20	Release push rod A	1
21	Release push rod B	1
22	Release arm pin	1
23	Clutch wire holder	1
24	6×10 A dowel	1
25	Ball	1

A. Construction

350 GTR has racing type dry discs instead of conventional wet discs to ensure quick and powerful action for better performance by eliminating resistance of oil film.

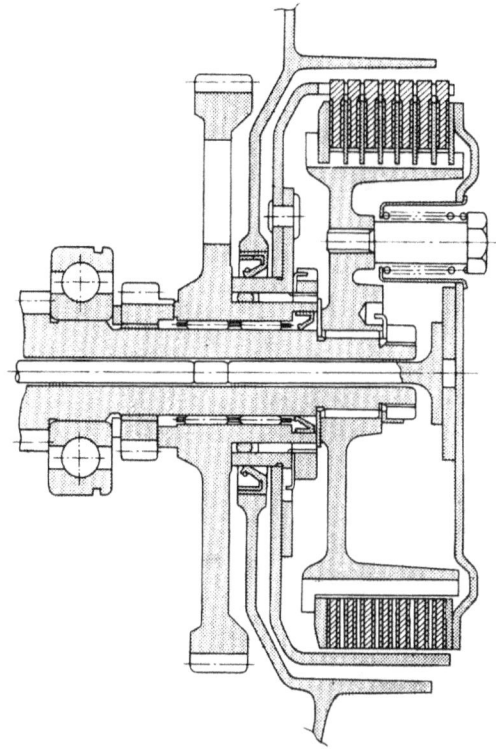

Fig. 50 General view of clutch

B. Operation.

1. Transmitting Engine Power

Engine power is transmitted through the drive pinion on the crankshaft and the driven gear. The driven gear is fitted to the clutch housing and clutch friction plates are fitted inside the clutch housing with teeth so that they turn together with the clutch housing and driven gear.

Clutch friction plates and inner plates are fitted alternately with the inner plates fitted to the clutch hub with teeth.

The clutch hub, friction plates and inner plates all fit inside the clutch housing and are pressed together tightly by the clutch springs. The clutch hub is spline fitted to the transmission countershaft, which turns the trasmission gears.

	Effective Serial No. 21 S 01021	After No. 21 S 01022
Clutch Friction Plate	7	7
Inner Plate	6	7
Outer Plate	1	none
Clutch Spring	8	8
Spring tension	100kg (220 lbs.)	100kg (220 lbs.)

2. Engine Power Cut Off

When the clutch lever is pulled, the clutch wire turns the clutch release arm so that the adjusting screw pushes the dowel (6×10), rod (6×236), push rod and presses the clutch pressure plate.

The clutch springs are then decompressed so that they do not press the clutch friction against the inner plates. As the friction plates and inner plates separate, the inner plates cease to turn so that engine power is cut off from the clutch hub and transmission countershaft.

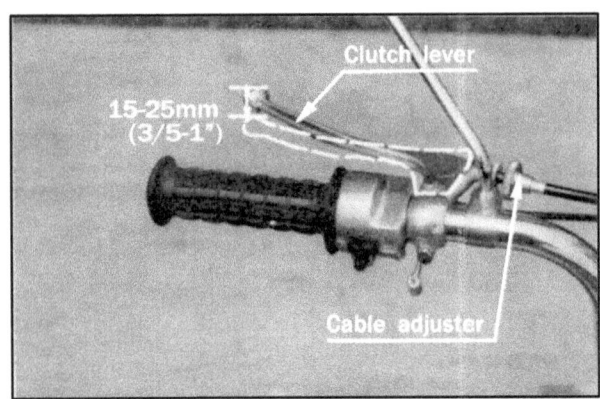

Fig. 51 Clutch cable adjuster

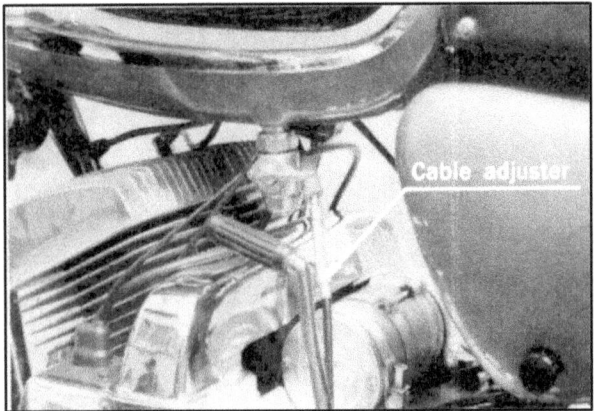

Fig. 52 Clutch cable adjust screw

Fig. 53 Clutch adjustment screw

Fig. 54 Unscrewing clutch hexagonal bolts

C. Clutch Adjustment

1. Adjustment is easily carried out with the cable adjuster and cable adjust screw. (Fig. 51, 52)
2. When satisfactory adjustmest cannot be made in this way; remove rubber cap from left crank case cover, loosen locknut, and adjust by holding down the lock nut and turning adjustment screw.

* The play of the lever is lessened by turning the screw right and increased by turning left. (Fig. 53)

D. Disassembling Clutch

1. Remove carburetor cover by unscrewing six screws of right carburetor cover, one (60×40), one (60×30), three (6×20) and one (6×8) screws.
2. Remove clutch springs and clutch facings and related parts by removing diagonally and evenly the hexagonal bolts of the clutch set plate. (Fig. 54)

3. Remove clutch hub nut (25mm) with clutch hub stopper (special tool) (Fig. 55)

Fig. 55 Removing clutch hub

4. Remove ring nut with clutch housing stopper and ring nut fitting tool (special tools), and then remove clutch housing. (Fig. 56, 57)

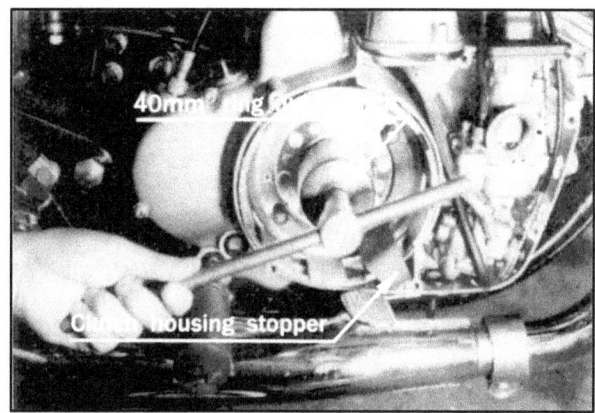

Fig. 56 Removing ring nut

E. Inspection

1. See if there are any damaged serrations on the inner plate, and worn or uneven plates.
2. Check for damaged arms on friction plates worn or uneven. (Fig. 58, 59)
3. Check release arm for wear, release screw, release push screw dowel and rod. Replace where necessary.

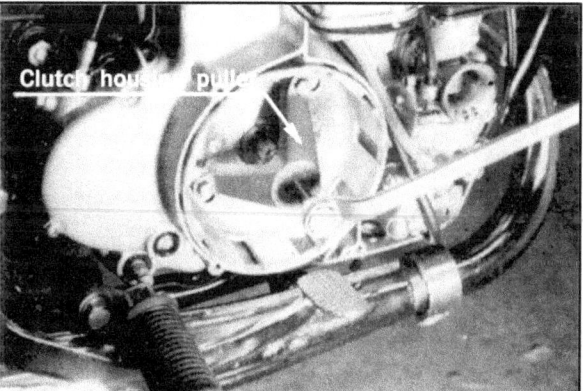

Fig. 57 Removing clutch housing

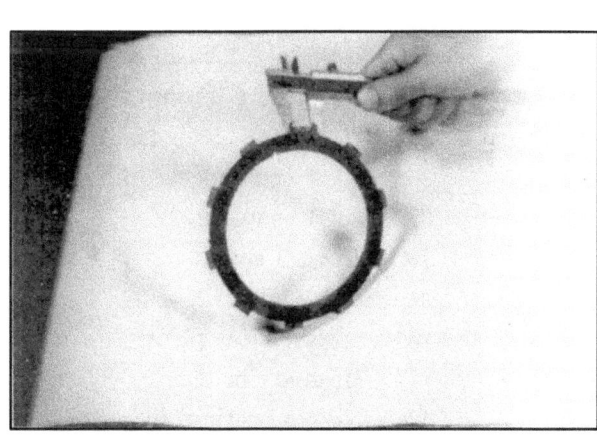

Fig. 58 Checking friction plate

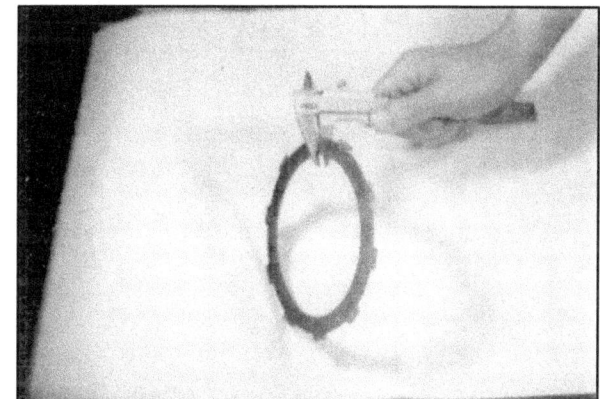

Fig. 59 Checking friction plate

7. TRANSMISSION

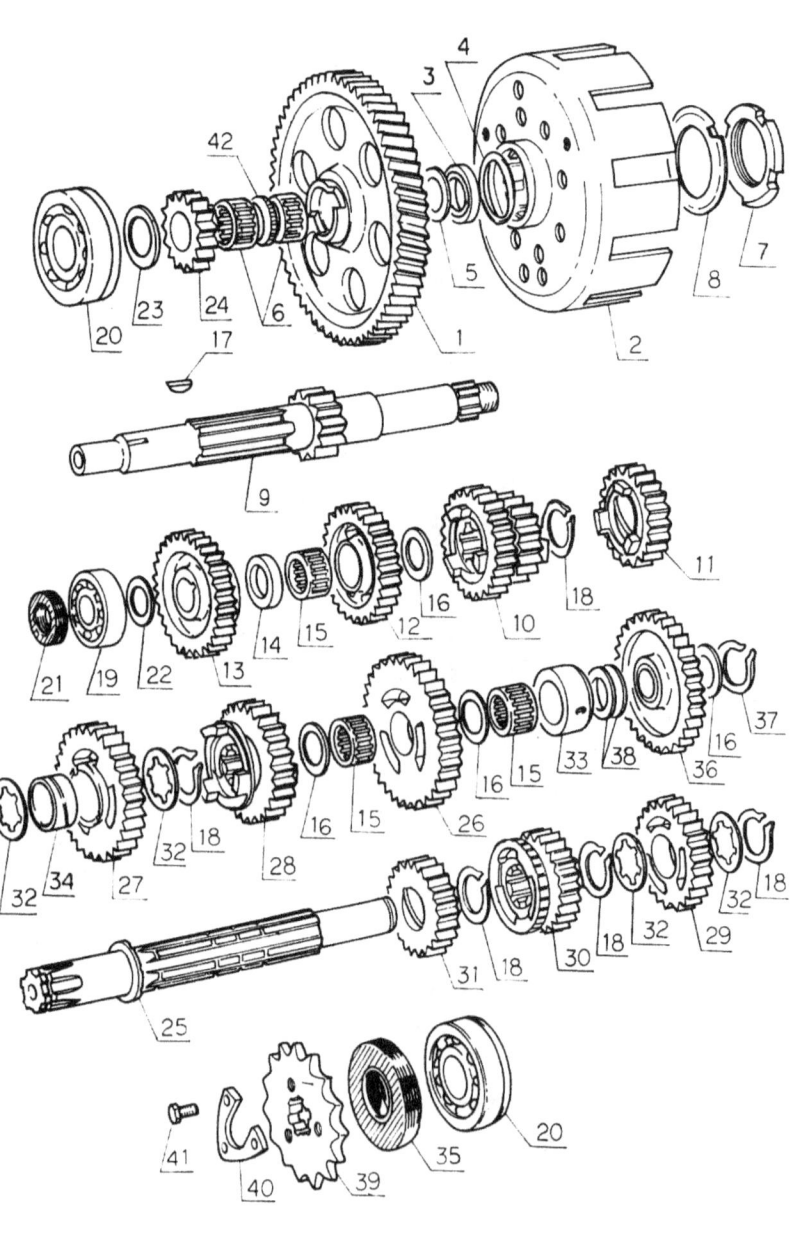

Components part of gear box

No.	Part Name	No. Req'd
1	Driven gear	1
2	Clutch housing	1
3	22 oil seal	1
4	35 O ring	1
5	22 thrust washer	1
6	Needle bearing	2
7	40 ring nut	1
8	40 lock washer	1
9	Counter shaft	1
10	2nd gear A	1
11	3nd gear A	1
12	5th gear A	1
13	6th gear A	1
14	Counter shaft spacer	1
15	Needle bearing	3
16	20 thrust washer	4
17	3×15 woodruff key	1
18	25 B snap ring	5
19	Ball bearing	1
20	Ball bearing	2
21	17 oil seal	1
22	17 thrust washer	1
23	22 thrust washer	1
24	Kick starter gear A	1
25	Drive shaft	1
26	1st gear B	1
27	2nd gear B	1
28	3rd gear B	1
29	4th gear B	1
30	5th gear B	1
31	6th gear B	1
32	25 thrust washer	4
33	Drive shaft bushing	1
34	2nd gear B bushing	1
35	25 oil seal	1
36	Kick starter gear B	1
37	20 B snap ring	1
38	20×0.3 shim	2–3
39	Drive sprocket	1
40	Sprocket set plate	1
41	Hexagon bolt A	3
42	Needle bearing spacer	1

A. Construction

350 GTR has 6 speeds return-change transmission.
(Fig. 60, 61)

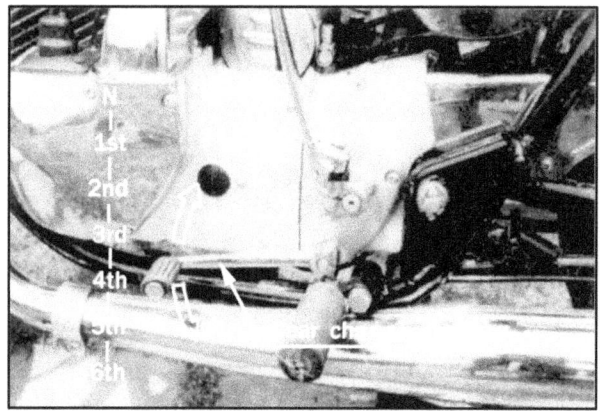

Fig. 60 Foot shift lever

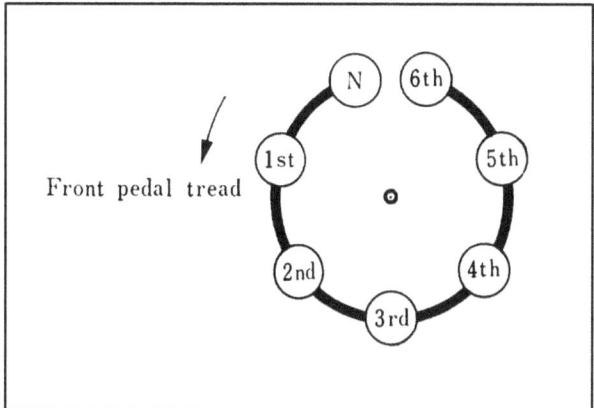

Fig. 61 Return-change transmission

B. Operation

When the gear shift pedal is depressed, the shift drum is turned by the shifter of change arm fixed on the gear change shaft.

Three shifting forks are fitted to the shift drum and travel along three grooves on the drum when it turns.

The gear shifting forks move the gears on the countershaft and drive shaft.

The operating angle of the gear shift pedal is 12 degrees and the gear shift drum turns 51 and a half degrees for each gear change.

C. Component parts of gear change pedal & shift drum

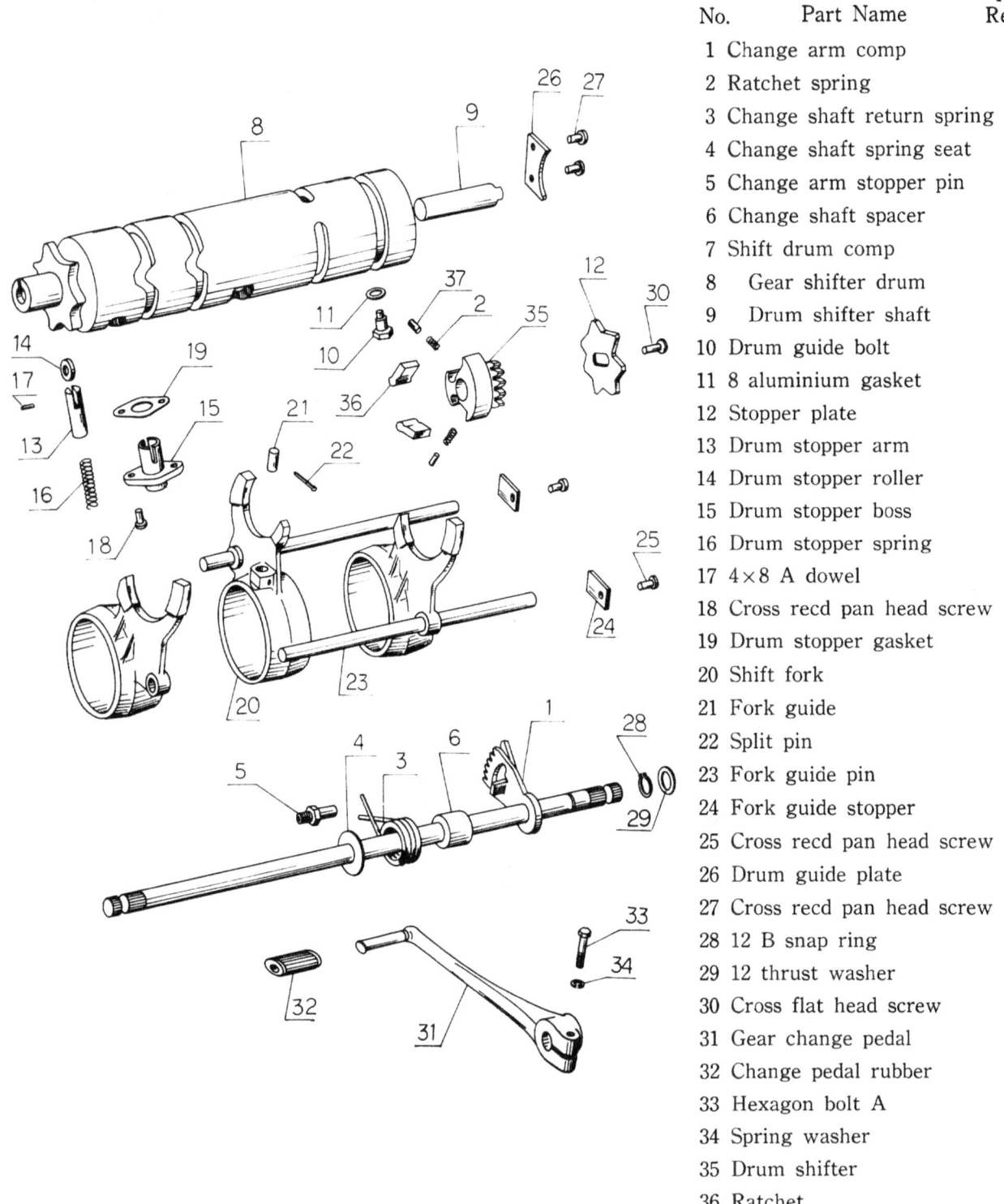

No.	Part Name	No. Req'd
1	Change arm comp	1
2	Ratchet spring	2
3	Change shaft return spring	1
4	Change shaft spring seat	1
5	Change arm stopper pin	1
6	Change shaft spacer	1
7	Shift drum comp	1
8	Gear shifter drum	1
9	Drum shifter shaft	1
10	Drum guide bolt	1
11	8 aluminium gasket	1
12	Stopper plate	1
13	Drum stopper arm	1
14	Drum stopper roller	1
15	Drum stopper boss	1
16	Drum stopper spring	1
17	4×8 A dowel	1
18	Cross recd pan head screw	2
19	Drum stopper gasket	1
20	Shift fork	3
21	Fork guide	3
22	Split pin	3
23	Fork guide pin	2
24	Fork guide stopper	2
25	Cross recd pan head screw	2
26	Drum guide plate	1
27	Cross recd pan head screw	2
28	12 B snap ring	1
29	12 thrust washer	1
30	Cross flat head screw	1
31	Gear change pedal	1
32	Change pedal rubber	1
33	Hexagon bolt A	1
34	Spring washer	1
35	Drum shifter	1
36	Ratchet	2
37	Ratchet pole	2

D. Gear shift mechanism

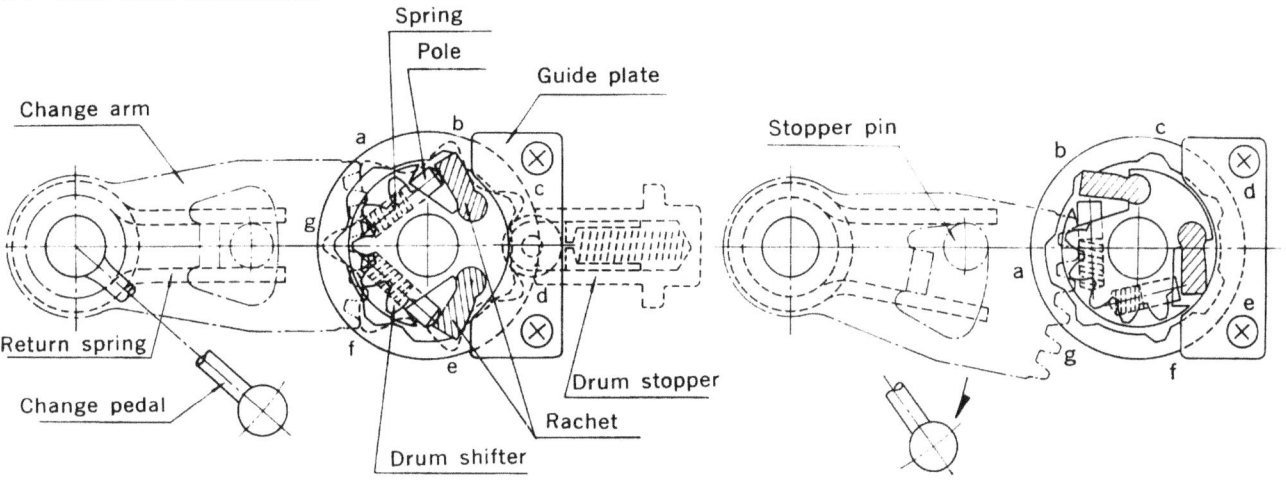

Fig. 62

Fig. 63 Operation of shift pedal pushed-down

C-1. Neutral gear position. (Fig. 62)

C-2. Operation of shift pedal pushed-down. (Fig. 63)

C-3. Operation of shift pedal lifted-up. (Fig. 64)

C-4. Operation of change arm stopper plate. (Fig. 65-1, 2)

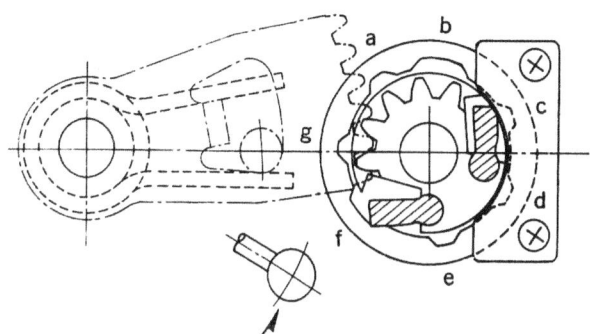

Fig. 64 Shift pedal lifted-up

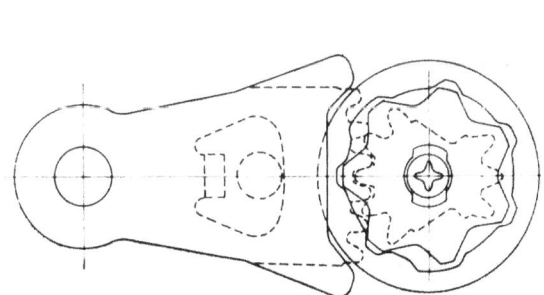

Fig. 65-1 Stopper plate

* To avoid missed gear shifting caused by excessive turning of the drum by inertia weight of the drum, the change arm stopper mechanism is equipped on 350 GTR.

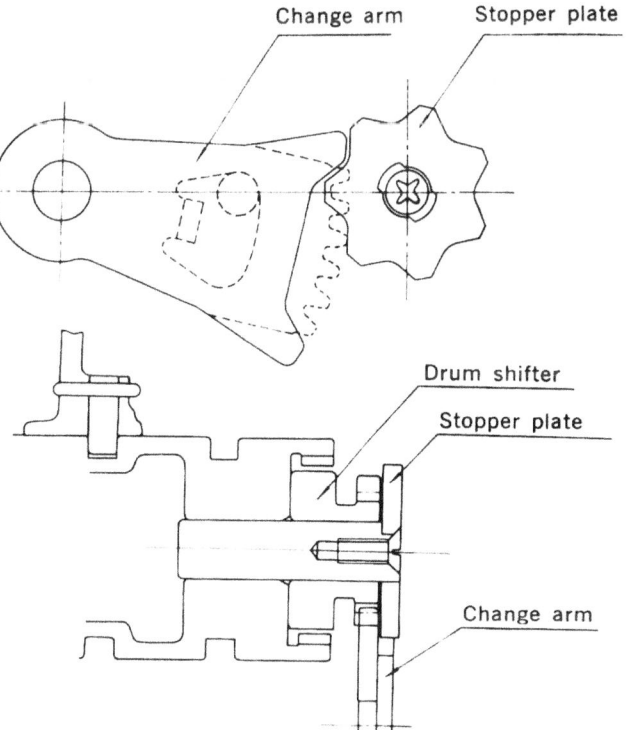

Fig. 65-2 Operation of charge arm stopper plate

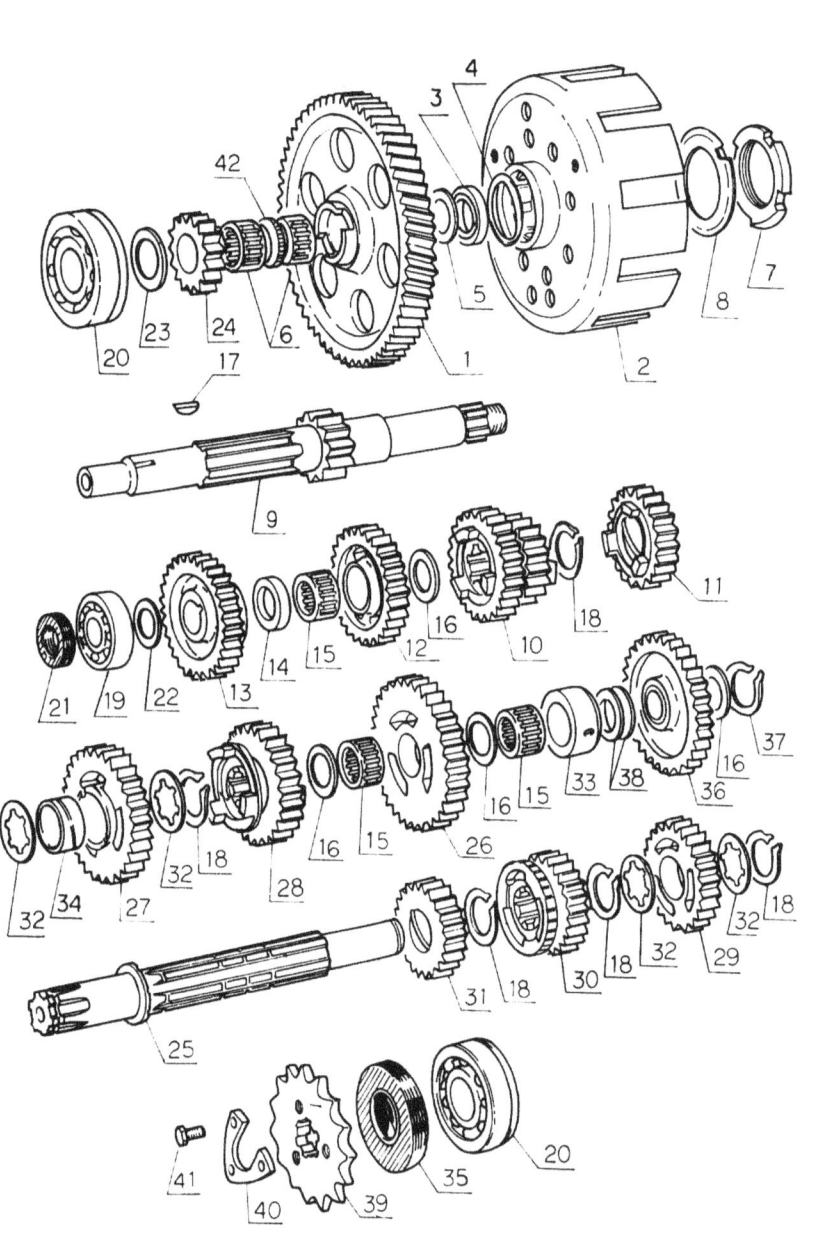

Components part of gear box

No.	Part Name	No. Req'd
1	Driven gear	1
2	Clutch housing	1
3	22 oil seal	1
4	35 O ring	1
5	22 thrust washer	1
6	Needle bearing	2
7	40 ring nut	1
8	40 lock washer	1
9	Counter shaft	1
10	2nd gear A	1
11	3nd gear A	1
12	5th gear A	1
13	6th gear A	1
14	Counter shaft spacer	1
15	Needle bearing	3
16	20 thrust washer	4
17	3×15 woodruff key	1
18	25 B snap ring	5
19	Ball bearing	1
20	Ball bearing	2
21	17 oil seal	1
22	17 thrust washer	1
23	22 thrust washer	1
24	Kick starter gear A	1
25	Drive shaft	1
26	1st gear B	1
27	2nd gear B	1
28	3rd gear B	1
29	4th gear B	1
30	5th gear B	1
31	6th gear B	1
32	25 thrust washer	4
33	Drive shaft bushing	1
34	2nd gear B bushing	1
35	25 oil seal	1
36	Kick starter gear B	1
37	20 B snap ring	1
38	20×0.3 shim	2-3
39	Drive sprocket	1
40	Sprocket set plate	1
41	Hexagon bolt A	3
42	Needle bearing spacer	1

E. Gear operation and gear ratios

1. Transmission Mechanism in Neutral Gear (Fig. 66)

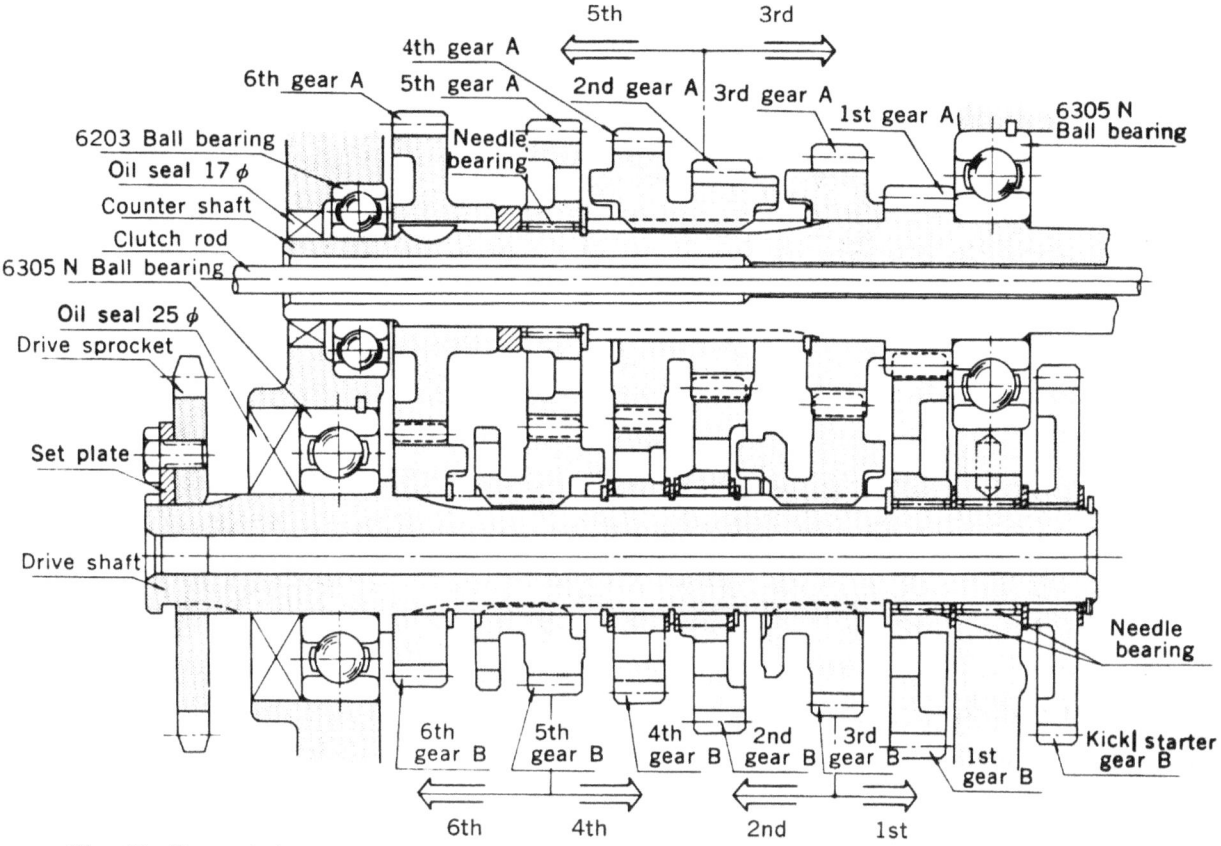

Fig. 66 Transmission

2. Gear ratios

Kinds of gears	Number of teeth		Transmission Gear Ratio
	"A" Gears Train (Countershaft)	"B" Gears Train (Driveshaft)	
1st gear (Low gear)	13	32	2.46
2nd gear	17	28	1.65
3rd gear	20	25	1.25
4th gear	23	23	1.00
5th gear	27	23	0.85
6th gear	29	22	0.76

3. Operation

The counter shaft and 1st gear A act as a unit. 2nd gear A and 4th gear A act as a unit and are spline fitted on the countershaft, and slide both way on the countershaft spline.

3rd gear A and 5th gear A turn freely on the countershaft.

6th gear A is knocked with woodruf key on the countershaft.

1st gear B, 2nd gear B, 4th gear B and 6th gear B turn freely on the driveshaft. 3rd gear B and 5th gear B are spline fitted on the driveshaft.

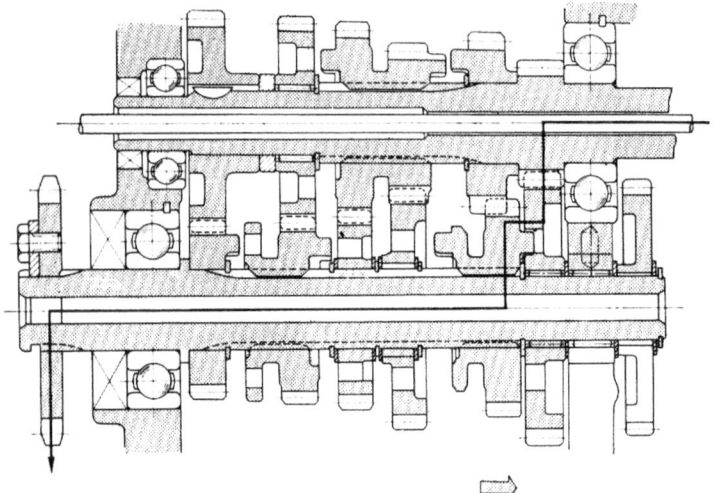

Fig. 67 In 1st gear position

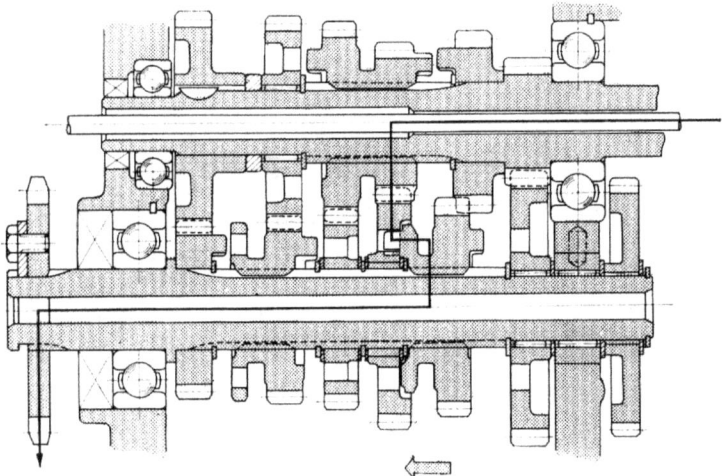

Fig. 68 In 2nd gear position

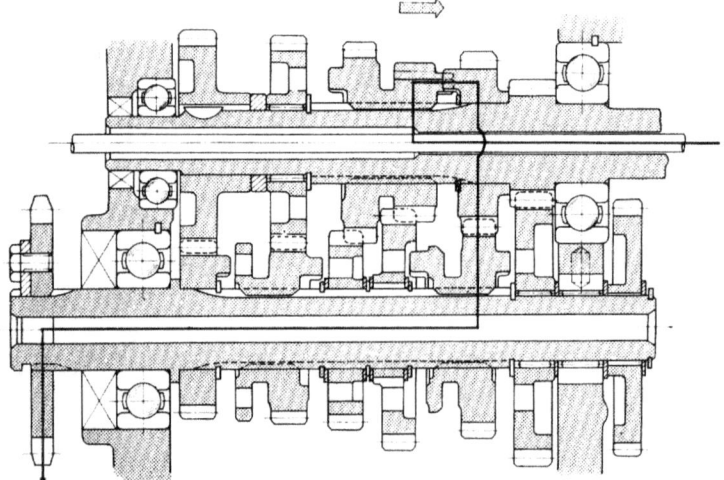

Fig. 69 In 3rd gear position

1st gear:

With the gears on the counter shaft remaining in position, the 3rd gear B on the drive shaft slides to the right and the claws on this gear engage with the 1st gear B.

● Engine power is transmitted in the order of driven gear—clutch—countershaft—First gear A—First gear B—3rd gear B—driveshaft and drive sprocket. (Fig. 67)

2nd gear:

With the 2nd gear A remaining in position, the 3rd gear B slides to the left and the claws on this gear engage with the 2nd gear B.

● Engine power is transmitted in the order of driven gear—clutch—countershaft—2nd gear A—2nd gear B—3rd gear B—driveshaft and drive sprocket. (Fig. 68)

3rd gear:

With the 3rd gear B on the drive shaft remaining in position, the 2nd gear A slides to the right and the claws on this gear engages with claws on the 3rd gear A.

● Engine power is transmitted in the order of driven gear—clutch—countershaft—2nd gear A—3rd gear A—3rd gear B—driveshaft and drive sprocket. (Fig. 69)

4th gear:

With the 4th gear A remaining in position, the 5th gear B slides to the right and the claws on this gear engages with the 4th gear B.
- Engine power is transmitted in the order of driven gear—clutch—countershaft—4th gear A—4th gear B—5th gear B—driveshaft and drive sprocket. (Fig. 70)

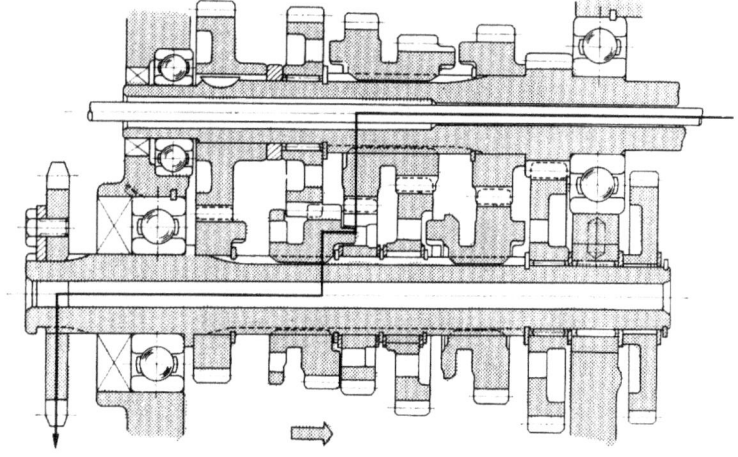

Fig. 70 In 4th gear position

5th gear:

With the 5th gear B remaining in position, 4th gear A slides to the left and the claw on this gear engages with the 5th gear A.
- Engine power is transmitted in the order of driven gear—clutch—countershaft—4th gear A—5th gear A—5th gear B—driveshaft and drive sprocket. (Fig. 71)

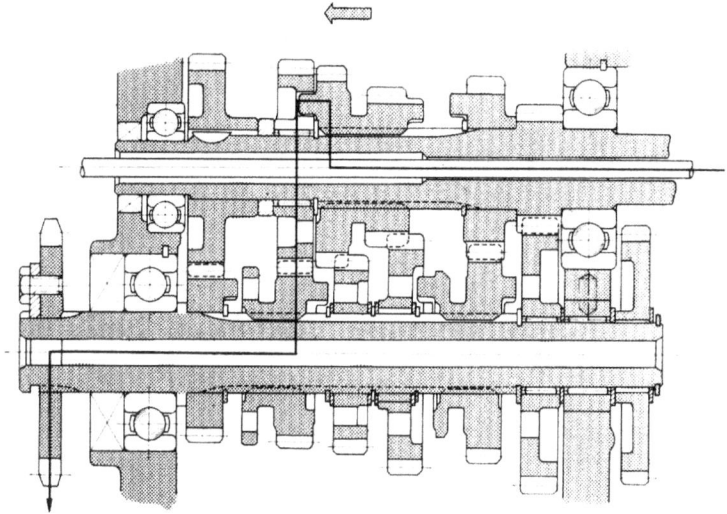

Fig. 71 In 5th gear position

6th gear:

With the 6th gear A remaining in position, 5th gear B slides to the left and engages with the claws on the 6th gear B.
- Engine power is transmitted in the order of driven gear—clutch—countershaft—6th gear A—6th gear B—5th gear B—driveshaft and drive sprocket. (Fig. 72)

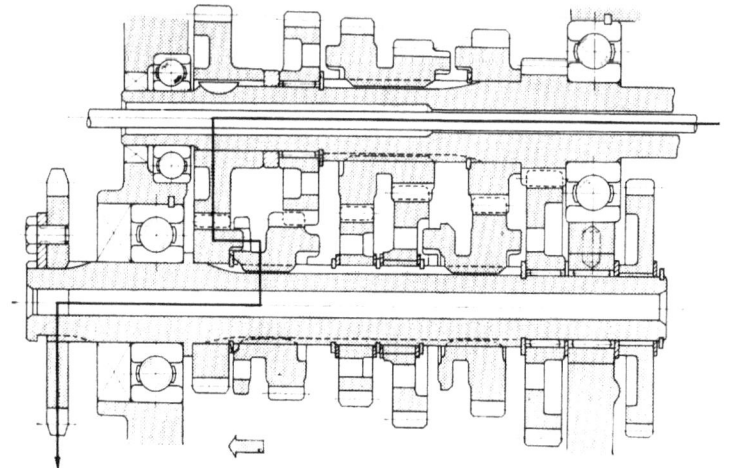

Fig. 72 In 6th gear position

F. Inspection:

1. Check for worn or damaged gears, splines, bearings and shafts.
2. Inspect shift fork and drum grooves.
3. Check for worn of change arm, ratchet and drum shifter spring.

8. KICK STARTER

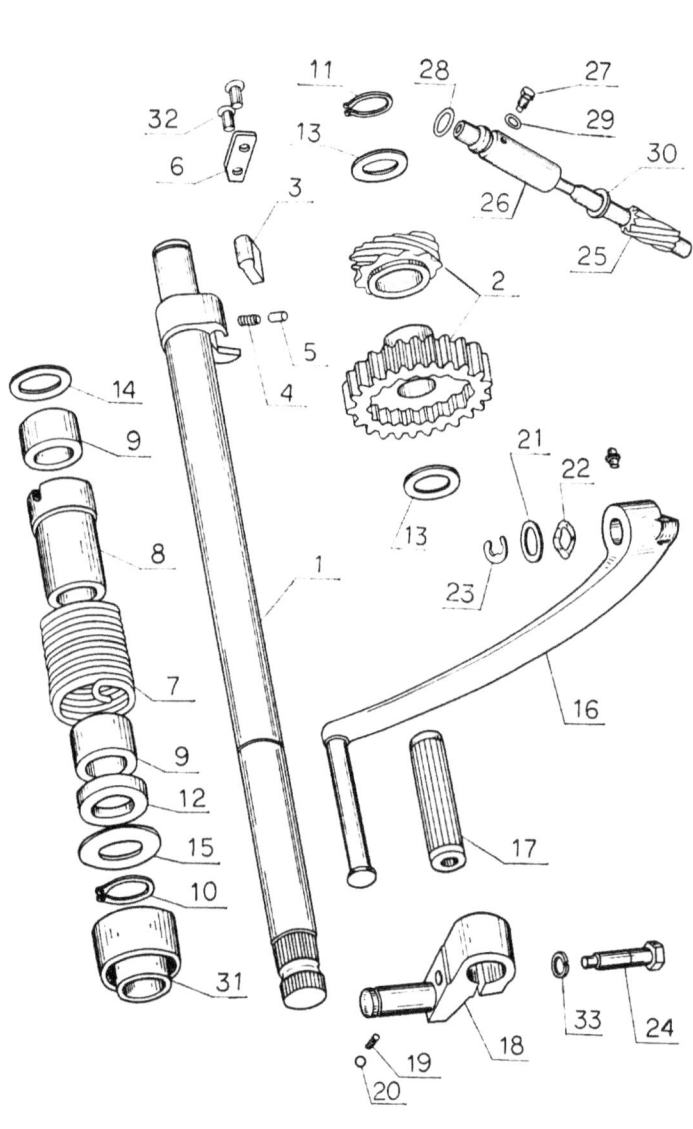

Component parts of kick starter

No.	Part Name	No. Req'd
1	Kick starter shaft	1
2	Kick gear C comp.	1
3	Ratchet	1
4	Ratchet spring	1
5	Ratchet pole	1
6	Kick starter ratchet stopper	1
7	Kick starter return spring	1
8	Return spring spacer	1
9	Kick starter shaft bush	2
10	18 B snap ring	1
11	15 F snap ring	1
12	18 oil seal	1
13	15 thrust washer	2
14	18 thrust washer	1
15	Plane washer A	1
	Kick starter arm assy	1
16	Kick starter arm	1
17	Kick starter pedal rubber	1
18	Kick starter arm boss	1
19	Kick starter set spring	1
20	Ball	2
21	15 plane washer	1
22	15 wave washer	1
23	10 D snap ring	1
24	Kick starter shaft bolt	1
25	Tachometer gear B	1
26	Tachometer gear bush	1
27	Tachometer bush bolt	1
28	12 O ring	1
29	6 fiber gasket	1
30	8 thrust washer	1
31	Chain guide	1
32	Cross rec'd round head screw	2
33	Spring washer	2

A. Construction:

A primary kick starter system such as installed on other Bridgestone models is used on the Bridgestone 350 GTR. As the kick starter does not operate through the clutch, the engine can be started even when the transmission gears are engaged, by simply pulling in the cluch lever. This is a very convenient system which has earned a good reputation and eliminates the need for finding neutral position, thus allowing quick starting of the engine. In the case of conventional kick starter, the kick gear engages with one of the transmission gears, but, with the primary type kick starter, three kick starter gears are installed independently in the transmission gear box. (Fig. 73)

B. Operation:

B-1 To start:

1. Kick shaft and rachet arm turn counterclockwise as shown in Fig. 74 and ratchet turns counter clockwise, resulting from the pressure of ratchet spring, and meshes with the kick gear. (Fig. 74)
2. Ratchet which is in mesh, turns kick gear clockwise.
3. Since kick gear is always in mesh with kick gear A & B, the force created by turning the kick shaft is transmitted from kick starter gear B, kick starter gear A, driven gear and pinion gear, to the crankshaft, and starts the engine.
4. When the kick shaft is released, it is returned to its original position by the return spring and ratchet is released automatically from the kick gear, and the kick gear rorates freely.

B-2 In cruising.

Ratchet arm is turned counter clockwise by the kick return spring, and ratchet and kick gear are held apart. (Fig. 75)

C. Inspection

Check for worn or damaged gears, kick return spring and ratchet.

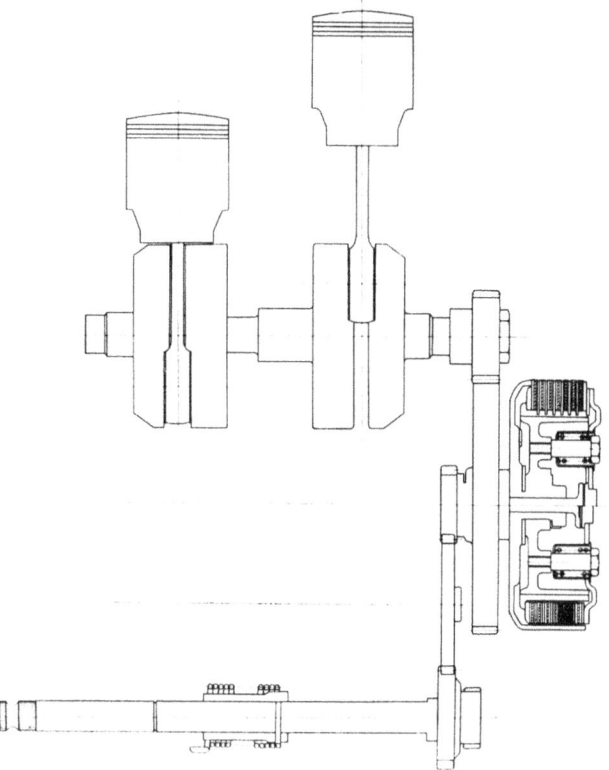

Fig. 73 Construction

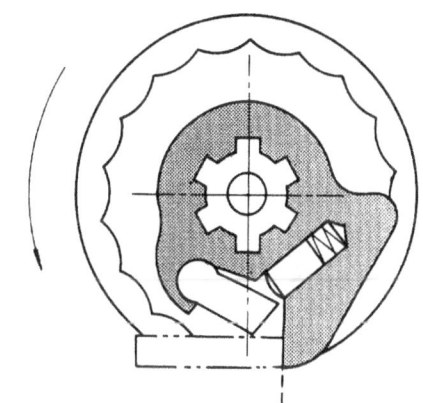

Fig. 74 In kicking position

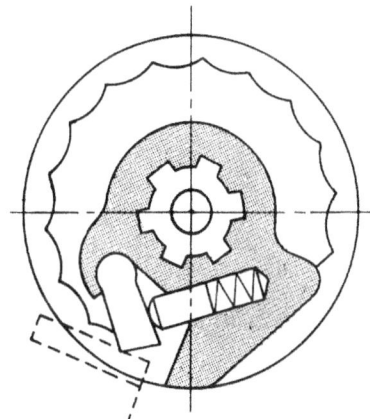

Fig. 75 In cruising position

9. CARBURETORS

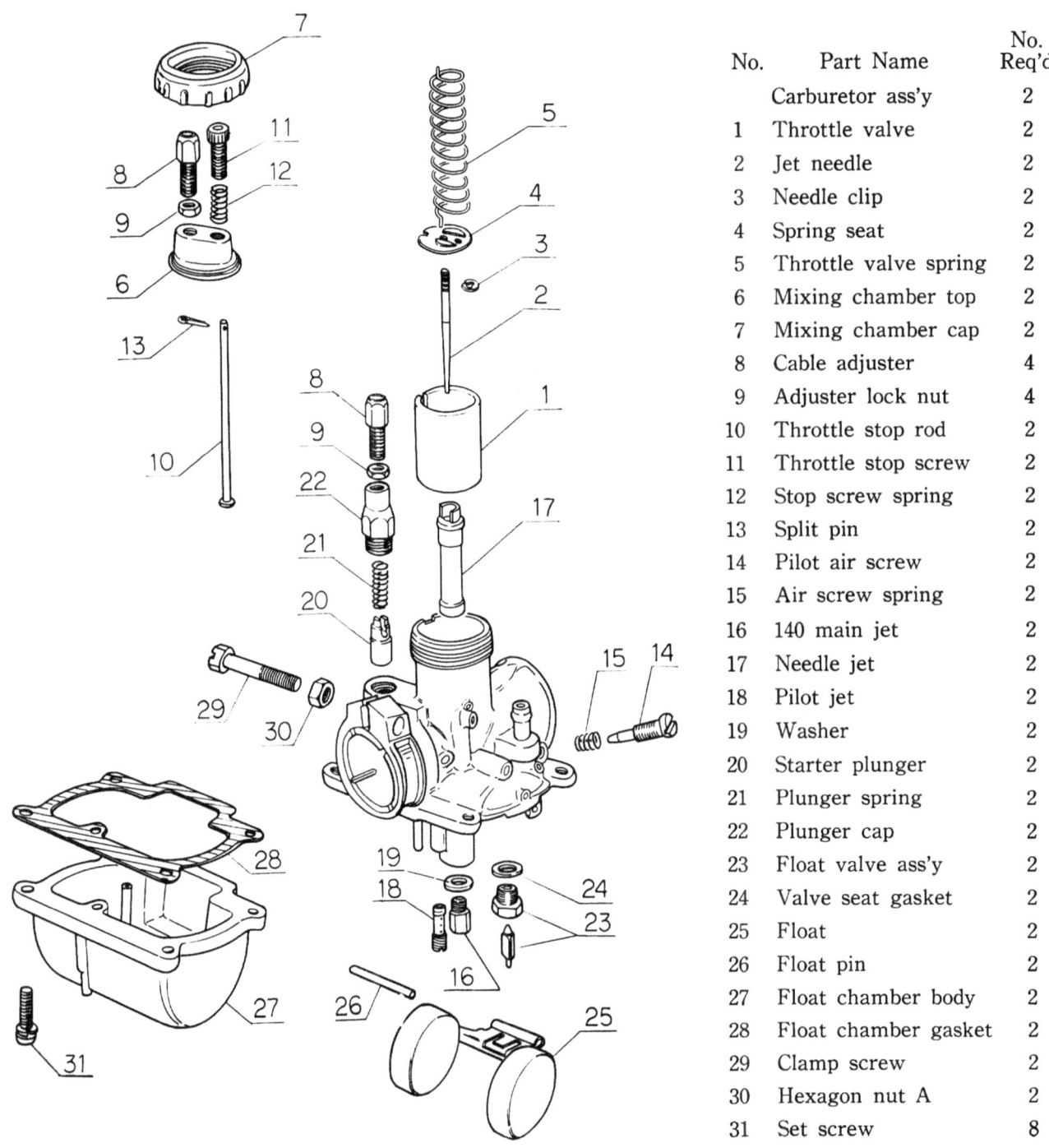

No.	Part Name	No. Req'd
	Carburetor ass'y	2
1	Throttle valve	2
2	Jet needle	2
3	Needle clip	2
4	Spring seat	2
5	Throttle valve spring	2
6	Mixing chamber top	2
7	Mixing chamber cap	2
8	Cable adjuster	4
9	Adjuster lock nut	4
10	Throttle stop rod	2
11	Throttle stop screw	2
12	Stop screw spring	2
13	Split pin	2
14	Pilot air screw	2
15	Air screw spring	2
16	140 main jet	2
17	Needle jet	2
18	Pilot jet	2
19	Washer	2
20	Starter plunger	2
21	Plunger spring	2
22	Plunger cap	2
23	Float valve ass'y	2
24	Valve seat gasket	2
25	Float	2
26	Float pin	2
27	Float chamber body	2
28	Float chamber gasket	2
29	Clamp screw	2
30	Hexagon nut A	2
31	Set screw	8

Component parts of carburetor

A. Synchronizing Carburetors

Opening the throttle grip slightly, match the mark "O" on both throttle valves with the top center line of ventilator of carburetor by adjusting throttle valve adjusters. (Fig. 76)

B. Indication of trouble at various engine speeds.

Indication of Too Rich Mixture

1. Engine speed fluctuates
2. Engine dose not run smoothly when starter lever is used.
3. Engine does not run smoothly after warming up
4. Spark plugs are apt to foul
5. Engine runs smoothly when carburetor cover is removed
6. Exhaust fumes are white or grey

Indication of Too Lean Mixture

1. Engine overheats
2. Engine runs smoothly when starter is used
3. Engine does not run smoothly when engine is cool
4. Spark plugs are apt to heat or burn
5. Engine runs smoothly when carburetor is choked
6. Exhaust fumes are light blue or colorless

C. Idling Adjustment (0-1/8 Throttle opening)

1. When the engine stops at engine idling speed, turn the slow adjuster on both carburetor until the engine runs smoothly while controlling engine speed with the throttle grip. (Fig. 77)
2. Turn the pilot air screws on the carburetors alternately.
   Both screws must be turned an equal amount. Set the screws at the point where the engine runs the most smoothly
   * When the pilot air screw is turned clockwise, the gasoline/air mixture becomes leaner and when it is turned counterclockwise the mixture becomes rich. Correct adjustment is 2 turns back. (Fig. 78)

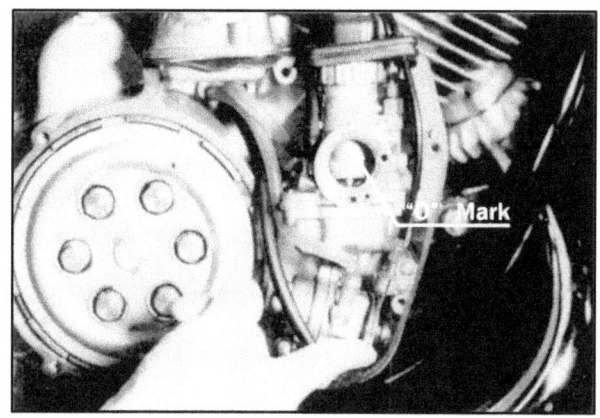

Fig. 76 Adjusting throttle valve

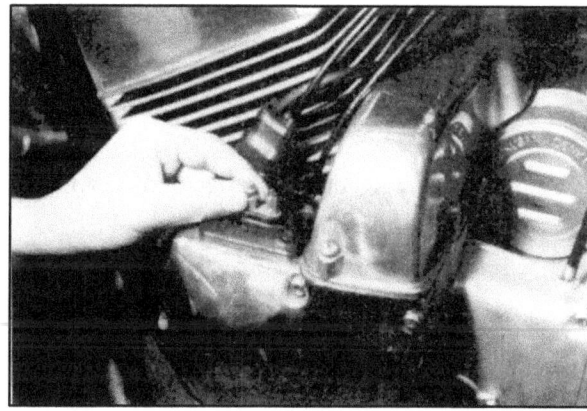

Fig. 77 Idling adjustment

Fig. 78 Pilot air screw adjustment

3. Regarding the setting of the pilot air screw, a fairly satisfactory method is to detach one spark plug, and set the air screw on the carburetor of the other cylinder, and reversing the process to the other cylinder.

   It may be found that when both spark plug are fitted, the engine runs slightly quicker than desirable, in which case, a slight readjustment of the throttle screw will put this right.

4. Trouble shooting

Possible causes	Remedies
1) Pilot air hole or breezer hole of pilot jet is checked	Clean and blow these holes
2) Loosening pilot jet	Set pilot jet securely
3) Starter plunger does not set in position when starter lever is not used.	Adjust starter cable to set plunger completely
4) The opening of pilot air screw is too small.	Adjust the turning of air screw. Correct adjustment is 2 turns back.

D. Medium Engine Speed Adjustment (1/8~3/4 throttle opening)

1. The gasoline/air mixture can be adjusted by raising or lowering the jet needle at 1/8~3/4 throttle opening for medium engine speed. Therefore, it is recommended to adjust jet needle within the range where acceleration is not adversely affected.

2. Trouble shooting

Possible causes	Remedies
1) Clogged main jet or needle jet	Clean
2) Loose fitting of needle jet or main jet	Screw in securely
3) Worn needle jet	Replace it with new one
4) Incorrect adjusment of needle jet position	Raise the jet needle when mixture is too lean and lower it when mixture is too rich. Standard jet needle position is in the third groove.

E. High Engine Speed Adjustment

1. The gasoline/air mixture can be adjusted by the main jet at 3/4 full throttle opening.
2. Trouble shooting

Possible causes	Remedies
1) Clogged needle jet hole	Clean
2) Loose fitting of needle jet or main jet	Screw in securely
3) Incorrect main jet size	Use a bigger main jet when mixture is too lean and a small one when mixture is too rich. Standard main jet is No. 140.

Caution: The main jet size should be decided considering the climate or temperature.

F. Adjustment of Carbureter Float Level

1. Check the float level as follows, because the float level affects the gas/air mixture sensitively.
   * Gas/air mixture becomes rich at high float level, and lean at low level.
2. Adjustment

    Dismount carburetor, detach float chamber body and hold mixing body upside down to the position where needle valve contacts the float arm. (Fig. 79)

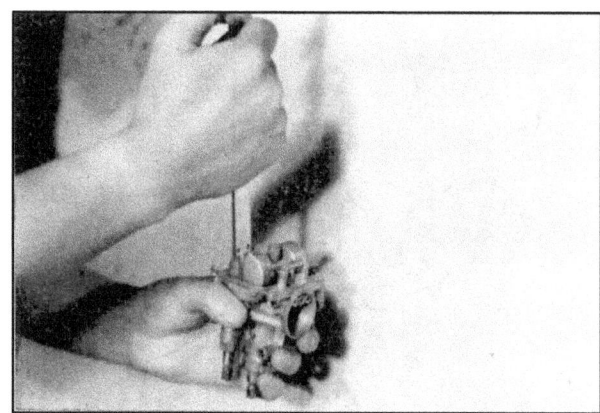

Fig. 79 Measuring float level

G. Trouble Shooting of Gasoline Leakage from Carburetor

Possible causes	Main causes of trouble	Remedies
Gas oozes out	Inadequate contact between needle valve and valve seat	Replace needle valve and valve seat with a new one.
Gas overflows at any time (even cruising or stopping)	Punctured or deformed float.	Replace the float with a new one.
Gas leakage occasionally	1. Operation of float or needle spring is not correct. 2. Clogged needle valve and valve seat with dirt.	Adjust float or replace needle valve with a new one. Clean needle valve or valve seat. Clean fuel cock bowl.

10. OIL INJECTION SYSTEM:

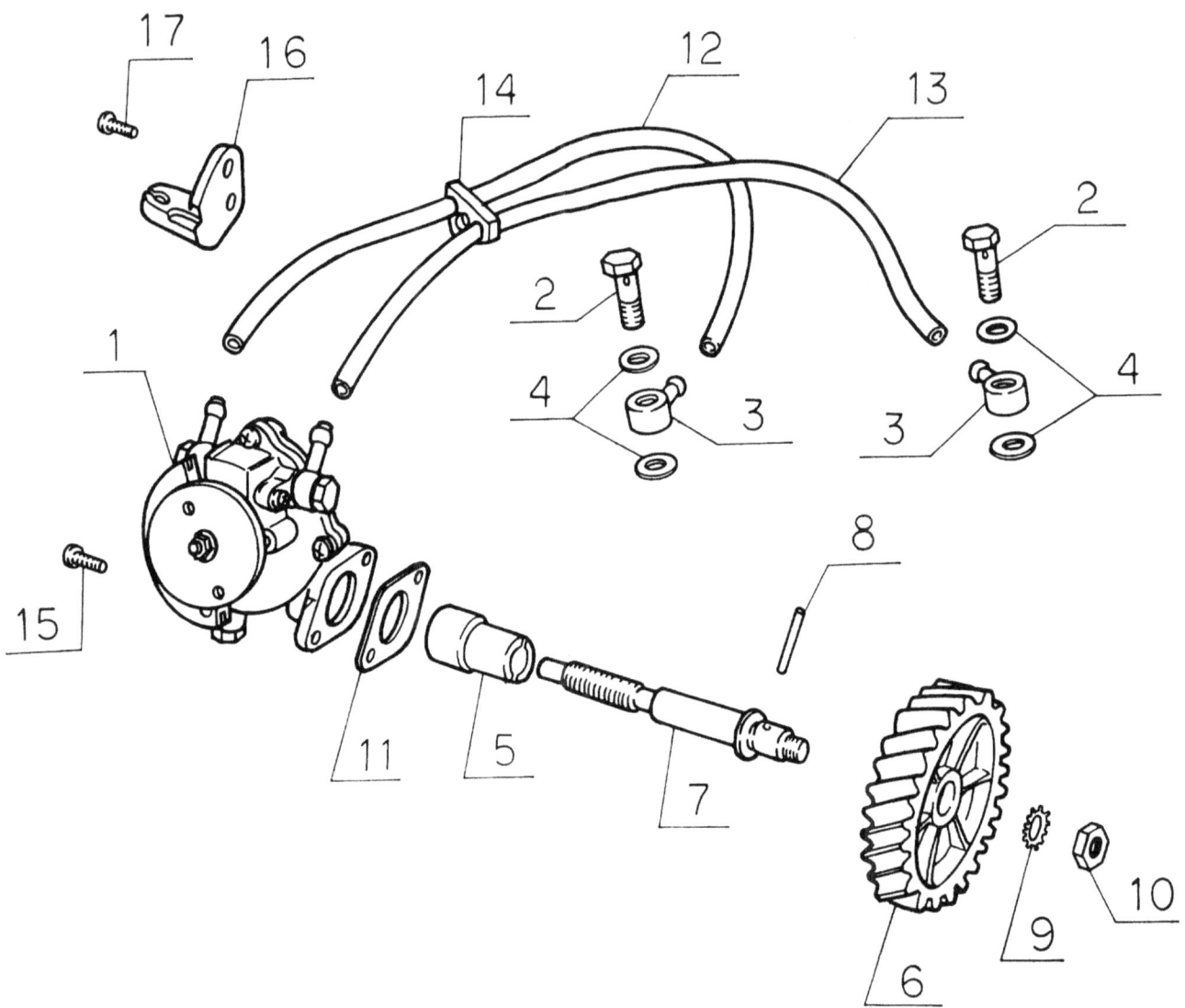

Component parts of oil injection system

No.	Part Name	No. Req'd	No.	Part Name	No. Req'd
1	Oil pump assy	1	10	Hexagon nut C	1
2	Check valve assy	2	11	Pump gasket	1
3	Union connection C	2	12	Oil tube A	1
4	8 Aluminium gasket	4	13	Oil tube B	1
5	Worm shaft bush B	1	14	Oil tube grommet	1
6	Pump gear B	1	15	Cross recd pan head screw	2
7	Worm shaft	1	16	Wire bracket	1
8	3×24 A dowel	1	17	Cross recd pan head screw	2
9	External toothed washer	1			

On 350 GTR, the oil injection mechanism, which precludes the necessity of pre-mixing gasoline and oil, inject lubricating oil direct to crankshaft bearings and other parts. (Fig. 80)

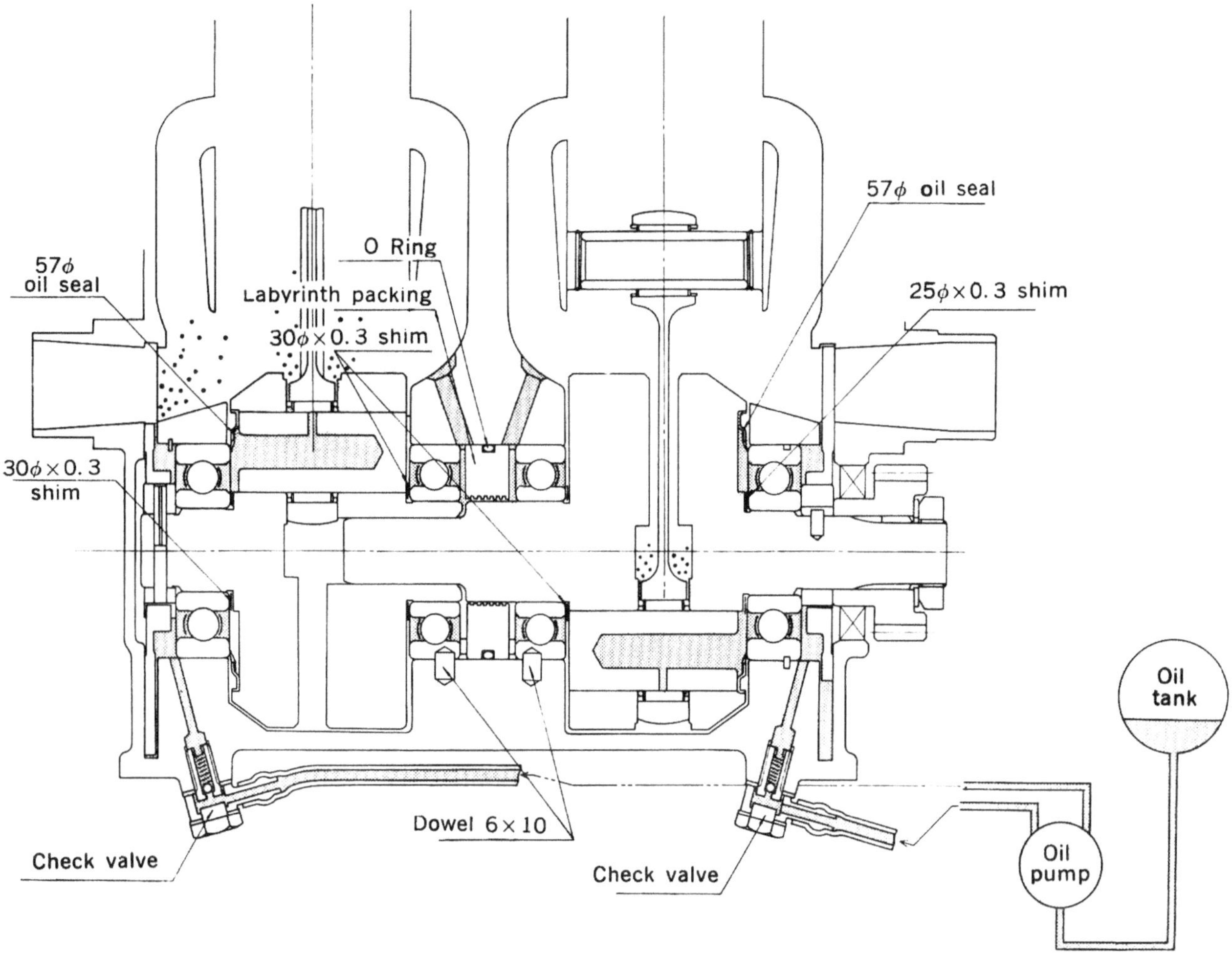

Fig. 80 Oil injection system

A. Operation

The worm wheel of pump is driven through Crankshaft→Driven pinion→Pump gear B.

The worm wheel, the boss of which is cam shaped, is pushed in direction A by the plunger spring and contacts the rod (c) as shown in (Fig. 81)

The worm wheel plunger slides both ways, following the cam height.

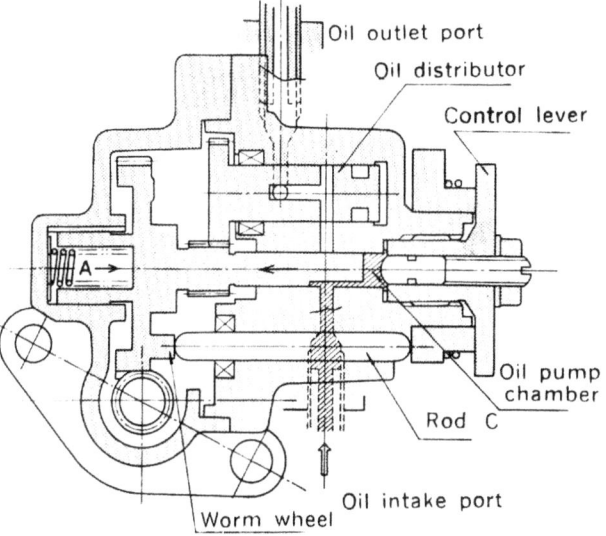

Fig. 81 Operation

B. Oil Intake:

When the worm wheel contacts rod at the highest point of the cam the volume of the pump chamber increases and the pressure in the chamber decreases. The inlet port opens and oil is sucked into the oil pump chamber. (Fig. 82-1, 2, 3)

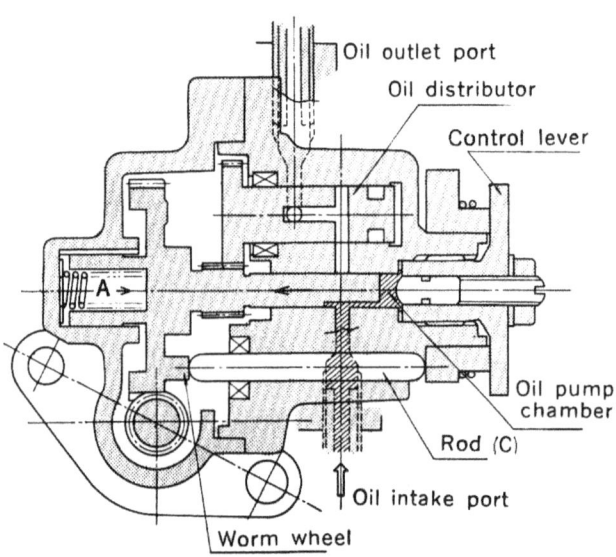

Fig. 82-1 Oil intake

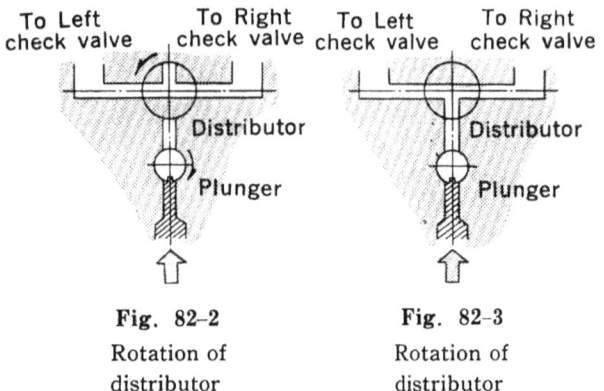

Fig. 82-2 Rotation of distributor

Fig. 82-3 Rotation of distributor

C. Oil Outlet:

When the worm wheel plunger slides in the direction A and contacts the rod at the lowest point of the cam, the pump chamber volume decreases, therefore oil is forced into the outlet port. (Fig. 83)

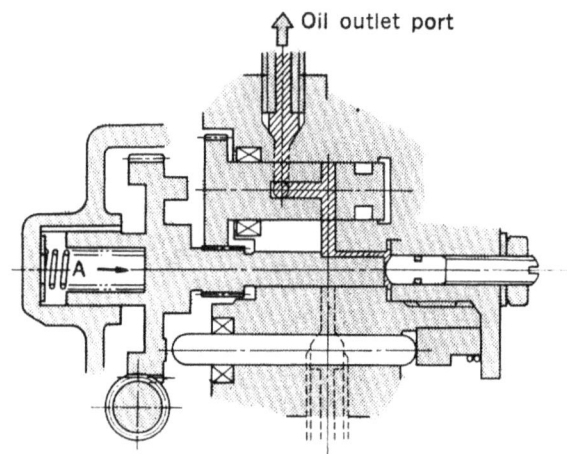

Fig. 83 Oil outlet

D. Distribution of oil to both cylinders

The rotation of distributor shaft is one half of that of worm wheel plunger and the distributor shaft has oil passage holes as shown in Fig. 84, therefore oil flows to each cylinder alternately. (Fig. 84-1, 2)

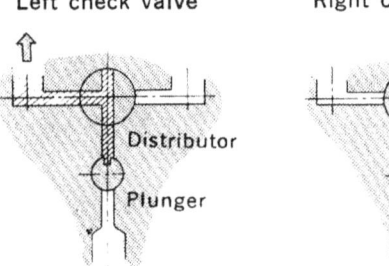

Fig. 84-1 Distribution of oil to left check valve

Fig. 84-2 Distribution of oil to right check valve

E. Operation of worm wheel plunger in relation to the throttle grip:

F-1 Engine Idling at slow speed

When the throttle grip is in zero position, i.e. throttle grip is in closed position, the rod contacts the control lever at its lowest position.

The worm wheel plunger slides to the right by spring tension and the plunger contacts the adjust screw before it contacts the rod. When the cam height is at the lowest point, plunger contacts the rod instead of adjust screw.

The distance of shift of the plunger to the adjust screw (D) is shortened to less than the height of the worm wheel cam, thereby reducing the volume of oil. (Fig. 85, 86)

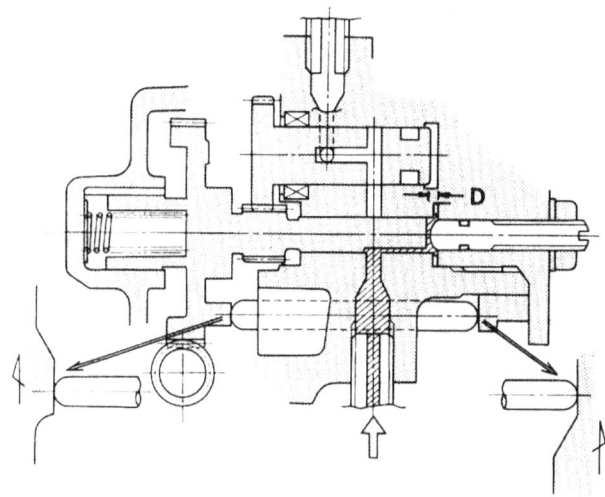

Fig. 85 Oil intake at the throttle grip is in zero position

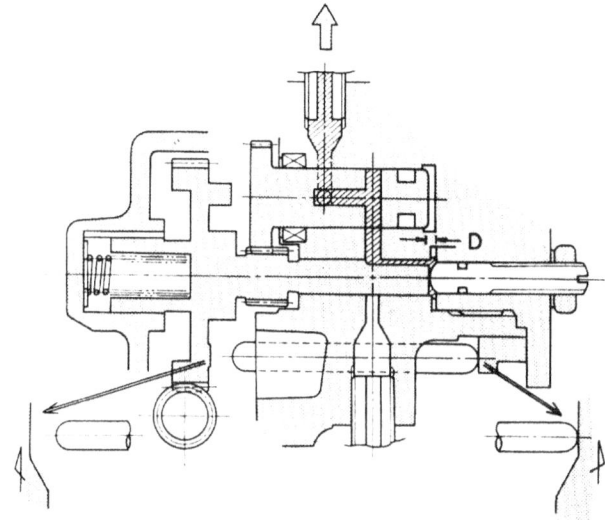

Fig. 86 Oil outlet at the throttle grip is in zero position

F-2. High Speed, wide open throttle

When the throttle grip is wide open, the cam of the control lever contacts the rod (c) at its highest point, thereby shifting the rod (c) to the left so that the distance of shift of the plunger is lengthened, and the volume of oil is increased. (Fig. 87, 88)

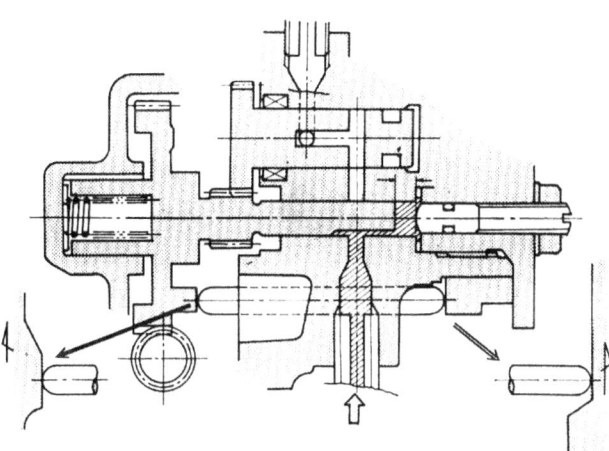

Fig. 87 Oil intake at the throttle grip is wide open

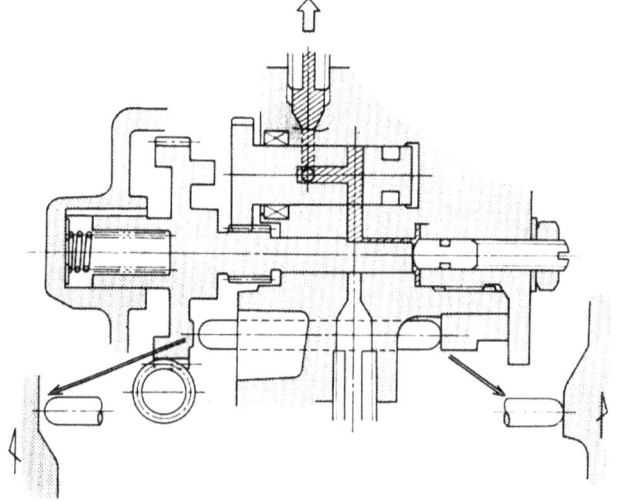

Fig. 88 Oil outlet at the throttle grip is wide open

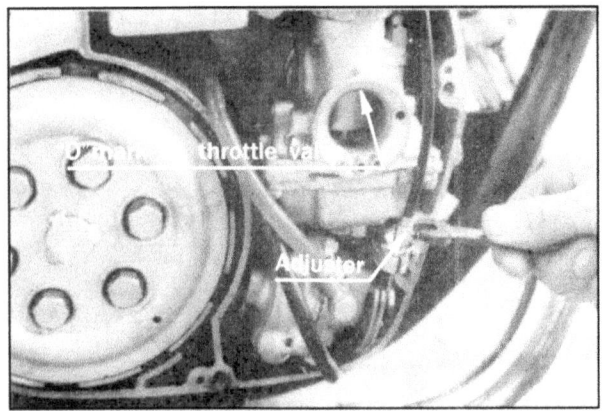

Fig. 89-1 Adjustment of oil pump wire

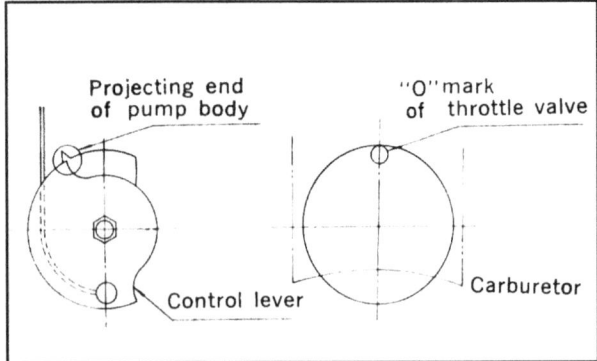

Fig. 89-2 Adjustment of oil pump

F. Adjustment of oil pump control wire

Open the throttle grip slightly, until the "O" mark of throttle valve matches the top center of ventilator of carburetor.

At this time, the edge of control lever of oil pump should match the projecting end of the oil pump body. (Fig. 89-1, 89-2)

Caution: Caution the customers, not to touch the adjusting screw because it is adjusted accurately at the factory.

Control lever is adjusted by turning the adjuster.

By turning the adjuster to left······lever is lifted up.

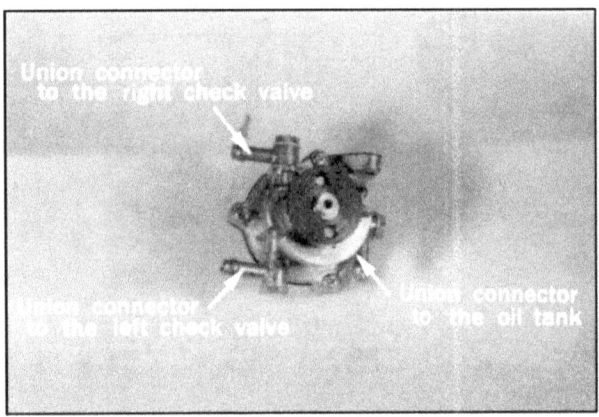

Fig. 90 Assembling the union connectors

G. Special Attention:

1. Assemble the union connectors to the pump body as shown in (Fig. 90)
2. Do not unscrew the union bolts to avoid bending the 6 mm aluminum gasket of union bolts.

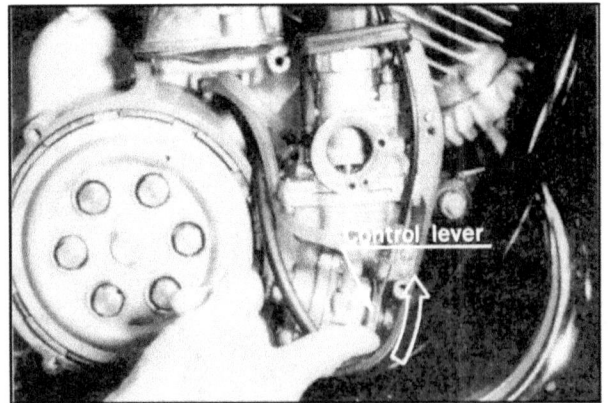

Fig. 91 Exhausting air bubbles

3. To exhaust air bubbles between oil tank and oil tube, disconnect the tube from oil pump ass'y. Then connect the tube to the pump and open control lever wide and crank the engine at idle revolution for about one minute. (Fig. 91)
4. Be sure of the position of the check balls when screwing in the check valves on crank case.

H. How to mesh the plunger gear with the distributor gear. (Fig. 92)

1. When the oil pump is disassembled, be careful to mesh the plunger gear with the distributor gear. Because the distributor gear has three oil passage holes, (Refer to Fig. 84······one hole is for oil intake, the others for lubrication of both cylinders) therefore it is necessary to match the holes of distributor with the plunger cam slot.

2. How to mesh both gears
   1) Blow air through the union connector by slowly turning the distributor gear anticlockwise.
      When air comes out from the plunger shaft hole, reverse the gear (clockwise) until the air stops coming through. (Fig. 92)
   2) Then insert the plunger shaft setting its position at shown in Fig. 93.

3. Covenient procedure
   1) Match the timing pin mark on the distributor gear with the center of the plunger shaft hole. (Fig. 92)
   2) Insert the plunger shaft by placing end of cam over the center of the distributor gear. (Fig. 94)

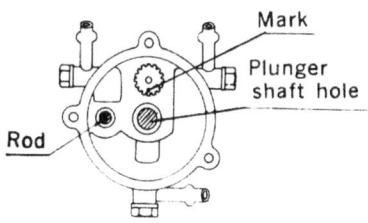

Fig. 92 Disassembled oil pump

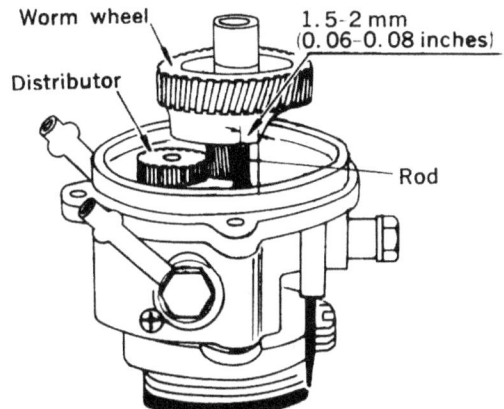

Fig. 93 Insert the plunger shaft as shown

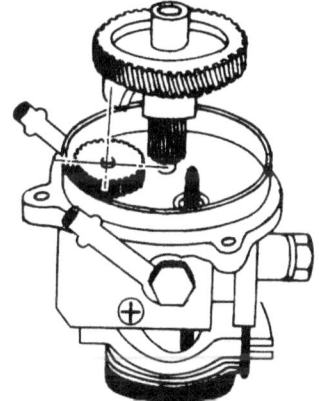

Fig. 94 Place the end of cam over the center of the distributor

11. FRAME

Component parts of frame and rear fender

No.	Part Name	No. Req'd
1	Frame comp	1
2	Rear fender comp	1
3	Hexagon bolt A	4
4	Hexagon bolt A	3
5	Hexagon nut A	4
6	Plane washer A	6
7	Plane washer A	3
8	Spring washer	2
9	Rear fender clamp	1
10	Fender mounting rubber	1
11	Outer race	2
12	Inner race	2
13	Race cap	1
14	Race lock nut	1
15	Race adjuster	1
16	Ball	38
17	Oil tank pad	1
18	Pivot shaft	1
19	14 hexagon sloted nut	1
20	15 Plane washer	1
21	Split pin	1
22	Front tank cushion rubber	2
23	Rear tank cushion rubber	1
24	Tank mounting bolt	1
25	18 Plane washer	4
26	Frame handle	1
27	Hexagon bolt A	1
28	Plane washer A	1
29	Cover pad	1
30	Tank cushion rubber	1
31	Number plate supporter	1
32	Supporter pad	3
33	Hexagon bolt	2
34	Engine cushion rubber A	2
35	Engine mounting bolt	1
36	Rear fender grommet	1
37	10×145 hexagon bolt	1
38	Hexagon nut A	6
39	Hexagon nut D	1
40	Left engine bracket	1
41	Right engine bracket	1
42	Engine cushion rubber B	4
43	Left engine hanger	1
44	Right engine hanger	1
45	10 plane washer	4
46	8 plane washer	4
47	Hexagon bolt A	4
48	Hexagon bolt A	2
49	Spring washer	2
50	Spring washer	10
51	Spring washer	3
52	10×38 hexagon bolt	2
53	Main switch bracket	1
54	Spacer A	1
55	Battery band	1
56	Battery pad	1
57	Battery seat	1

11-1 Handlebar

A. Removing Handlebar

1. Loosen clutch cable to the limit of adjusting nut and remove from clutch lever.
2. Remove adjusting nut of front brake and pull out brake lever.
3. Take off (6×45) hexagonal nut of starter lever and remove starter cable from lever.
4. Unscrew head light rim fitting screw at bottom of the rim, and disconnect wiring harness connections from terminals. (Fig. 95)
5. Take off four handle holder fitting (8×36) and remove handlebar assembly from front fork.

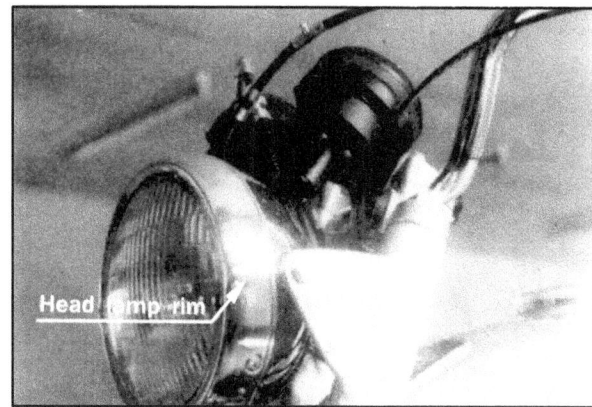

Fig. 95 Removing head light rim

B. Assembling:

Assembling is done in the reverse order of removing.

C. Inspecion:

1. Adjust clutch and brake levers properly.

   Brake lever

   Front brake lever should be so adjusted to allow a play of 15~30 mm (3/5″−1.1/4″) before the brake acts. (Fig. 96)

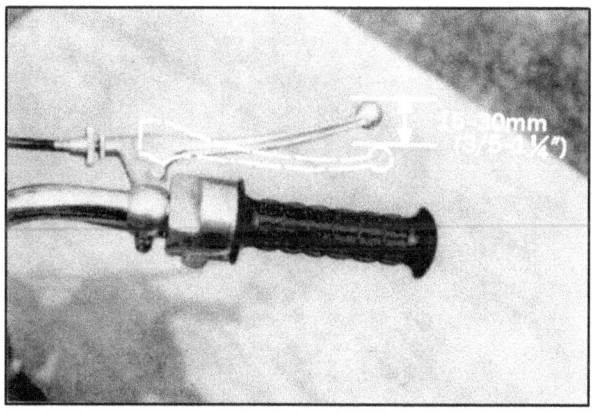

Fig. 96 Adjustment of brake lever

   Clutch lever

   When properly adjusted, there will be approximately 15~20 mm (3/5″~3/4″) free play in the clutch control before the clutch disengages. (Fig. 97)

2. Check for damaged or cracked wire in the grip holders of dimmer switch and horn switch, and replace it necessary.

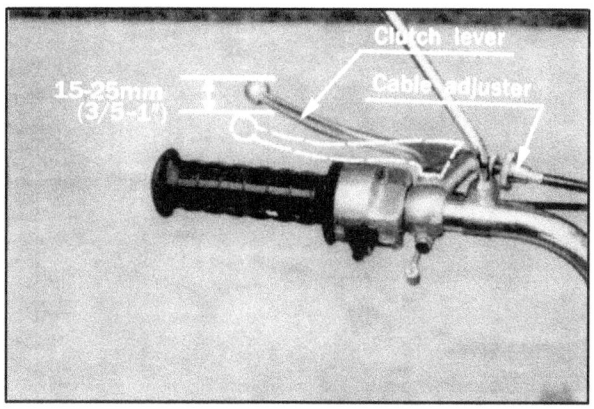

Fig. 97 Adjustment of clutch lever

FRONT FORK

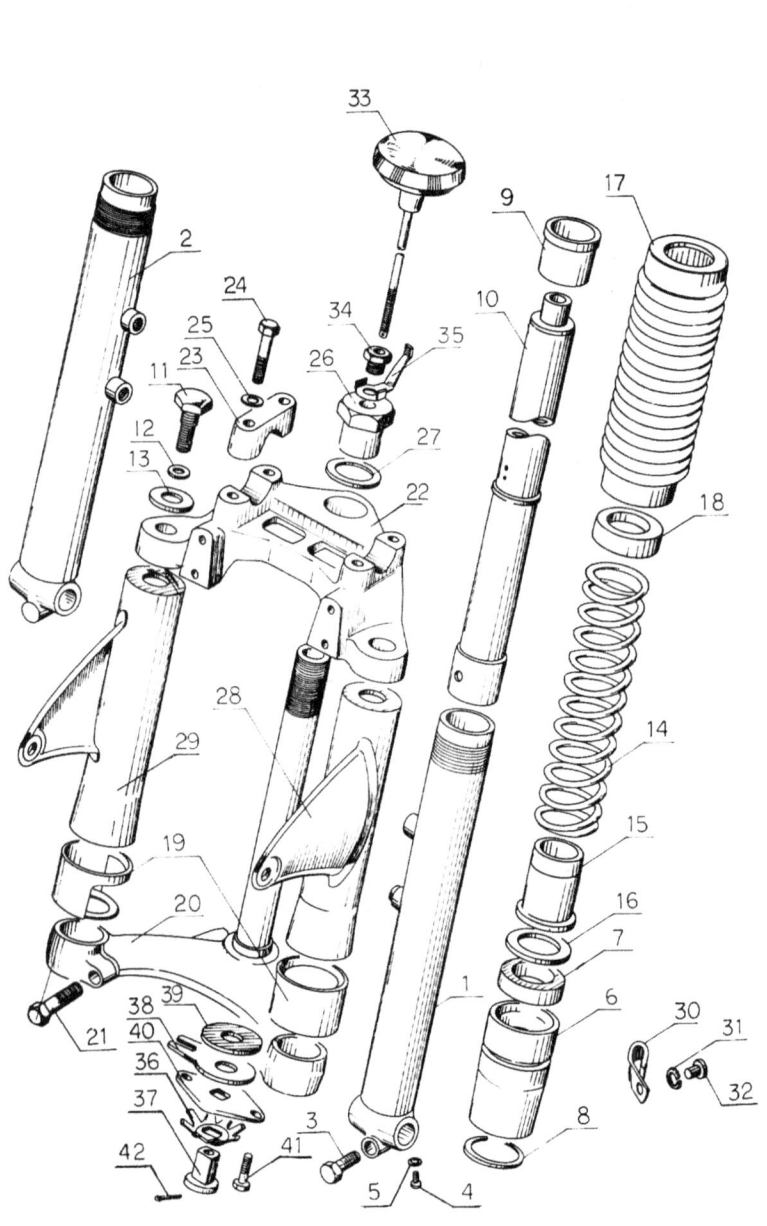

No.	Part Name	No. Req'd
1	Outer tube B	1
2	Outer tube A	1
3	8×26 hexagon bolt	1
4	4×7 cross pan head screw	2
5	Drain plug gasket	2
6	Outer tube nut	2
7	34 oil seal	2
8	40 O ring	2
9	Cushion slide metal	2
10	Inner tube A	2
11	Upper bridge bolt	2
12	9 O ring	2
13	Upper bridge washer	2
14	Front main cushion spring	2
15	Dust seal	2
16	Main spring seat	2
17	Front fork boot	2
18	Upper boot holder	2
19	Fork cover guide	2
20	Lower bridge	1
21	10×32 hexagon bolt	2
22	Upper bridge	1
23	Handle holder	2
24	Hexagon bolt C	4
25	Plane washer B	4
26	Steering head nut	1
27	Steering head washer	1
28	Left fork cover	1
29	Right fork cover	1
30	Cable clip	1
31	Spring washer	1
32	Cross recd pan head screw	1
33	Steering damper knob	1
34	Damper knob guide	1
35	Damper lock spring	1
36	Steerig damper spring	1
37	Damper spring guide	1
38	Friction plate	1
39	Damper facing	1
40	Damper guide plate	1
41	6×18 hexagon bolt	2
42	Split pin	1

A. Operation

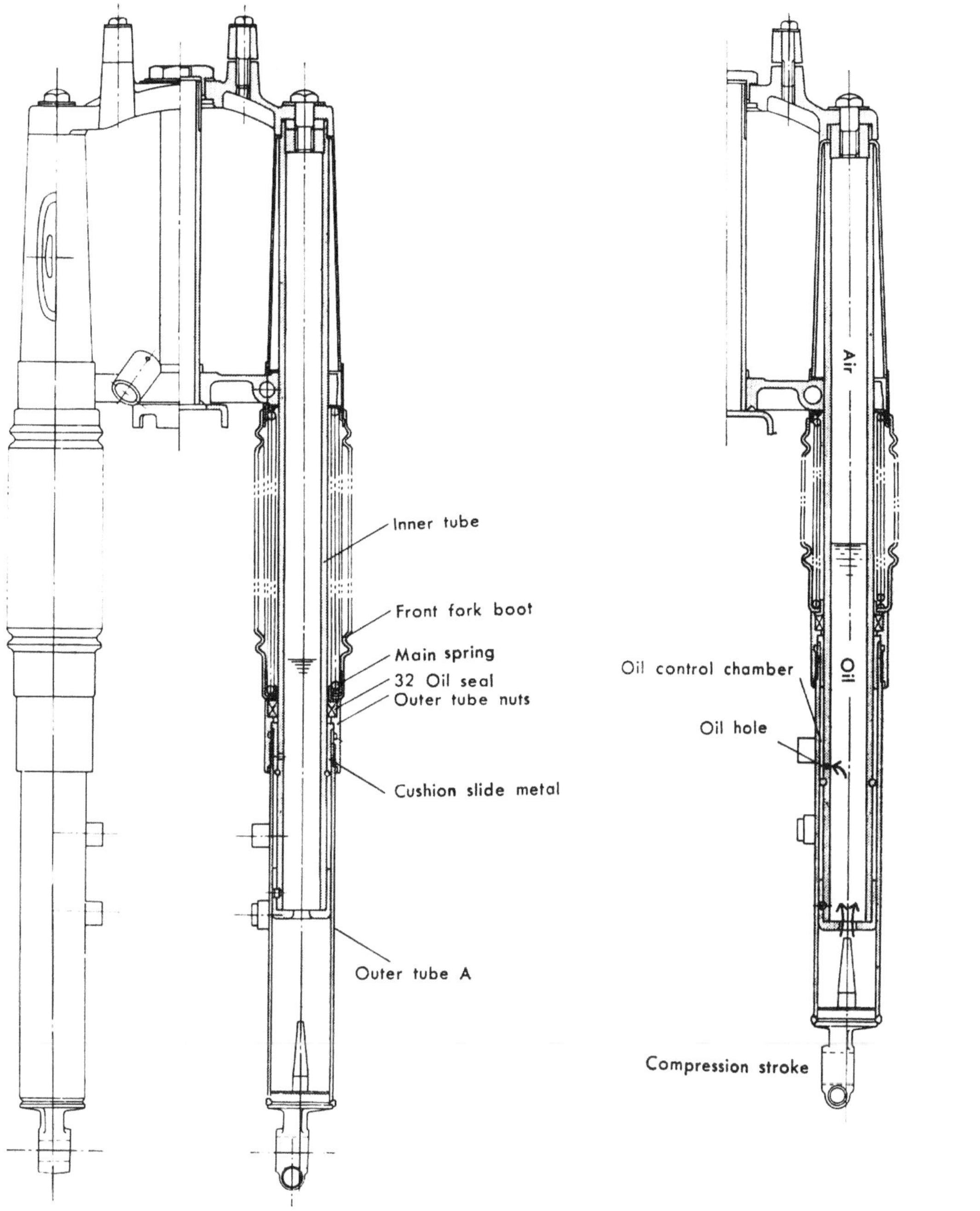

Fig. 98 Operation of front fork

When load is applied to the front fork, the load is taken by the fork spring. At the same, oil in the oil chamber flows into the oil control chamber and the load is held by resistance of the compressed oil and air, and the shock is absorbed.

Oil lock bars are installed inside of the bottom of the lower forks, to prevent the fork from bottoming when receiving severe shocks.

When oil passes through the passage between the piston oil hole and the oil lock bar, shock is absorbed by resistance of the oil.

The oil lock bar is tapered so that oil resistance increases as the front fork compresses.

When the fork rises, rebound is absorbed by oil resistance generated by the oil flow from the oil control chamber through the oil hole to the oil chamber and by the oil flow through the passage between the oil lock bar and piston oil hole. (Fig. 98)

B. Disassembling:

1. Prop up the machine on the mainstand and place a supporting block under the engine before disassembling front fork and front wheel.
2. Take off front fender by loosening four hexagonal bolts (8×12) and then turning the outer tube of fender.
3. Front fork is removed separately by removing upper bracket bolts and lower bracket bolts.

C. Assembling and Inspection

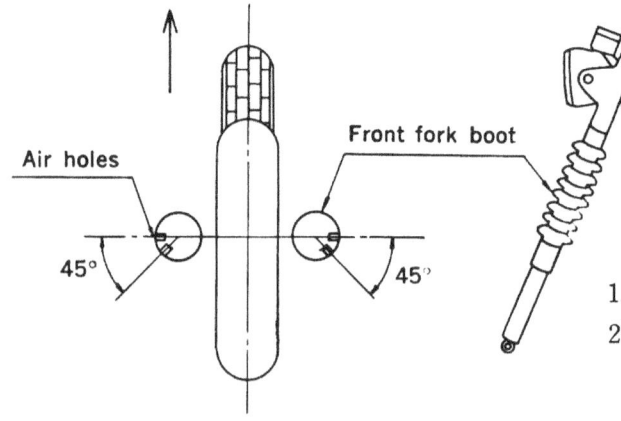

Fig. 99 Assembling front fork

1. Assembling is done in the reverse order of removing.
2. Place the air holes on the rubber boot facing back to prevent dust entering as shown in Fig. 99.
3. Fill each fork tube with 220cc fork oil. (Fig. 100) The oil level is checked with an oil gauge: Correct level depths is 45 mm (1.77 inches)

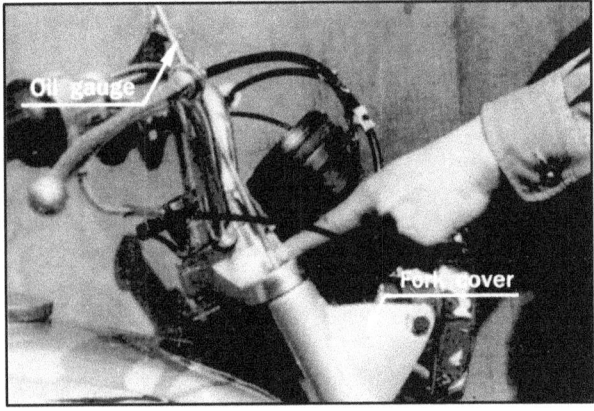

Fig. 100 Checking oil level

D. Removing the steering damper.

1. The steering damper is disassembled by taking off the split pin at the bottom of the steering damper knob, and loosen the steering damper knob by removing the fitting bolt of damper guide plate. (Fig. 101)

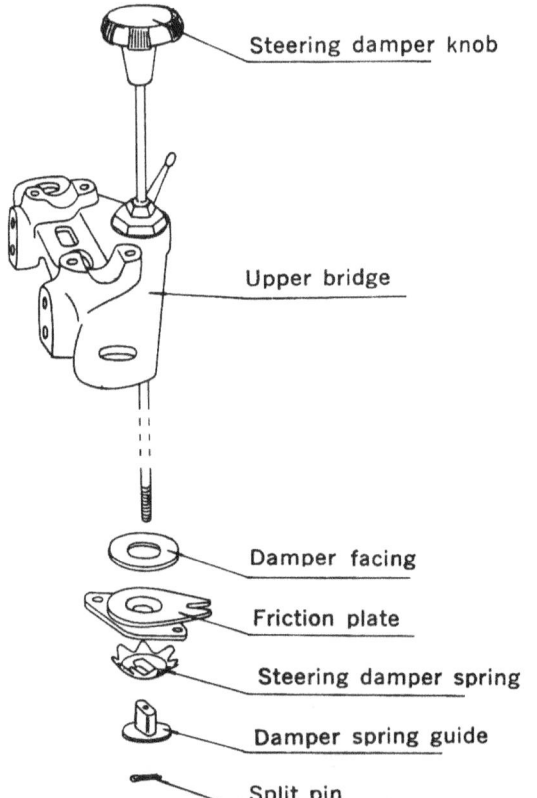

Fig. 101 Component part of steering damper

11-3 Rear suspension:

A. Constructon:

The rear suspension of 350 GTR is adjustable for load or road conditions by changing the mounting position at the top end of the shock absorber as shown in Fig. 102. The vertical positin is stiffer.

Fig. 102 Adjustment of rear suspension

B. Operation: (Fig. 103)

1. When depressed by shock or load:

When the unit is subjected to shock or load, the spring is compressed, oil enters the oil passage and pushes open the valve and flows into the oil control chamber. Oil flows through the oil hole on the inner tube into the passage between the inner tube and the outer tube. Shocks are absorbed by this spring action and oil flow.

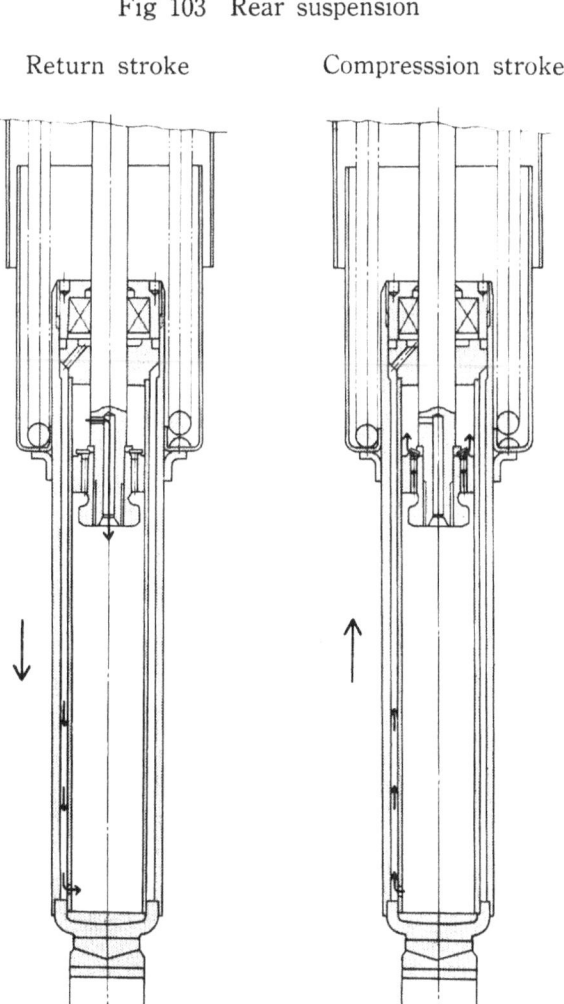

Fig 103 Rear suspension

Return stroke   Compresssion stroke

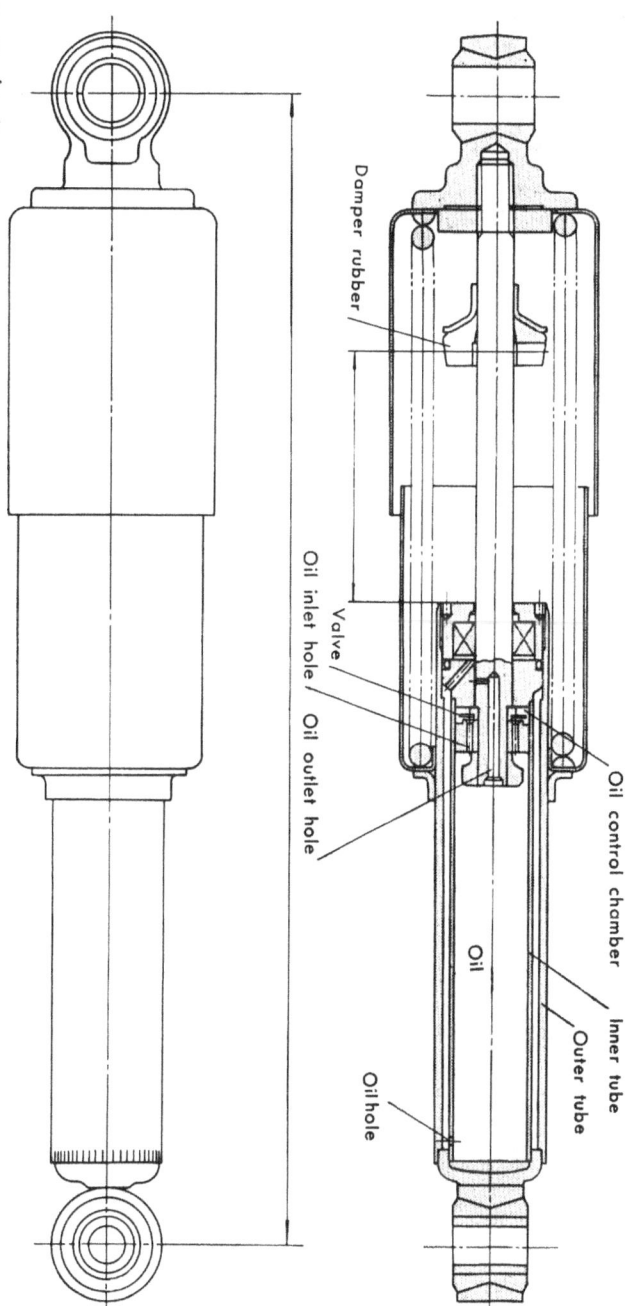

2. Return stroke:

On the return stroke of the unit, the valve on the oil control chamber closes and the damping oil flows out of the oil passage.

The oil overcomes strong resistance when it begine to flow in the passage between the inner tube and the outer tube and flows back into the damping oil chamber. Rebound is absorbed by this oil flow resistance.

C. Adjustment of rear suspension

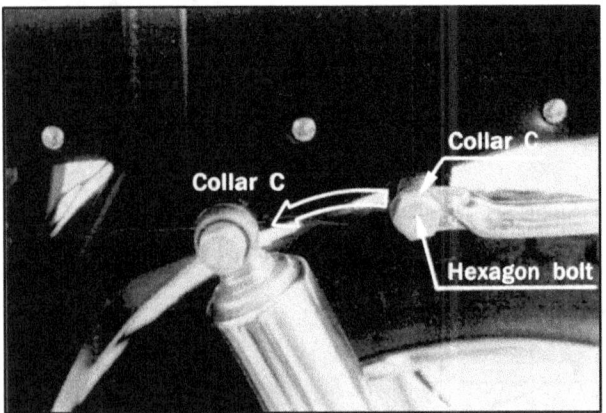

Fig. 104 Adjustment of rear suspension

To adjust the suspension, remove the hexagonal bolt and collar C of frame handle.

This collar C should be replaced after the suspension is moved to position. (Fig. 104)

11-4 Wheels:

A. Construction:

Tires:	Front:	3.25-19, 4ply	
	Rear:	3.25-19, 4ply	
Drums:	Front:	180mmφ	(7.09 inches)
	Rear:	180mmφ	(7.09 inches)

B. Checking of Tire Pressure and Balance

Since 350 GTR has excellent acceleration and high speed performance, correct tire pressure should always be maintained. It is advisable to make a thorough weekly check.

Recommended tire pressure:

Front tire   2.0kg/cm² (28 lbs/cub-inches)

Rear tire   2.2kg/cm² (31.3 lbs/cub-inches)

Balance:

1. Tire balance is very important to minimize vibration at high speeds.
2. When replacing tires or repairing punctures, check carefully the yellow spot on the side wall of the tire which indicates tire balance, so to see that the tube valve is lined up with this mark. When this yellow mark is not recognizable, mark the the position of tube valve on the tire before removing the tire.
3. Balance weights clamped to the spokes should be attached to the original position. (Fig. 105)

Fig. 105 Balance weights

4. To check the wheel balance, spin the wheel several times. A balanced wheel will stop in any position. If the wheel regularly stops in the same position, clamp a balancing weight to the top spoke (the lightest part) in the stopped position. (Fig. 106)
Be sure to check the wear and air pressure of tires, bent or deformed rim, looseness of spokes and wear of shafts or bearings before balancing tire.
5. There are two balancing weight of 10 and 30 gram.
6. To fit the weights, tap them lightly onto the the nipples by hand.

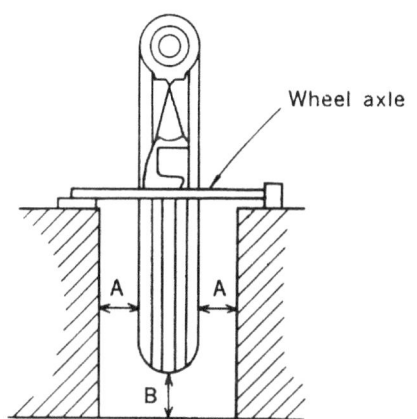

Fig. 106 Wheel balancing

FRONT WHEEL

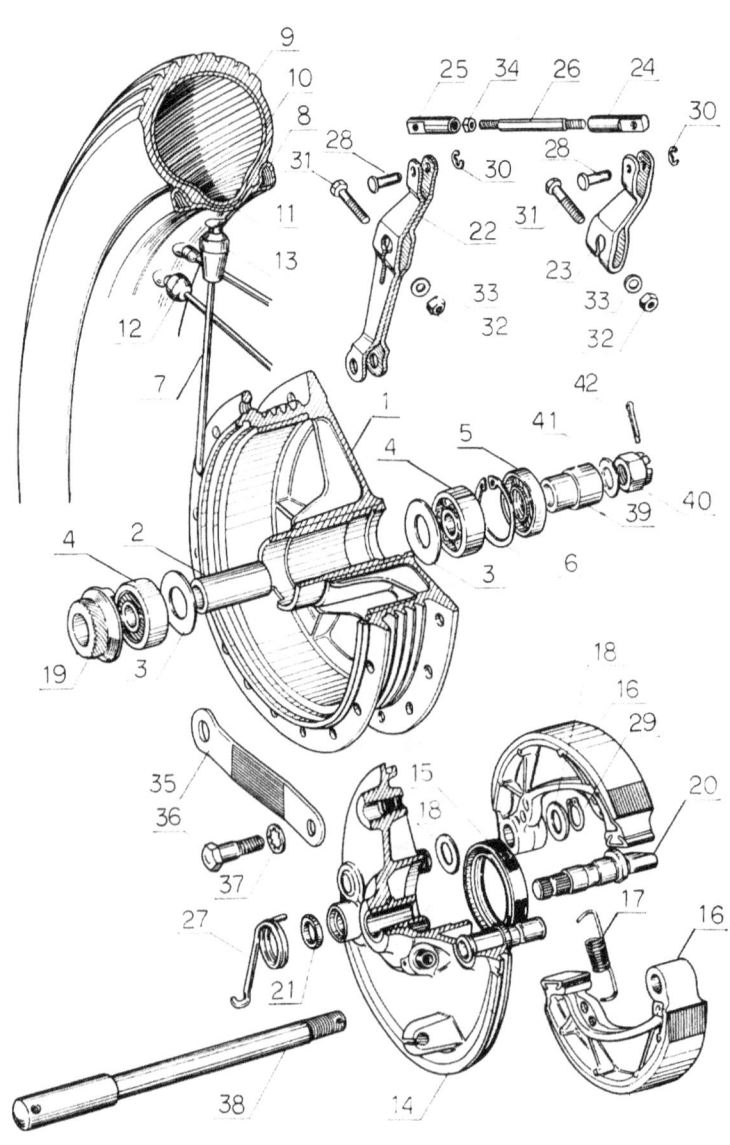

Component parts of front wheel

No.	Part Name	No. Req'd
1	Front brake drum	1
2	Front drum collar	1
3	Collar supporter	2
4	Ball bearing	2
5	22 oil seal	1
6	42 A snap ring	1
7	Front spoke assy	1
8	Front wheel rim	1
9	Front wheel tire	1
10	Wheel tube	1
11	Tire flap	1
12	Wheel balancing weight A	1
13	Wheel balancing weight B	1
14	Front panel comp	1
15	48 oil seal	1
16	Brake shoe comp	2
17	Brake shoe spring	2
18	14 thrust washer	4
19	Speedometer gear	1
20	Front brake cam	2
21	Cam dust seal	2
22	Brake arm A	1
23	Brake arm B	1
24	Rod end A	1
25	Rod end B	1
26	Brake arm rod	1
27	Front arm return spring	1
28	Brake arm pin	2
29	14 A snap ring	2
30	5 D snap ring	2
31	Hexagon bolt A	2
32	Hexagon nut A	2
33	Plane washer A	2
34	Hexagon nut C	1
35	Front torque link	1
36	Front link bolt	1
37	Internal toothed washer	1
38	Front wheel axle	1
39	Front axle collar	1
40	14 sloted hexagon nut	1
41	14 plane washer	1
42	Split pin	1

REAR WHEEL

No.	Part Name	No. Req'd
1	Rear brake drum	1
2	Rear drum collar	1
3	Collar supportor B	1
4	Collar supportor B	1
5	Ball bearing	1
6	Ball bearing	1
7	28 oil seal	1
8	Rear wheel damper	6
9	Driven sprocket	1
10	10×35 hexagon bolt	6
11	Hexagon nut C	6
12	Spring washer	6
13	78 B snap ring	1
14	Front spoke assy	1
15	Front wheel rim	1
16	Rear wheel tire	1
17	Wheel tube	1
18	Tire flap	1
19	Wheel balancing weight A	1
20	Wheel balancing weight B	1
21	Rear panel comp	1
22	Brake shoe comp	2
23	Brake shoe spring	2
24	14 thrust washer	4
25	Rear brake cam	1
26	Cam dust seal	1
27	Brake arm C	1
28	Rear arm return spring	1
29	14 A snap ring	2
30	Hexagon bolt A	1
31	Spring washer	1
32	Rear torque link	1
33	Rear link bolt	1
34	Latch clip	1
35	Hexagon nut A	1
36	Plane washer A	1
37	Spring washer	1
38	Rear wheel axle	1
39	Rear axle collar	1
40	Oil seal collar	1
41	14 sloted hexagon nut	1
42	14 plane washer	1
43	Split pin	1
44	Roller chain ass'y	1
45	Chain joint comp	1

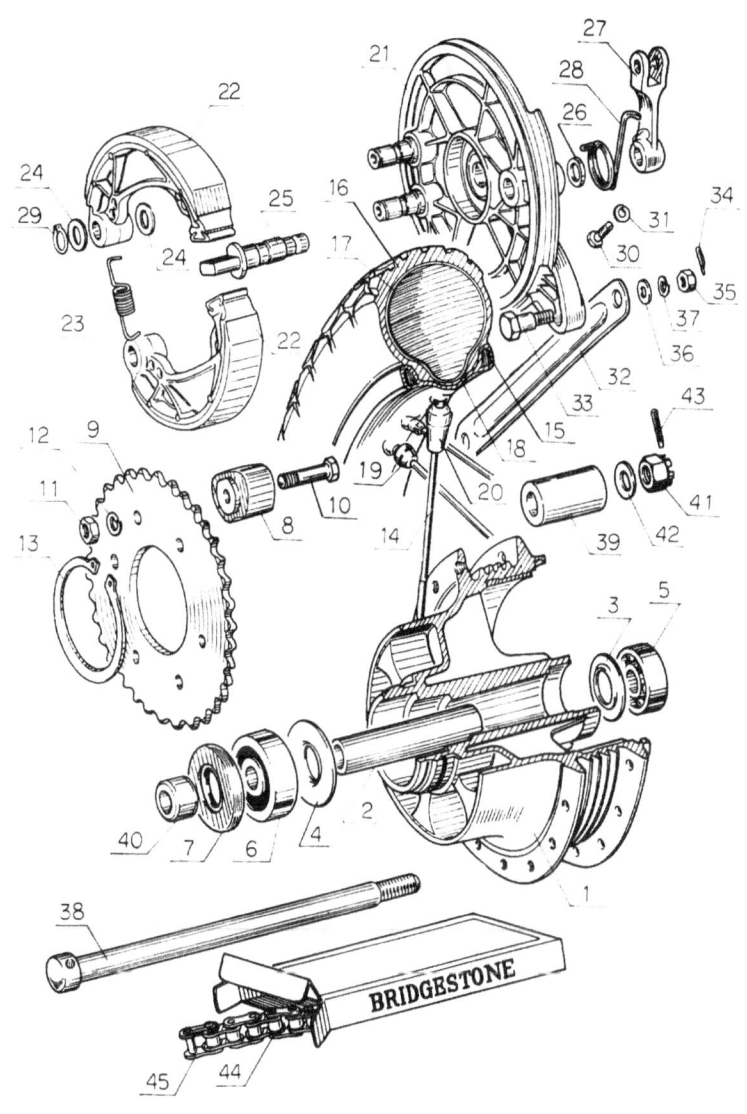

Component parts of rear wheel

12. ELECTRICAL EQUIPMENT:

Dynamo & Neutral Switch

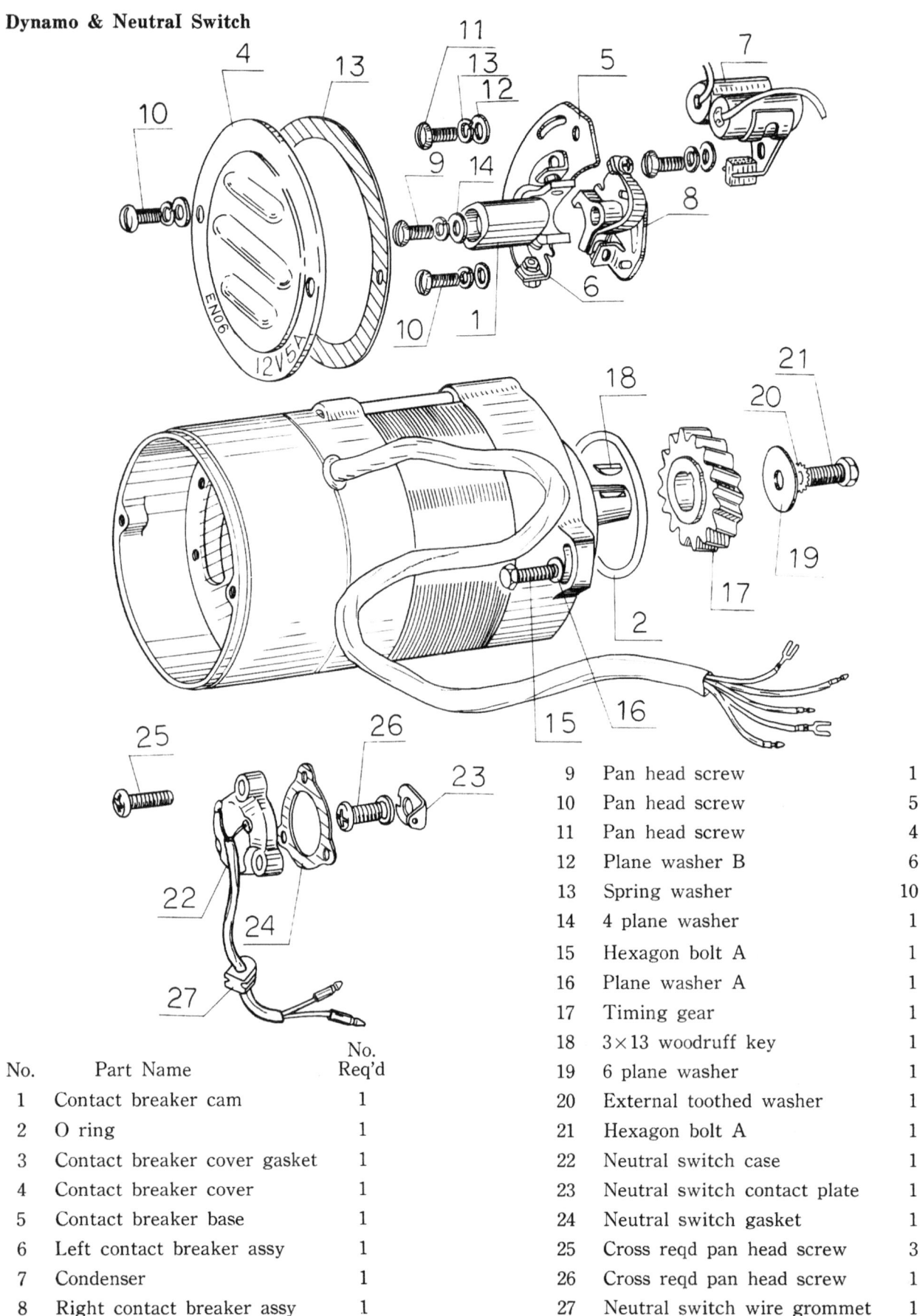

No.	Part Name	No. Req'd
1	Contact breaker cam	1
2	O ring	1
3	Contact breaker cover gasket	1
4	Contact breaker cover	1
5	Contact breaker base	1
6	Left contact breaker assy	1
7	Condenser	1
8	Right contact breaker assy	1
9	Pan head screw	1
10	Pan head screw	5
11	Pan head screw	4
12	Plane washer B	6
13	Spring washer	10
14	4 plane washer	1
15	Hexagon bolt A	1
16	Plane washer A	1
17	Timing gear	1
18	3×13 woodruff key	1
19	6 plane washer	1
20	External toothed washer	1
21	Hexagon bolt A	1
22	Neutral switch case	1
23	Neutral switch contact plate	1
24	Neutral switch gasket	1
25	Cross reqd pan head screw	3
26	Cross reqd pan head screw	1
27	Neutral switch wire grommet	1

12-1 A.C. Generator:

A. Description: The generator fitted to 350 GTR is a six pole, magnetic, inner rotor type A.C. dynamo. The dynamo consists of a rotor into which magnets are cast and a stator consisting of an iron core and wires wound around the iron core. The timing gear is fitted on one end of the rotor and a cam which operates the contact breakers is fitted at the other end.

A six pole parmanent magnet is contained in the center of the rotor. Its rated output of 88 watts is produced at an engine speed of 5000 r.p.m. and the peak output of 98 watts at 8000 r.p.m. The rated output therefore is obtained at the following speeds. (m.p.h.)

B. Charging current: The following table shows the engine speed which charges the battery.

Operation of Engine			Speed M.P.H. (K.M.H.)		
	lighting	rpm	4 th gear	5 th gear	6 th gear
Daytime	0%	1850	19 (30)	22 (35)	25 (40)
	10%	2550	26 (41)	30 (48)	34 (55)
Upper beam	0%	2300	23 (37)	27 (43)	30 (48)
	10%	2850	29 (46)	34 (54)	39 (62)
Lower beam	0%	2250	23 (37)	27 (43)	30 (48)
	10%	3200	32 (52)	38 (61)	43 (69)

12-2 Voltage Regulator

The voltage regulator is equipped on the 350 GTR. (Fig. 107)

The charging current generated by A.C. dynamo is regulated by the voltage regulator and the regulated current is shown below. (Fig. 108)

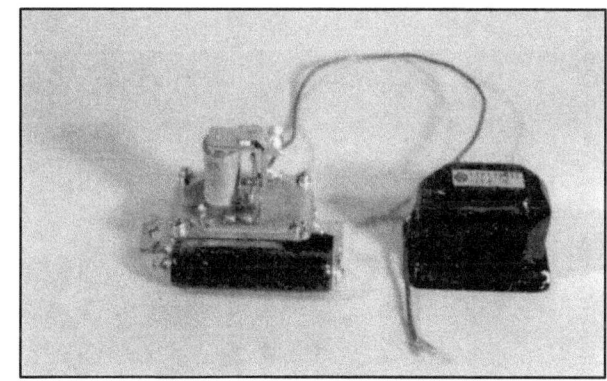

Fig. 107 Voltage regulator

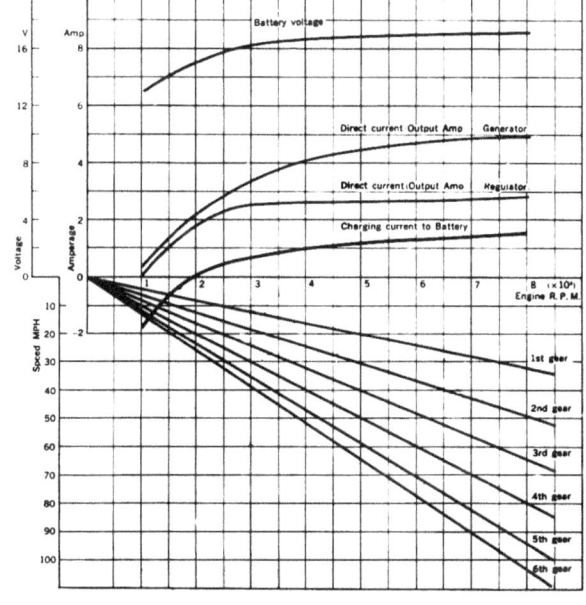

Fig. 108-1 Daytime driving

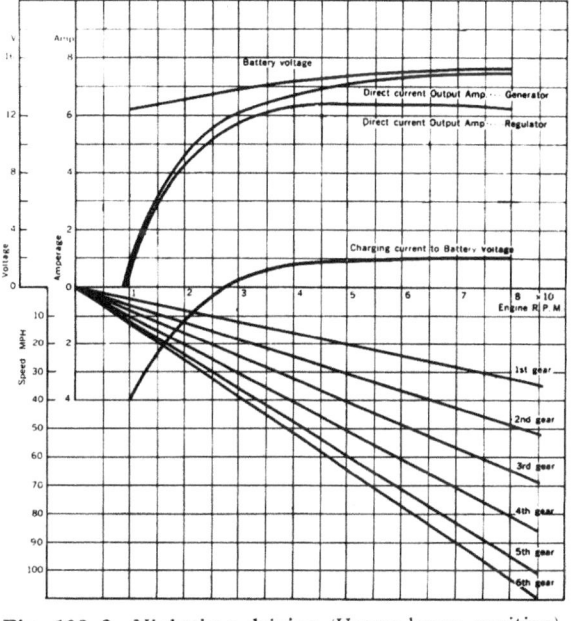

Fig. 108-2 Nighttime driving (Upper beam position)

12-3 Ignition system

A. Contact Breakers:

1. Description:

Two contact breakers are fitted on the A.C. dynamo. The A.C. dynamo is turned by the pinion gear, through the driven and timing gears.

The timing gear turns two complete revolution when the crankshaft turns one full revolution. The timing gear and point cam are fixed on the dynamo shaft and turns with it.

As the speed of the A.C. dynamo is one-half of that of the crankshaft, contact point must give four sparks to each revolution of the dynamo, so two cams and two sets of contact breakers are installed.

One contact breaker opens every 90° (1/4 turn) of cam rotation and high voltage current is induced in the ignition coil.

2. Maintenance:

Contact breaker points should be kept bright and smooth.

If the points are rough or pitted, smooth them with a point file. If the point are very rough or pitted, rub lightly and evenly with an oil stone, and wash with gasoline or thinner.

B. Adjusting the gap:

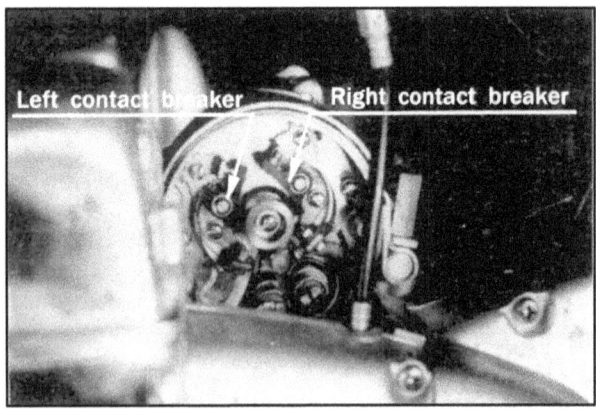

Fig. 109 Contact breakers

Loosen two lock screws of breaker and adjust gap to the correct gauge of 0.3–0.4 mm (0.012–0.016 inches) with a thickness gauge, by sliding breaker base slowly. (Fig. 109)

C. Checking and Adjusting Ignition Timing

Checking

Push the timing button by taking off 8×12 hexagon bolt on the crank case. Remove the left spark plug and earth it to the cylinder fin.

Rotate rear wheel counterclockwise. If the spark fires when the timing button snaps into the hole in the crankshaft, the ignition timing is correct.

Adjustment

Fit a dial guage on the right cylinder head after removing the spark plug. Connect the black wire from the A.C. dynamo to a timing tester and the other terminal to a bolt on the frame for grounding. (Fig. 110)

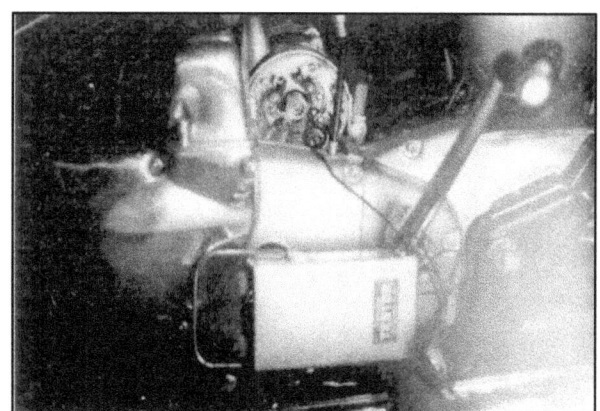

Fig. 110 Checking ignition timing

Find top dead center with the dial guage by putting the motorcycle in gear and turning the rear wheel in the forward direction.

Then turn back the rear wheel until the piston is backed to 3.33mm below top dead center. (Fig. 111)

Fig. 111 Finding igntion timing

This is 25° before top dead center. Contact breaker points should just begin to open at this point. Permissible timing is between 2.82mm (0.11 inches) and 3.6mm (0.14 inches) position distance below top dead center.

When ignition timing is advanced:

Loosen the fittings of the A.C. dynamo and turn counter-clockwise.

When ignition timing is retarded:

Turn the A.C. dynamo clockwise.

Note:

B.T.D.C.	23°	24°	25°	26°
Piston distance (m/m)	2.82	3.07	3.33	3.60
(inches)	0.11	0.12	0.13	0.14

12-4 Selenium Rectifier:

The selenium rectifier converts A.C. current generated by the generator into D.C. current and charges the battery. (Fig. 112, 113)

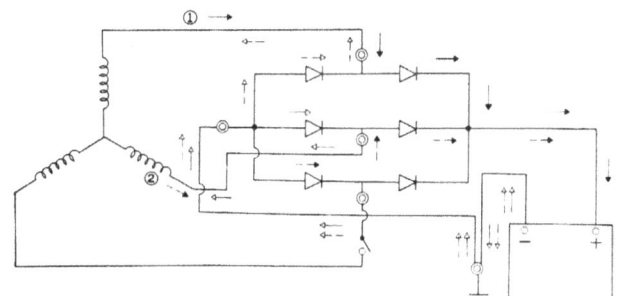

Fig. 112 Key position 1

When ① is positive cycle, ② changes into negative cycle and vice versa.

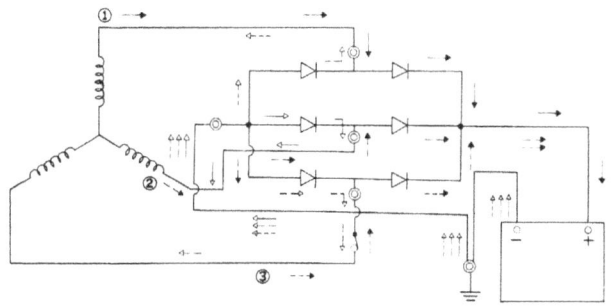

Fig. 113 Key position 2

When ① is positive cycle, ② or ③ changes into negative cycle.

② is positive cycle, ① or ③ negative.

③ is positive cycle, ① or ② negative.

A. **Special Attention:**

Take care not to wet the rectifier when washing the motorcycle or run the engine with rectifier disconnected.

B. **Inspection**

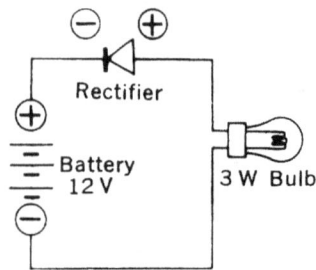

1. Inspection is carried out easily by flowing 12 voltage current in the reverse direction as shown in Fig. 114.
   If the bulb lights in the circuit, the function of rectifier is damaged.
2. Insulation resistance should be more than 10 Meg ohm with a 500V megger.

Fig. 114 Inspection of rectifier

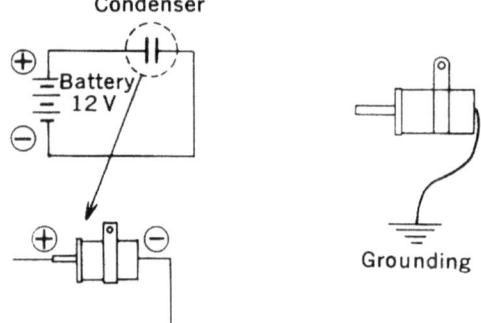

Fig. 115 Inspection of condenser

12-5 Condenser

A. **Inspection**

The capacity and insulation resistance of condenser should be checked with an electric tester, but it can also be checked easily in following manner.

Pass the current to the condenser by connecting the wire of the battery, and then earth the condenser wire.

If there is sharp spark between the wire and the earth, the condenser is in good condition. (Fig. 115)

Condenser capacity 0.2–0.3μF

Insulation resistance more than 5MΩ

12-6 Ignition coil

A. **Inspection**

When testing the ignition coil, perform with an electro tester.
If the spark jumps 9mm or more, the coil is in good condition.

Checking	Standard figure
Sparking	Over 9mm at 1500 rpm
Insulate resistance	500MΩ
Resistance of secondary coil	1 MΩ

12-7 Spark plug

A. Description

The standard spark plug used is N.G.K. B-8H whose sectional struture is shown in Fig. 116.

The gap of the spark plug should be adjusted to 0.5-0.6mm (0.020-0.024 inches).

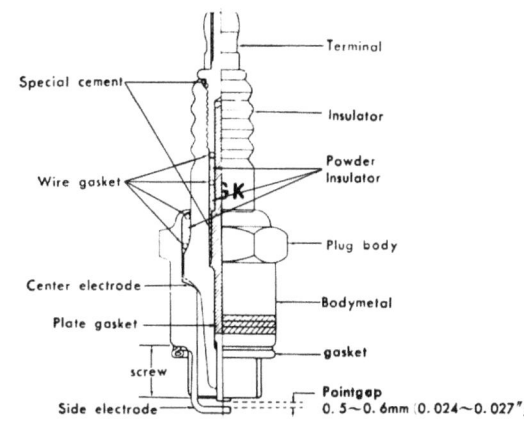

Fig. 116 Spark plug

B. Inspection and Adjustment

Check the spark plug every 3,000km (2,000 miles).

When the electrode becomes coated with carbon deposit or is worn out, clean or replace it as the case may be.

Worn or dirty plug affects sparking, and causes hard starting and lose of engine power.

1. If a "cold" type plug is used.

    Oil or heavy carbon deposit on the electrode will result.

    Change to a "hotter" type plug. (**Lower number**)

2. When a correct plug is used.

    The electrode burns light brown.

3. When too hot a plug is used.

    There will be absence of deposit, and shows bleached insulator, sometimes blistered.

    Change to a colder plug. (**Higher number**)

4. See chart below for plugs recommended.

BRAND	STANDARD	IF PLUG FOULS EASILY (Slow Speed)	IF PLUG OVERHEATS EASILY (High Speed)
NGK	B-8H	B-7H	B-9H
CHAMPION	L-58R	L-5	L-56T
BOSCH	W310T16	W240T	W340T16
LODGE	R47	3HN	R49

12-8 Battery

The capacity of the battery is 12V–6AH.

The battery should be checked periodically by the rider or dealer. Check the level of the electrolyte and the specific gravity. Specific gravity of the solution should be 1.260–1.280 at 20° centigrade (68° F) when the battery is fully charged.

A. Inspection of Specific Gravity

The condition of the battery can be determined by measuring the specific gravity of the electrolyte solution. If the gravity is below 1.220, the battery should be charged without delay.

Specific gravity at 20°C (65°F) (Solution Temperature)	Amount of charge
1.260	100%
1.220	75
1.160	50
1.105	25
1.050	None

Caution

Take care of the following points when checking the specific gravity.

1) Do not let the hydrometer float touch the side of wall.
2) Read the hydrometer at A (upper level of contact) instead of B (lower level) as shown in Fig. 117.

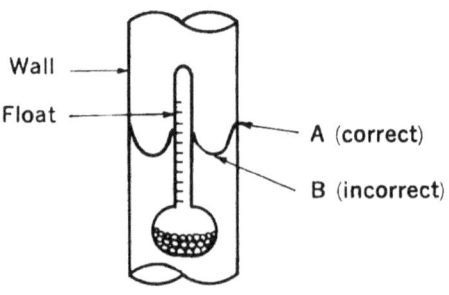

Fig. 117 Hydrometer

3) As specific gravity varies according to the temperature of the solution, apply the following conversion table based on standard 20°C (68°F) for the different temperatures.

Relation between specific gravity and temperature of solution.

0°C 30°F	5°C 42°F	10°C 50°F	15°C 59°F	20°C 68°F	25°C 77°F	30°C 86°F	35°C 95°F	40°C 104°F	45°C 113°F
1.218	1.215	1.212	1.208	1.205	1.202	1.198	1.195	1.191	1.188
1.228	1.225	1.222	1.218	1.215	1.212	1.208	1.205	1.202	1.198
1.238	1.235	1.232	1.228	1.225	1.222	1.218	1.215	1.211	1.208
1.249	1.246	1.242	1.239	1.235	1.231	1.228	1.224	1.221	1.217
1.259	1.256	1.252	1.249	1.245	1.241	1.238	1.234	1.231	1.227
1.269	1.266	1.262	1.259	1.255	1.251	1.248	1.244	1.240	1.237
1.274	1.271	1.267	1.264	**1.260**	1.256	1.253	1.249	1.245	1.242
1.276	1.276	1.272	1.269	**1.265**	1.261	1.258	1.254	1.250	1.247
1.284	1.281	1.277	1.274	**1.270**	1.266	1.263	1.259	1.255	1.252
1.289	1.286	1.282	1.279	**1.275**	1.270	1.268	1.264	1.260	1.257
1.294	1.290	1.287	1.284	**1.280**	1.276	1.273	1.269	1.265	1.261

B. Storage of dry charged battery.

Dry charged battery, if stored in a relatively dry place, will remain in good condition for a considerable period, but if the cells absorb moisture during storage, the negative plates will discharge slowly and the charging rate will be longer as shown in the following table.

Storage period	Decreased Capacity	Capacity	Charging Rate
One Month	0%	100%	0.6 Ampere × 10 Hour
Three Month	15	85	0.6 × 12
Six Months	30	70	0.6 × 14
One Year	50	50	0.6 × 20

C. Initial Charging Rate

1) Fill the battery with sulfuric acid.
2) Leave battery from 2 to 12 hours after filling before charging.
   When the level of electrolyte has dropped, add more electrolyte until the proper level is reached.
3) Charge at the proper rate as given below until all cells are gassing freely and cell voltage and specific gravity stop rising and remain constant.
   The total charging time will be 10 hours.
   During charging, battery temperature should be kept below 45°C (113°F).
   When the temperature excess 45°C., stop charging for a time until the temperature falls below 45°C.

   Proper charging 0.6 Ampere × 12 hour
   Quick charging   3 Ampere × 1 hour

12-9 Lights

A. Head lamp · Tail lamp

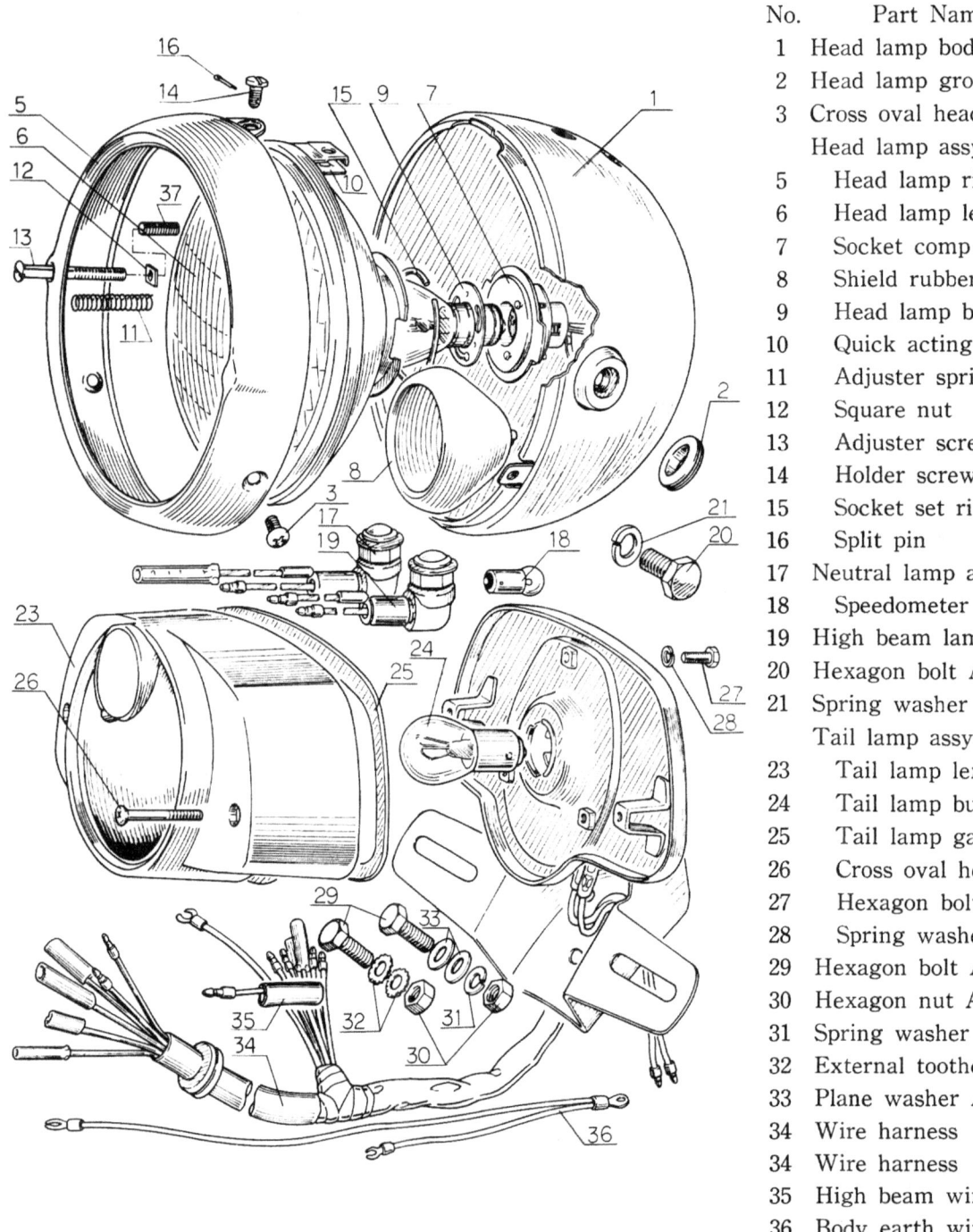

No.	Part Name	No. Req'd
1	Head lamp body	1
2	Head lamp grommet	1
3	Cross oval head screw	2
	Head lamp assy	1
5	Head lamp rim comp	1
6	Head lamp lens comp	1
7	Socket comp	1
8	Shield rubber	1
9	Head lamp bulb	1
10	Quick acting nut	2
11	Adjuster spring	1
12	Square nut	1
13	Adjuster screw	1
14	Holder screw	2
15	Socket set ring	1
16	Split pin	2
17	Neutral lamp assy	1
18	Speedometer bulb	2
19	High beam lamp assy	1
20	Hexagon bolt A	2
21	Spring washer	2
	Tail lamp assy	1
23	Tail lamp lens	1
24	Tail lamp bulb	1
25	Tail lamp gasket	1
26	Cross oval head screw	2
27	Hexagon bolt A	3
28	Spring washer	3
29	Hexagon bolt A	3
30	Hexagon nut A	3
31	Spring washer	2
32	External toothed washer	2
33	Plane washer A	8
34	Wire harness	1
34	Wire harness	1
35	High beam wire	1
36	Body earth wire	1
37	Cover tube	1

B. Speedometer · Ignition coil · Main switch

No.	Part Name	No. Req'd
1	Speedometer assy	1
2	Speedometer bulb	3
3	Tachometer assy	1
4	Left meter holder	1
5	Right meter holder	1
6	Speedometer washer	2
7	Speedometer set spring	2
8	Meter cushion rubber	2
9	Hexagon bolt A	4
10	Plane washer A	4
11	Horn assy	1
12	Hexagon bolt A	2
13	Spring washer	2
14	Left ignition coil assy	1
15	Right ignition coil assy	1
16	Plug cap comp	2
17	Hexagon bolt A	4
18	Spring washer	4
19	Main switch assy	1
20	Stop switch comp	1
21	Stop switch spring	1
22	Battery	1
23	Rectifier assy	1
24	Pan head screw	5
25	Plane washer A	5
26	Plane washer A	2
27	Spring washer	5
28	Spring washer	1
29	Hexagon nut C	1
30	Regulator assy	1
31	Hexagon bolt A	2
32	Spring washer	2
33	Fuse assy	1
34	Fuse	2

C. Bulbs

Lamps	Wattage	Lamps	Wattage
Head lamp	12V-35/30W	5th Gear Indicator lamp	12V-3W
Speedometer lamp	12V-3W	Headlight Beam lamp	12V-3W
Tachometer lamp	12V-3W	Tail lamp	12V-7W
Neutral Indicator lamp	12V-3W	Stop lamp	12V-23W

D. Adjustment of head light beam

The headlamp setting for high and low beams is of vital importance and must therefore be carefully adjusted.

For this purpose, a cross should be marked on a light wall at the same height as the center of headlamp.

The motorcycle should stand on its wheels about 33 feets (10 meters) from the wall, carrying a rider.

Switch on the high beam and set the headlamp so that the beam strikes the center of the cross.

Switch to low beam; the upper edge of the illuminated area should be about 3.5 inches (9 cm) below the cross: Adjust as required. (Fig. 118)

For centering the beam, screw in or out the screw located at the left side of the head right rim.

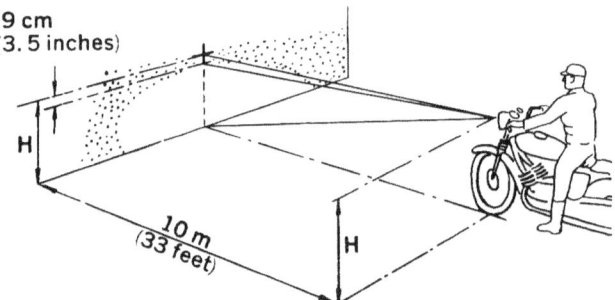

Fig. 118 Adjustment of head light beam

12-10 Main Switch

Ignition switch is combined with the lighting and horn switches and divided into four positions and operated as follows.

Combination Table

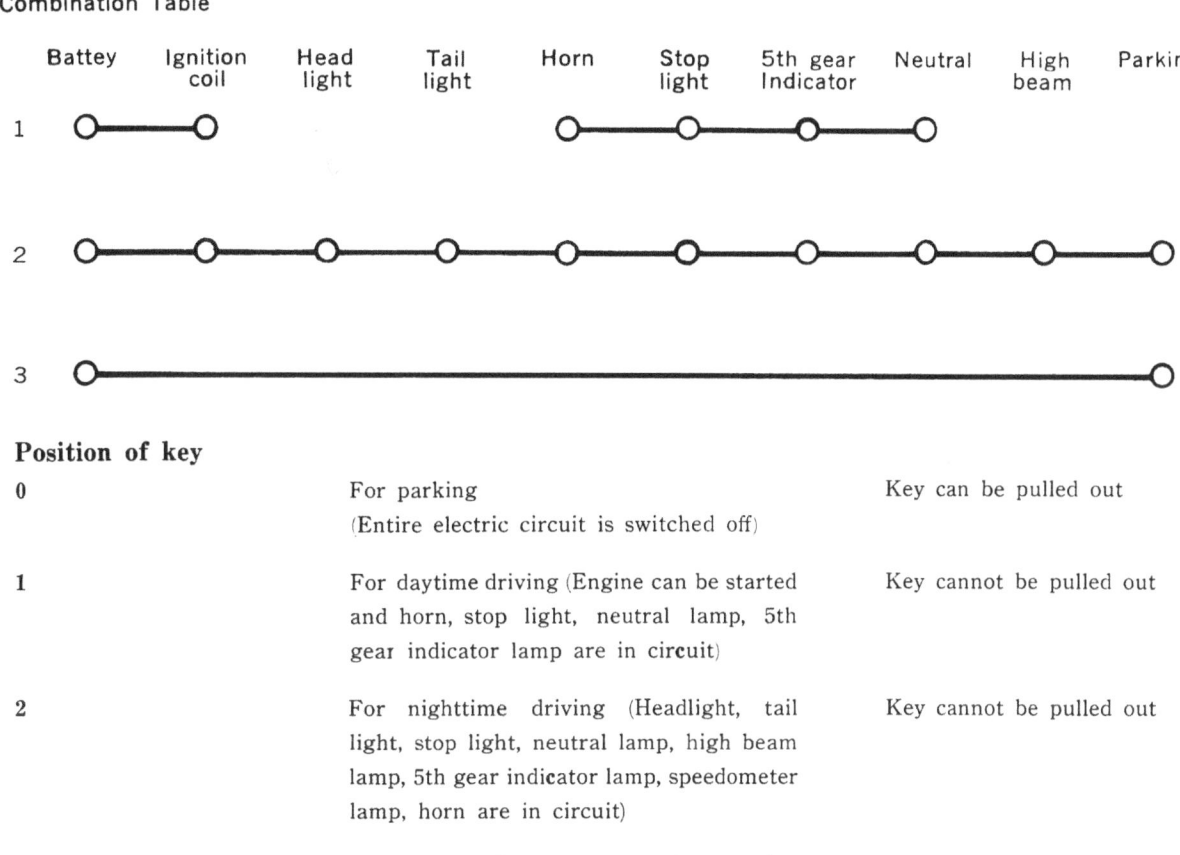

Position of key

0	For parking (Entire electric circuit is switched off)	Key can be pulled out
1	For daytime driving (Engine can be started and horn, stop light, neutral lamp, 5th gear indicator lamp are in circuit)	Key cannot be pulled out
2	For nighttime driving (Headlight, tail light, stop light, neutral lamp, high beam lamp, 5th gear indicator lamp, speedometer lamp, horn are in circuit)	Key cannot be pulled out
3	For parking (Parking light is in circuit)	Key can be pulled out

12-11 Horn

Volume of sound is adjusted by the adjusting screw. (Fig. 119)
When horn does not work correctly, the trouble is due to disconnected wires, damaged contact points or short circuited coil in the horn.

Fig. 119 Adjustment of horn volume

13. TROUBLE SHOOTING:

13-1 Engine is hard to start.

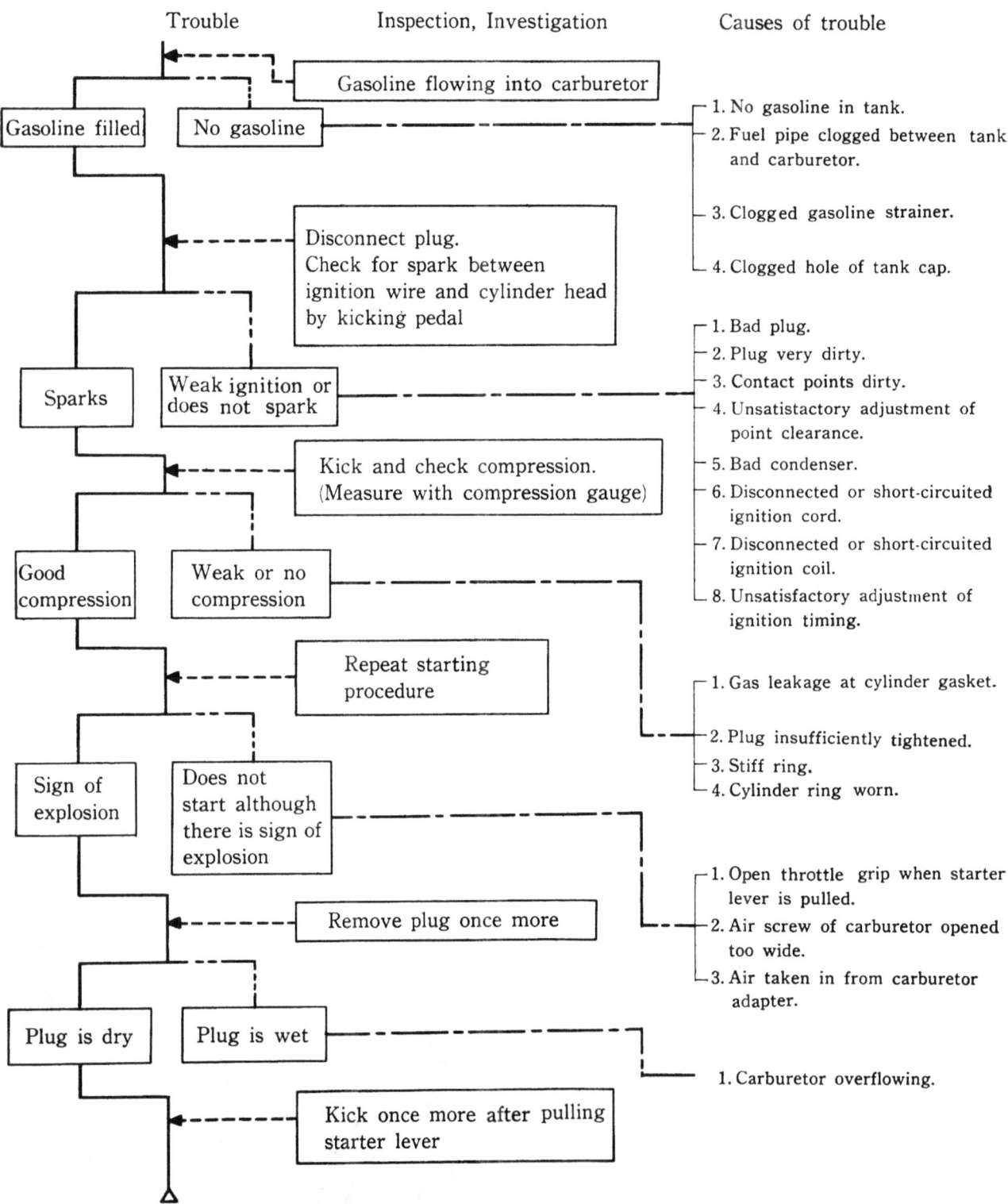

Fuel, spark and compression are basic points for engine operation.
To locate engine trouble first check these points.

13-2 High engine revolution cannot be obtained. Insufficient power.

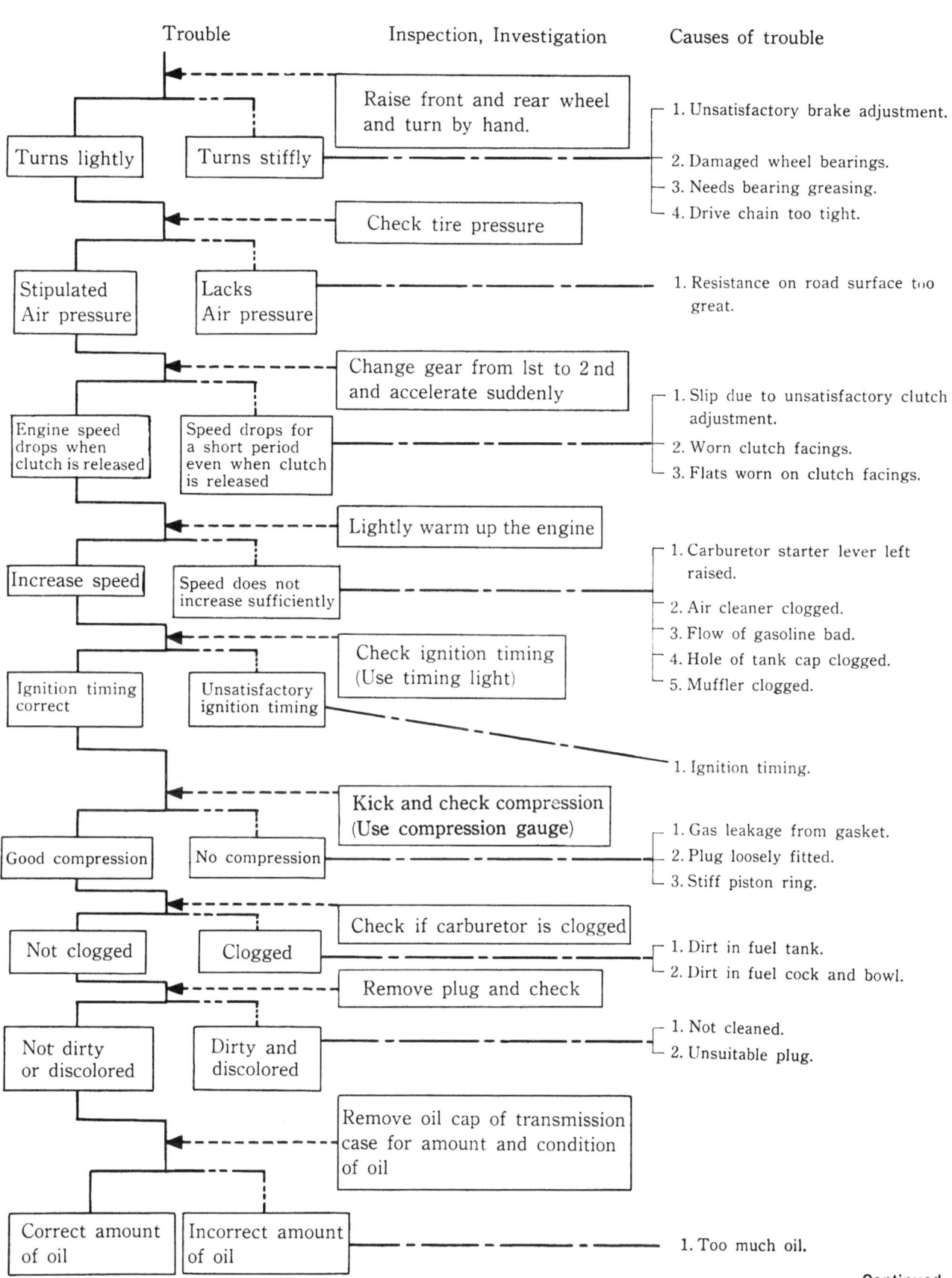

Continued

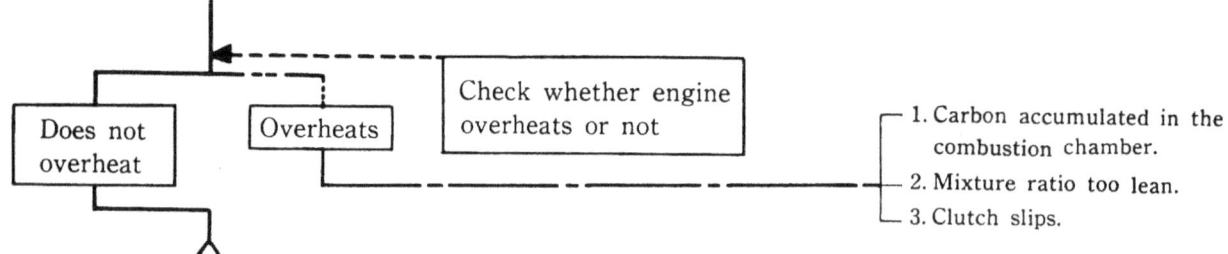

Check whether engine overheats or not
Does not overheat
Overheats
1. Carbon accumulated in the combustion chamber.
2. Mixture ratio too lean.
3. Clutch slips.

13-3 Unsatisfactory R. P. M. (Chiefly at low speed and idling).

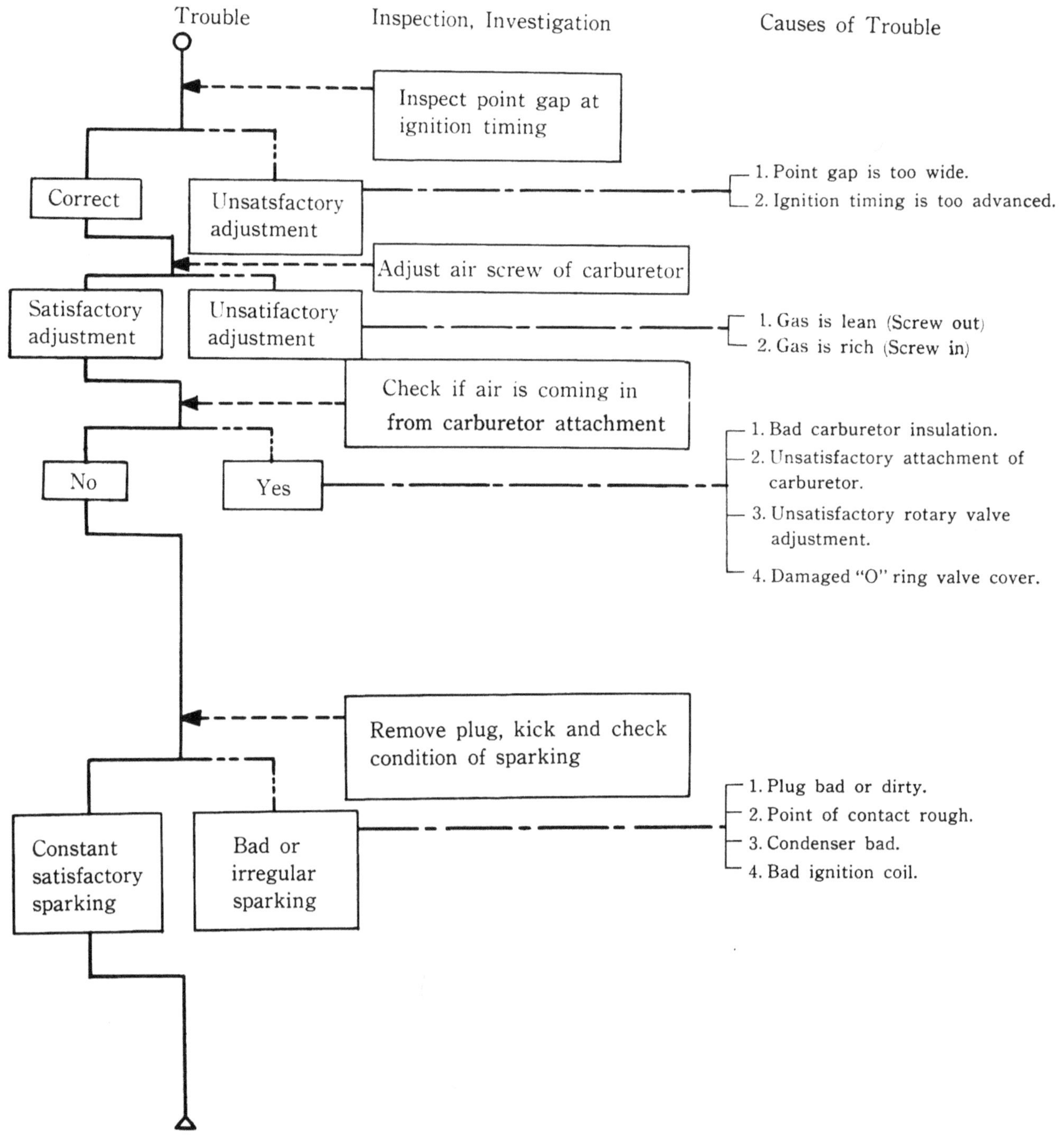

Trouble
Inspection, Investigation
Causes of Trouble
Inspect point gap at ignition timing
Correct
Unsatsfactory adjustment
1. Point gap is too wide.
2. Ignition timing is too advanced.
Adjust air screw of carburetor
Satisfactory adjustment
Unsatifactory adjustment
1. Gas is lean (Screw out)
2. Gas is rich (Screw in)
Check if air is coming in from carburetor attachment
No
Yes
1. Bad carburetor insulation.
2. Unsatisfactory attachment of carburetor.
3. Unsatisfactory rotary valve adjustment.
4. Damaged "O" ring valve cover.
Remove plug, kick and check condition of sparking
Constant satisfactory sparking
Bad or irregular sparking
1. Plug bad or dirty.
2. Point of contact rough.
3. Condenser bad.
4. Bad ignition coil.

13-4 Iregular Revolutions (At medium and high speeds).

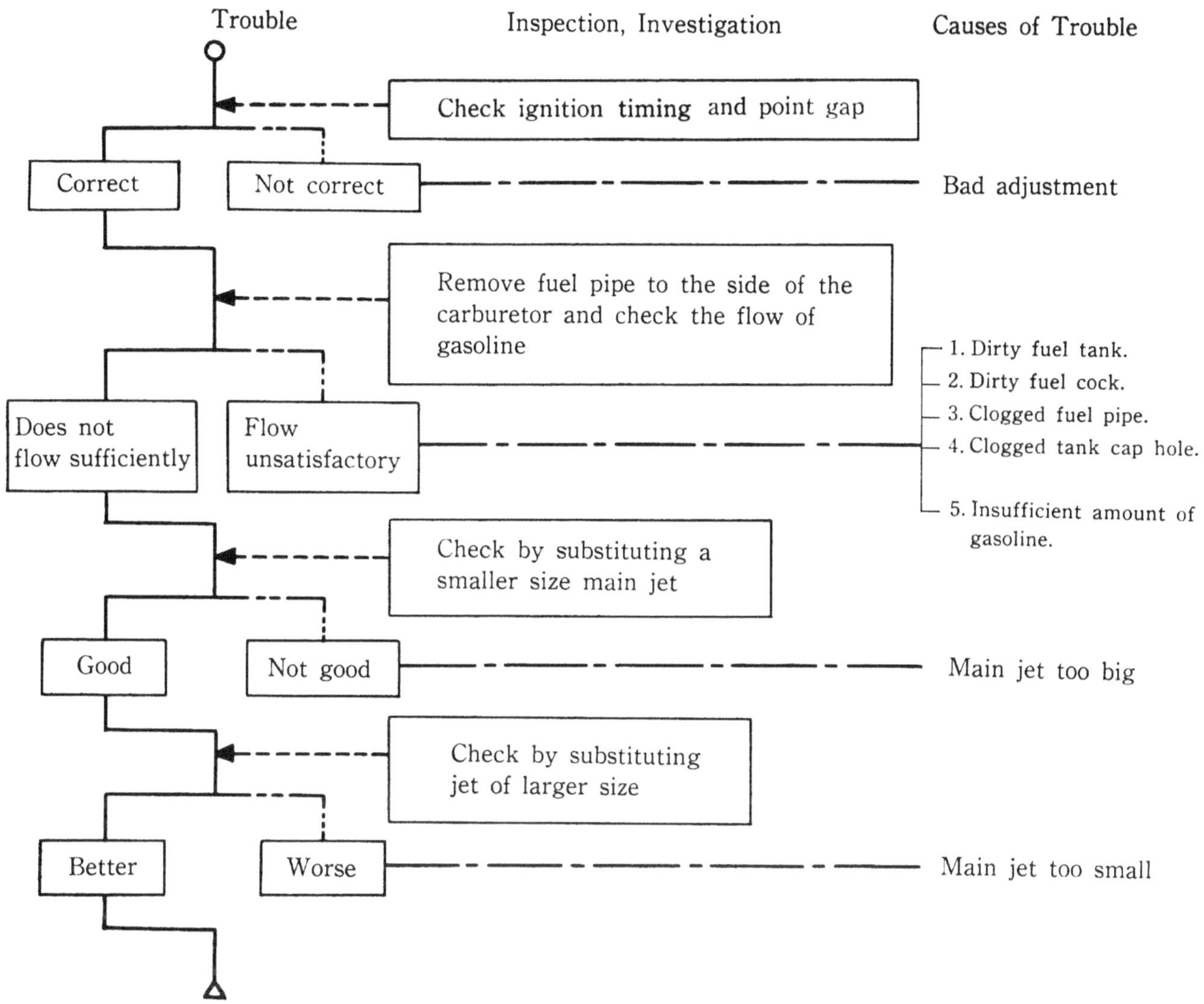

Trouble — Inspection, Investigation — Causes of Trouble

- Check ignition timing and point gap
  - Correct
  - Not correct — — — Bad adjustment

- Remove fuel pipe to the side of the carburetor and check the flow of gasoline
  - Does not flow sufficiently
  - Flow unsatisfactory — — —
    1. Dirty fuel tank.
    2. Dirty fuel cock.
    3. Clogged fuel pipe.
    4. Clogged tank cap hole.
    5. Insufficient amount of gasoline.

- Check by substituting a smaller size main jet
  - Good
  - Not good — — — Main jet too big

- Check by substituting jet of larger size
  - Better
  - Worse — — — Main jet too small

13-5 Unsatisfactory Gear Shifting.

Trouble — Causes of Trouble

Gears cannot be shifted smoothly
1. Improper working gear shift drum.
2. Bent shift fork.
3. Improper working clutch.
4. Worn claws of drum shifter.

Change pedal does not return smoothly
1. Broken change return spring.
2. Drum shifter touching some part.
3. Bent change shaft.

Gears disengage
1. Bent and worn out shift fork.
2. Worn out claws of drum shifter.
3. Worn out drum stopper.

13-6 Common Failures, Their Causes and Correction

One cylinder goes dead. This is generally due to in electrical, fuel or mechanical failure.

A. Possible causes of electrial failure
1. Spark plug fouled or in poor condition.
2. Contact breaker point fouled or out of adjustment.
3. Fouled condenser.
4. Fouled ignition coil.
5. Wrong ignition timing.
6. Cable disconnected between spark plug cap and high tension wire of ignition coil.
7. Damaged or short circuited wiring.

B. Possible causes of fuel failure.
1. Throttle valves not opening synchronously.
2. Clogged fuel line (fuel pipe, fuel cock bowl, tank cap, etc.)
3. Improperly adjusted air screw of carburetor.
4. Clogged jet holes of carburetor.

C. Possible causes of mechanical failure.
1. Worn cylinder, piston or piston rings.
2. Loosely fitted carburetor.
3. Cracked rotary disc valve.

A. Electrical failure

Possible causes	Remedies
1. Spark plug fouled or in poor conditon	Remove spark plug and earth it to cylinder fin, and crank engine. Spark must then flash. If spark plugs fouled, replace it with the plug of the other cylinder and recheck.
2. Fouled ignition coil	Defective ignition should be checked carefully with an electrotester. Before this test, remove spark plug, pull ignition cable out of spark plug adapter, hold cable at a distance of about 6 mm (0.236 inches) from the cylinder fin; If no sparks flash between cable and fin, the failure may be due to other causes including ignition coil.
3. Incorrect contact breaker point gap	Correct gap is 0.3~0.4 mm (0.012~0.016 inches).
Breaker points dirty, oxidized or burned	Clean both points with a fine file.
4. Excessive contact firing or badly burned contacts due to defective condenser	Check capacity of condenser with tester, replace it with new one when necessary. Correct capacity: $0.25 \pm 0.3\,\mu\mathrm{F}$ (micro-Farad) Insulation resistance: Over $5\,\mathrm{M}\Omega$ (Meg-ohm)
5. Checking ignition timing.	The main cause of failure is incorrect ignition timing.

B. Failures in fuel system

* Engine does not run smoothly at low and middle speeds.

	Possible causes	Remedies
1.	Clogged fuel line	Check the fuel flow from fuel tank to carburetor.
2.	Improperly adjusted pilot air screw	Correct adjustment is 2 turns back.
3.	Throttle valves not opening synchronously	Adjust both slow adjuster screws and then open the throttle grip slightly, until the "O" mark of throttle valve matches the upper line of ventilator.
4.	Defective carburetor	Air-blast all passages and jets and reassemble parts properly. Replace gasket with a new one.

* Engine does not run smoothly at high speeds.

1.	Fuel tank air vent hole plugged	Air blast the hole
2.	Clogged main jet	Air blast the hole
3.	Loosely fitting of carburetor to the engine	Tighten

C. Mechanical failures

1.	Insufficient compression	Check the compression Standard: 8.5–9.5 kg/cm^2 (121–135 lbs/in^2) Permissible Limit: 6.3 kg/cm^2 (90 lbs/in^2)
2.	Damaged rotary disc valve	Replace
3.	Worn crankshaft bearings	Replace
4.	Worn oil seals of crankcase	Replace

14. TOLERANCE AND FITS

A. Engine

		Standard	Permissible Limit
1.	Cylinder compression	8.5~9.5 kg/cm² (121–135 lbs/in²)	6.3 kg/cm² (90 lbs/in²)
2.	Maximum speed	Over 160 km/h (100 mph)	

B. Cylinder

		Standard	Permissible Limit
1.	Inside diameter	61.005~61.025 mm (2.4018~2.4026 inches)	61.1 mm (2.4055 inches)

Measure at 4 points along the wall

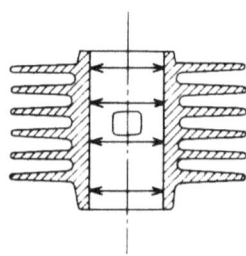 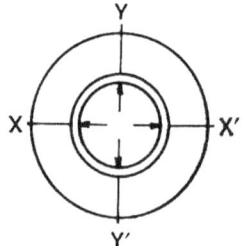

2.	Thickness of cylinder head gasket	0.95~1.05 mm (0.037~0.041 inches)	
3.	Nuts (Fitting torques)	250~300 kg/cm² (217~260 lbs/in²)	

C. Piston

		Standard	Permissible Limit
1.	Maximum diameter at skirt	60.956~60.985 mm (2.3959~2.3967 inches)	60.85 mm (2.3914 inches)
2.	Maximum clearance between piston & cylinder	0.04~0.05 mm (0.0016~0.0019 inches)	0.15 mm (0.0059 inches)

(Select piston and cylinder to get above clearance when replacing with new one)

		Standard	Permissible Limit
3.	Outside diameter of the piston pin	16.994~17.00 mm (0.6678~0.6681 inches)	16.90 mm (0.6288 inches)
4.	Piston ring free gap	0.15~0.35 mm (0.0059~0.0138 inches)	1.0 mm (0.0393 inches)

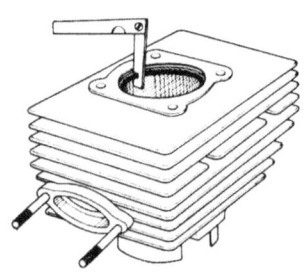

D. Crankshaft & Rotary Disc Valve

		Standard	Permissible Limit
1.	Inside diameter of big end of connecting rod	30.008~30.017 mm (1.1793~1.1797 inches)	30.057 mm (1.1812 inches)
2.	Inside diameter of small end of connecting rod	21.00~21.013 mm (0.8253~0.8258 inches)	21.053 mm (0.8274 inches)
3.	Thrust side play of small end of connecting rod		4.2 mm (0.1654 inches)
4.	Thrust side play of big end of connecting rod	0.1~0.3 mm (0.004~0.012 inches)	
5.	Outside diameter of left crankshaft (A)	24.004~25.009 mm (0.9434~0.9829 inches)	23.98 mm (0.9424 inches)
6.	Outside diameter of right crankshaft (B)	21.99~22.005 mm (0.8642~0.8648 inches)	21.97 mm (0.8634 inches)
7.	Up and down play of crankshaft	Less than 0.02 mm (0.0008 inches)	0.15 mm (0.0059 inch)
8.	Thickness of rotary disc valve	3.95~4.00 mm (0.1552~0.1572 inches)	

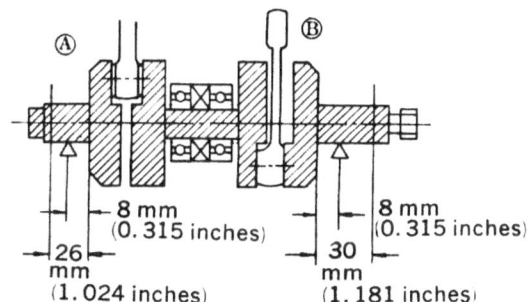

E. Clutch

		Standard	Permissible Limit
1.	Type	Multiple discs (seven facings), dry type	
2.	Distortion of clutch friction plate	Less than 0.1 mm (0.0039 inches)	0.2 mm (0.0078 inches)
3.	Thickness of friction plate	2.95~3.00 mm	(0.1161~0.1181 inches)
4.	Width of friction plate teeth	14.76 mm	(0.581 inches)

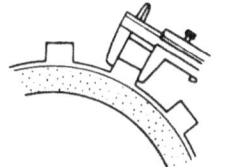

Inspecting width of teeth of friction plate   Inspecting distortion of inner plate

		Standard	Permissible Limit
5.	Distortion of inner plate	Less than 0.2 mm (0.0078 inches)	
6.	Distortion of outer plate	Less than 0.2 mm (0.0078 inches)	
7.	Free length of clutch spring	30.3~30.9 mm (1.1908~1.2144 inches)	29 mm (1.1397 inches)

F. **Number of teeth**

1.	Drive pinion gear	21	14.	6th gear B	22
2.	Driven gear	65	15.	Drive sprocket	15
3.	1st gear A	13	16.	Driven sprocket	36
4.	2nd gear A	17	17.	Kick gear	22
5.	3rd gear A	20	18.	Kick starter gear A	15
6.	4th gear A	23	19.	Kick starter gear B	30
7.	5th gear A	27	20.	Oil pump gear B	25
8.	6th gear A	29			
9.	1st gear B	32			
10.	2nd gear B	28			
11.	3rd gear B	25			
12.	4th gear B	23			
13.	5th gear B	23			

Correct pattern of teeth

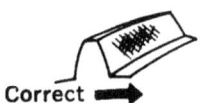 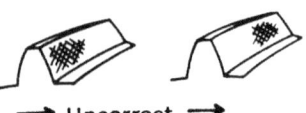

Correct ➡   ➡ Uncorrect ➡

G. **Fork guide**

		Standard	Permissible Limit
1.	Thickness of fork guide	5.35~5.45 mm	5.1 mm
		(0.2103~0.2142 inches)	(0.2004 inches)

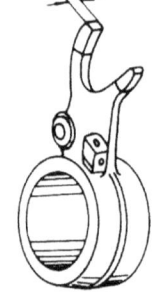

Measuring thickness of fork guide

H. **A.C. Generator & Ignition coil**

1. Rated output of A.C. Generator — 62 Watt/2000 Engine rpm
   88 Watt/5000 〃
   98 Watt/8000 〃
2. Ignition timing — 23~26° Before Top Dead Center (B.T.D.C.)
3. Contact breaker point gap — 0.3~0.4 mm (0.012~0.016 inches)
4. Condenser capacity — 0.22~0.28 micro Farad (μF)
5. Ignition coil
   Type — HS-12B
   Sparks — Over 9 mm at 1,500 Engine rpm
   Insulate resistance — Over than 500 Meg Ohm (MΩ)
6. Spark plug
   Type — B-8H or B-9H
   Plug gap — 0.5~0.6 mm
   (0.020~0.024 inches)

I. **Carburetor**

1. Type — Mikuni VM 26 SC
2. Throttle valve cut away — 2.0 mm
3. Main jet — No. 140 (130 for high temp)
4. Jet needle — 4D 3-2/5
5. Pilot jet — No. 30
6. Air screw turn-back — 2
7. Float level — 24±1.0 mm (0.98~0.91 inches)

J. Oil pump

		Standard	Permissible Limit
1.	Min. plunger stroke	0.40~0.45 mm (0.016-0.018 inchss) (60 cc/h~68 cc/h) at 5000 Engine rpm	Plunger stroke is measured with a dial gauge
2.	Max. plunger stroke	3.6~3.73 mm (0.142-0.147 inches) (600 cc/h~626 cc/h) at 5000 Engine rpm	

K. Frame

1.	Caster	63°	
2.	Trail	105 mm (4.13 inches)	
3.	Fuel tank capacity	15 litre (3⅘ US. gal) Including 3.2 litre (4/5 US. gal reserve)	
4.	Oil tank capacity	2.5 litre (3/5 US. gal)	
5.	Brake lining thickness	4.5 mm (0.1772 inches)	2 mm (0.079 inches)
6.	Brake shoes thickness	179.6~179.9 mm (7.07~7.08 inches)	177 mm (6.97 inches)
7.	Brake drum inside diameter	180~180.2 mm (7.09~7.095 mm)	181 mm (7.13 inches)

L. Suspension

1. Front fork
   - Stroke — 120 mm (4.716 inches)
   - Oil capacity — 220 cc (1/2 pint)
   - Oil surface — 405 mm (15.92 inches) — 435 mm (17.09 inches)
2. Rear suspension
   - Stroke — 80 mm (3.14 inches)

M. Lighting equipment

1. Battery
   - Capacity — 12V~6AH
   - Acid capacity — 390 cc (4.5 pint)
   - Specific gravity — 1.280 at 20°C (68°F) — 1.220
2. Main switch
   - Insulate resistance — over than 1 MΩ
3. Selenium rectifire
   - Capacity — 2.7 Amp. — 10 mm Amp.
4. Head lamp — 12V~35/30 W
5. 5th gear indicator lamp — 12V~3W
6. Speedometer lamp — 12V~3W
7. Stop lamp — 12V~23W
8. Tail lamp — 12V~7W
9. Horn volume — 95~115 phone
10. Fuse — 10 A
11. Speedometer error — +10% −0

N. Adjusting Torque

Size	Kg-cm	Lbs-inch
Stud (8×50) Exhaust	250~300	217~260
Stud (6×40) Dynamo	100~120	86~104
Stud (8×156) Cylinder	350~400	304~345
5 mm Hexagon bolt A	40~50	35~43
6 mm Hexagon bolt A	60~90	52~78
8 mm Hexagon bolt A	140~200	122~174
6 mm Clutch set bolt	70~90	61~78
8 mm Drum guide bolt	150~200	130~174
8 mm Change arm stopper pin	200~250	174~217
6 mm Tachometer bushing bolt	70~90	61~78
5 mm Cross pan head screw	35~45	30~39
6 mm Cross pan head screw	60~90	52~78
6 mm Cross flat head screw	60~80	52~69
40 mm Ring nut (clutch)	400~500	347~434
8 mm Cylinder head nut	250~300	217~260
20 mm Left thread nut (Pinion gear)	900~1000	780~868
8 mm Hexagon nut C (worm shaft)	150~200	130~174
16 mm Hexagon nut (Counter shaft)	400~500	347~434
Spark plug	200~300	174~260
8 mm Check valve ass'y	60~80	52~69
16 mm Drain plug	400~500	347~434
17 mm Hexagonal nut	500~700	434~610
10 mm Hexagonal nut	200~350	174~304

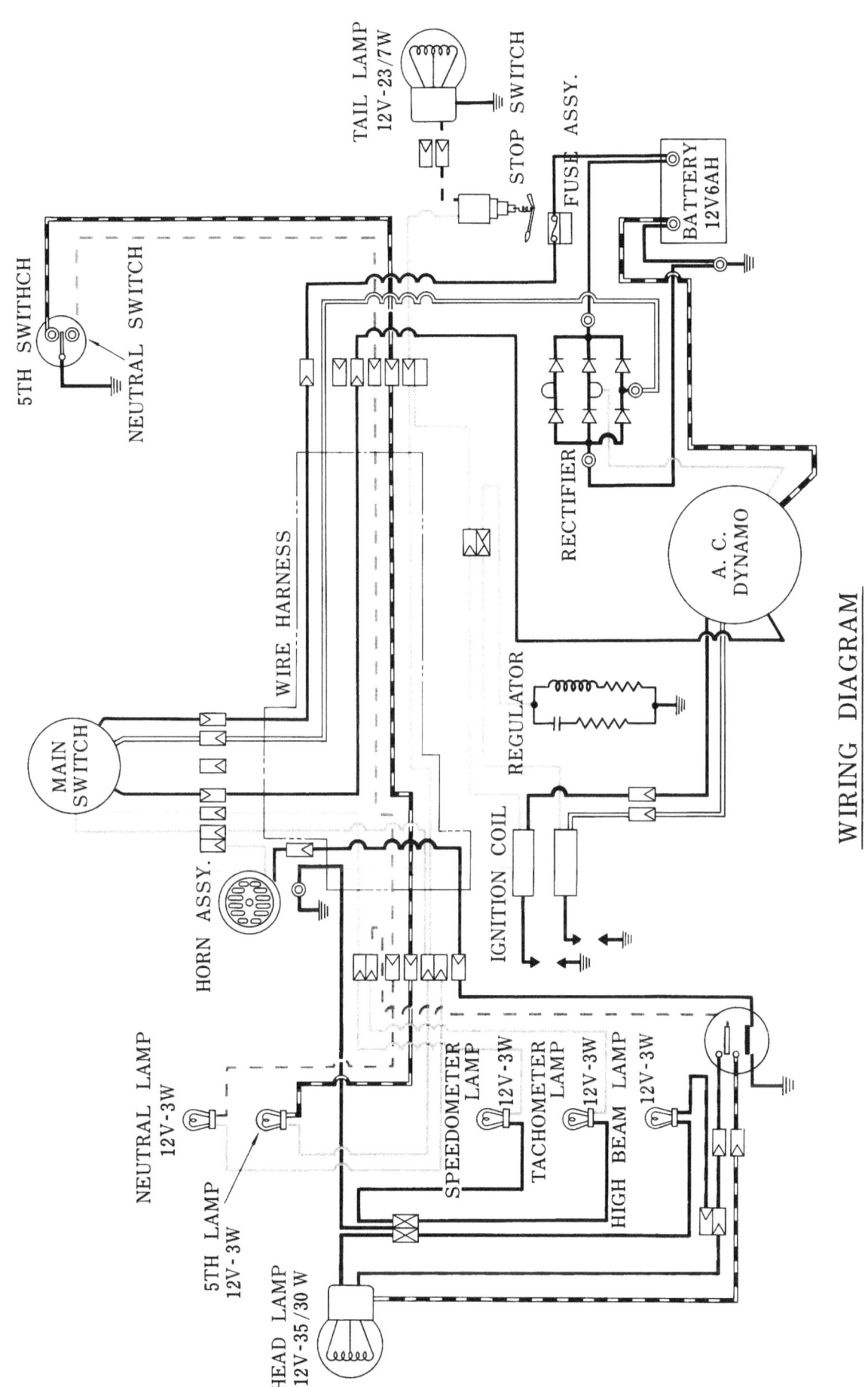

SERVICE MEMO

BRIDGESTONE MOTORCYCLES

TUNING UP FOR COMPETITION

QUALITY MACHINE FROM JAPAN

TUNING-UP 350 GTR FOR ROAD RACING

BRIDGESTONE
350 *GTR*
For ROAD RACING

3. DESIGN OF MUFFLER

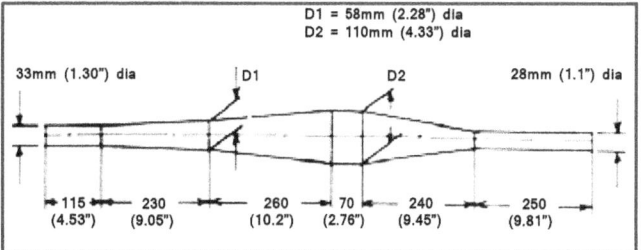

4. ENLARGE TWO TRANSFER PORTS

1. MODIFICATION OF ROTARY DISC VALVES

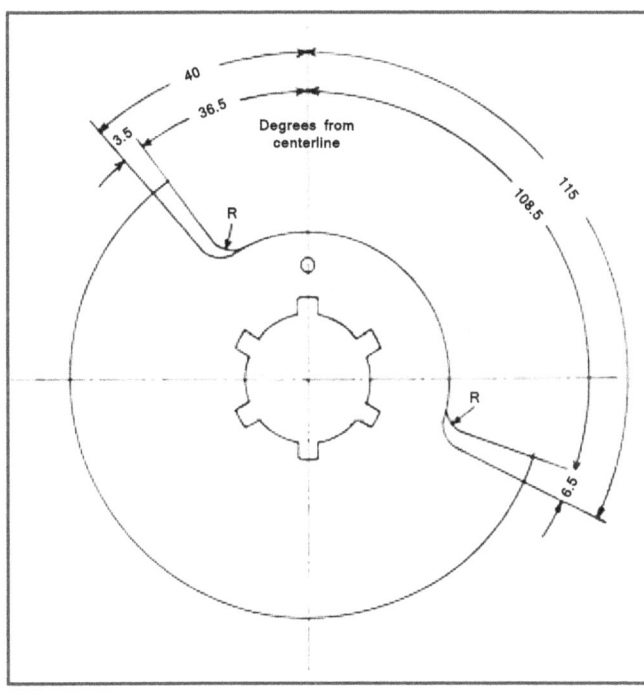

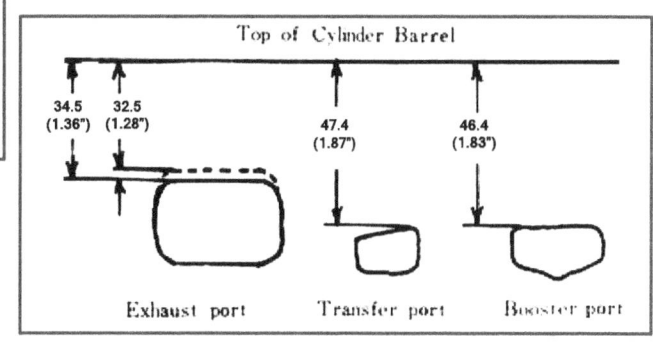

Enlarge both transfer ports with a fine electric grinder as shown, to eliminate flow friction of gas.

5. CYLINDER PORT TIMING

Enlarge valve gap at the disc as shown. Finish the cut corners (R) carefully to prevent cracking of the disc at high speed.

2. CARBURETOR SETTING

Standard size carburetor will be effective for races, except main jet size from No. 90 (original size) to No. 100.

Raise exhaust port 2 mm (0.079 inches) with an electric grinder as shown. Transfer port & Booster port are not required to be changed.

6. INCREASE COMBUSTION CHAMBER PRESSURE

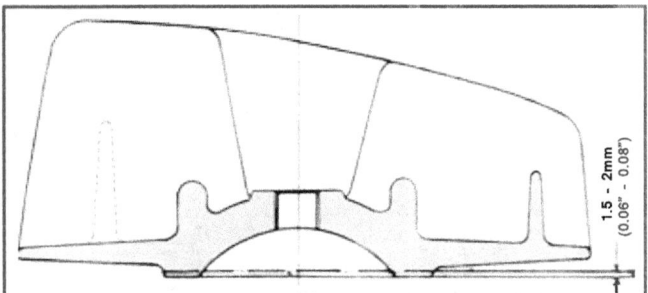

Raise combustion chamber compression by shaving down the cylinder head base as shown.

7. MODIFICATION OF ROTARY DISC VALVE COVER

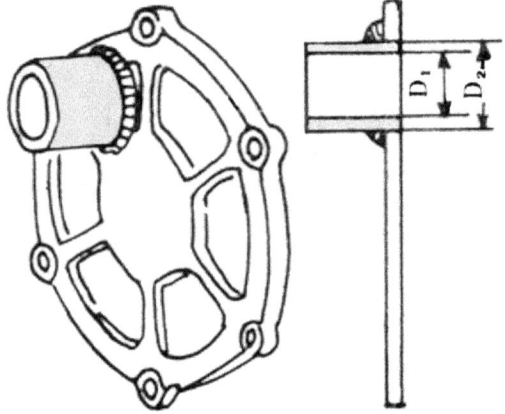

D_1 = 30mm Dia. (1.2")
D_2 = 34mm Dia. (1.34")
D_2 = D_1 + 4 mm (0.16")

To suit the 30 mm bore carburetor, make and weld a larger tube, as shown.

8. IGNITION TIMING

8-1. Ignition Timing: 25° Before Top Dead Center same as standard timing.

8-2. Piston Displacement Before Top Dead Center: 3.6 mm (0.142 inches) same as standard displacement.

8-3. Point Gap of Contact Breaker: 0.25-0.3 mm (0.01-0.012 inches) instead of 0.3-0.4 mm (0.012-0_016 inches) of original gap

8-4. Spark Plug: NGK B-8HN-IOHN

Performance of Standard Engine

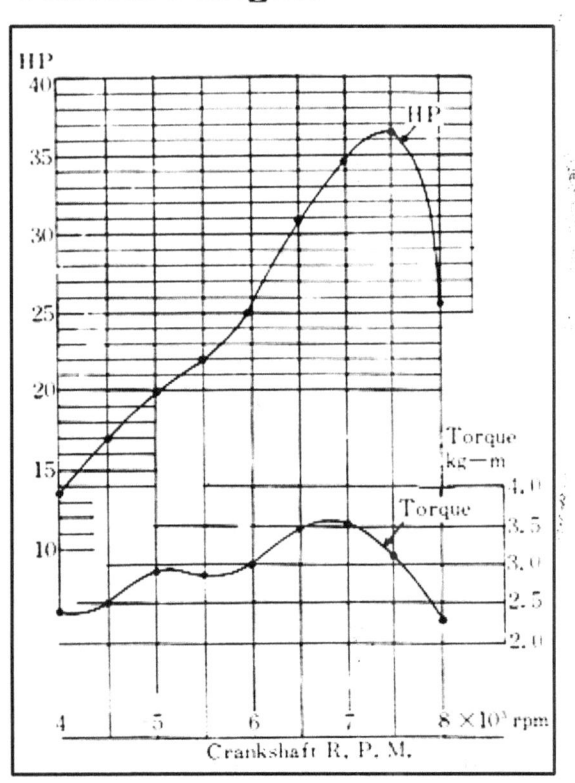

Performance after Tune-up

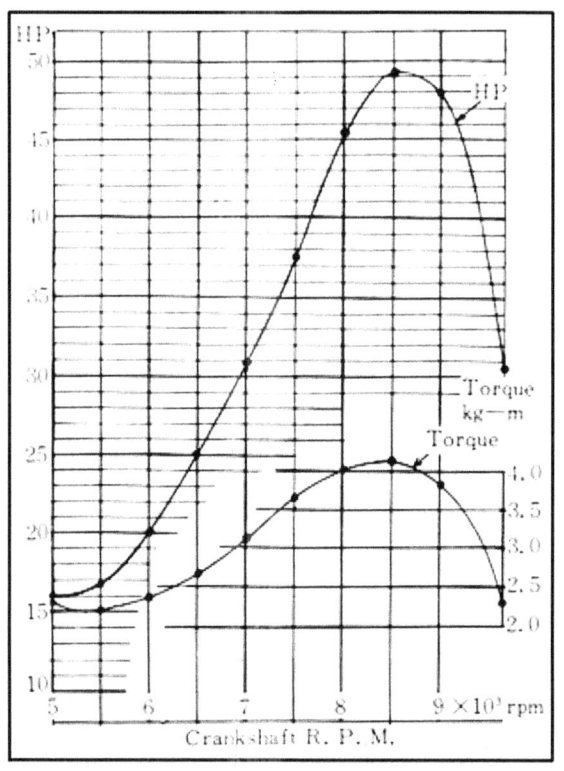

TUNING-UP 350GTR FOR SCRAMBLING

BRIDGESTONE
350 GTR
For SCRAMBLING

For tuning, it is only necessary to make the following modifications:

1. DESIGN OF MUFFLER

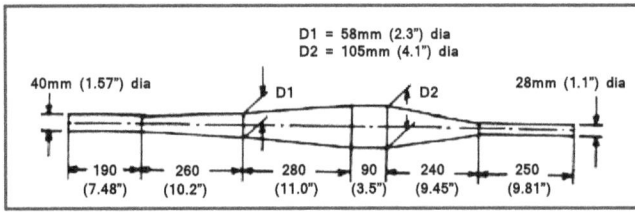

2. INCREASE COMBUSTION CHAMBER COMPRESSION

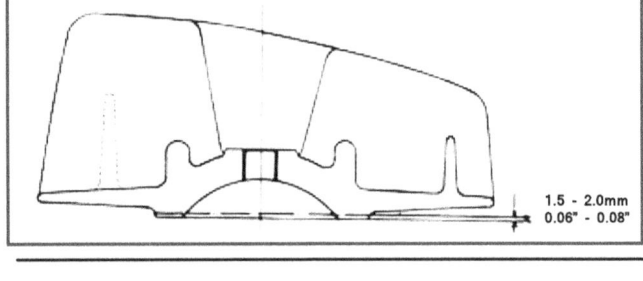

Raise combustion chamber compression by shaving down the cylinder head base as shown.

3. CARBURETOR SETTING

To obtain higher power output at high speed, the AMAL racing type carburetor 26mm main bore and with a separate float chamber is preferable to VM 26 mm bore originally equipped.

4. REMARKS

The following items do not require any modification except the point gap of contact breaker and spark plug.

4-1. Point Gap of Contact Breaker:
 0.25-0.3 mm (0.010-0.012 inches) instead of 0.3-0.4 mm (0.012-0.016 inches) of original gap.

4-2. Spark Plug: NGK B-8HN~B-9HN

Performance of Standard Engine

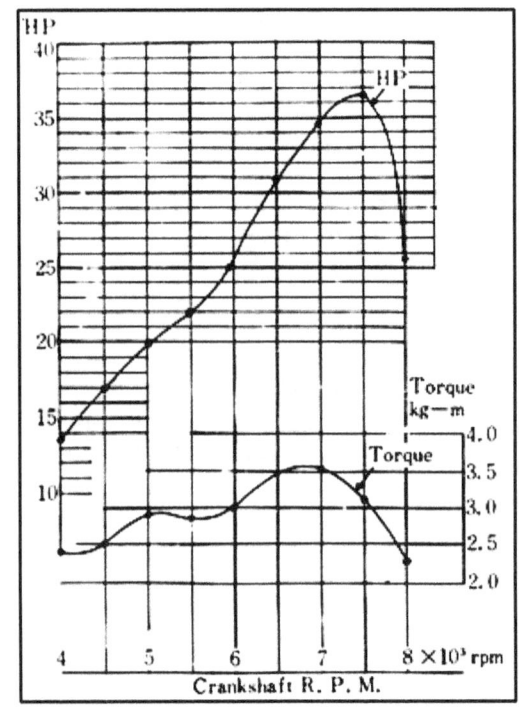

Performance after Tune-up

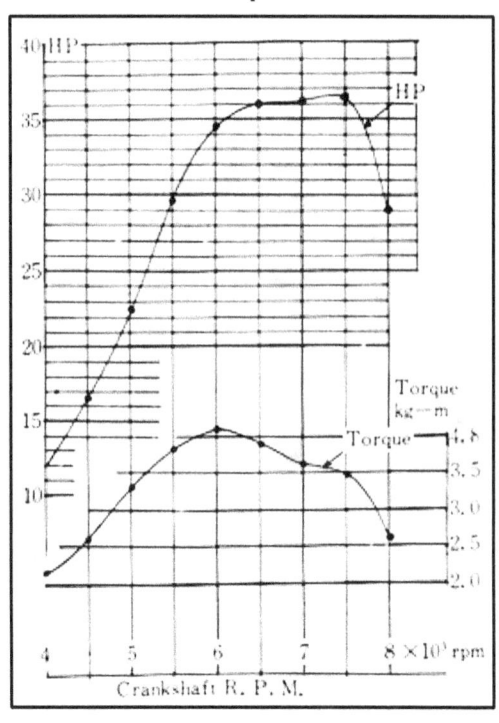

PARTS CATALOGUE

BRIDGESTONE 350 GTR

P7350WO

 BRIDGESTONE TIRE CO., LTD.

Printed in Japan. July. '67

INSTRUCTIONS FOR USING THE PARTS CATALOGUE

1. This catalogue covers all the items of genuine parts and tools of BRIDGESTONE 350GTR motorcycle.
2. Please note the following when placing orders.
   a. Be sure to state accurately the index No., part No., and name of each part.
   b. All the items recessed (set-back) under individual "assembly item" represent a group of parts comprising the "Assembly"
   c. The numbers shown in the column "No. Req'd" represent the quantities required for one unit.
   d. The numbers shown in the column "Min. lot" represent the quantities to be ordered in one lot, and in the event of larger quantities, order in multiple quantities of the minimum specified.
   e. Symbols FAR, CBK, MS and XCl following the Part Number indicate Flamboyant red, Black, Metallic silver and chrome plating finish respectively.
   f. Dimensions of the parts listed in this catalogue are in millimeters.

CONTENTS

Index No.	Description	Page
	Engine Group	
1)	Cylinder · Cylinder Head	2~ 3
2)	Crankshaft · Piston · Rotary Valve	4~ 5
3)	Oil Pump · Pump Gear · Air Cleaner	6~ 7
4)	Carburetor	8~ 9
5)	Dynamo · Neutral Switch	10~11
6)	Crank Case	12~13
7)	Left Crank Case Cover	14~15
8)	Right Crank Case Cover	16~17
9)	Clutch	18~19
10)	Transmission	20~21
11)	Gear Change Pedal · Shift Drum	22~23
12)	Kick Starter	24~25
	Body Group	
13)	Frame	26~29
14)	Main Stand · Brake Pedal	30~31
15)	Front Fork	32~35
16)	Front Fender · Handle Bar	36~37
17)	Rear Fork · Rear Cushion	38~39
18)	Fuel Tank · Oil Tank	40~41
19)	Clutch Grip	42~43
20)	Throttle Grip · Winker Lamp	44~45
21)	Speedometer Cable · Wires	46~47
22)	Muffler · Exhaust Pipe	48~49
23)	Dual Seat · Winker Relay	50~51
24)	Front Wheel	52~55
25)	Rear Wheel	56~59
26)	Head Lamp · Tail Lamp	60~61
27)	Speedometer · Ignition Coil · Main Switch	62~63
28)	Service Tool Set · Special Tool Set	64~65

1) CYLINDER · CYLINDER HEAD

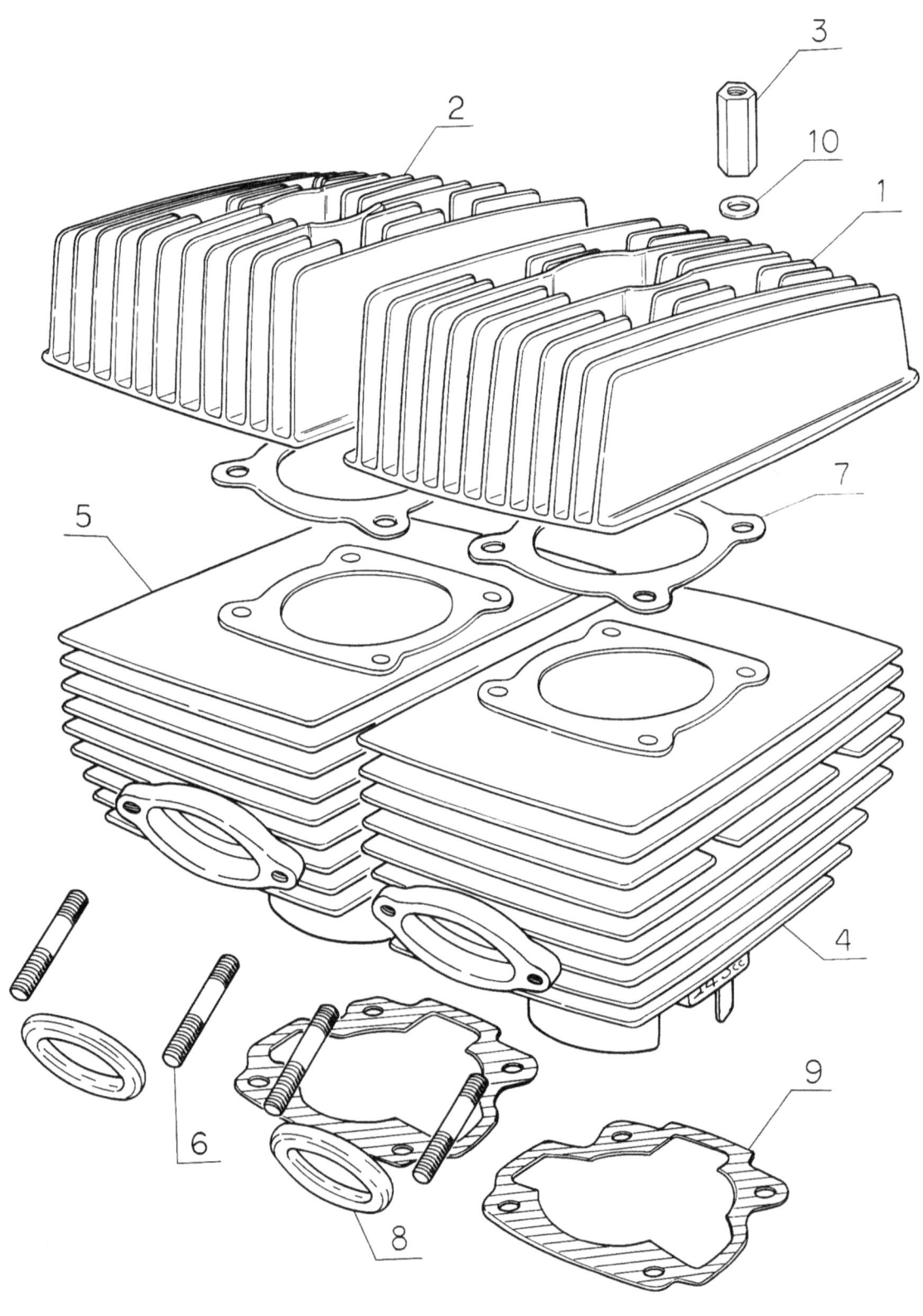

1) CYLINDER · CYLINDER HEAD

Index No.	Part No.	Part Name	No. Req'd	Unit Price	Min. Lot	Remarks
1- 1	1112-9000	Left cylinder head	1			
1- 2	1113-9000	Right cylinder head	1			
1- 3	1115-5400	Cylinedr head nut	8		10	100SP/OI
1- 4	1122-9000	Left cylinder	1			
1- 5	1123-9000	Right cylinder	1			
1- 6	09016-113	8×50 Stud	4		10	
1- 7	1141-9000	Cylinder head gasket	2		10	
1- 8	1142-9000	Exhaust pipe gasket	2		10	
1- 9	1143-9000	Cylinder base gasket	2		10	
1-10	0421-0816	Plane washer B	8		50	

MEMO

1000-9000 Engine ass'y.

2) CRANK SHAFT · PISTON · ROTARY VALVE

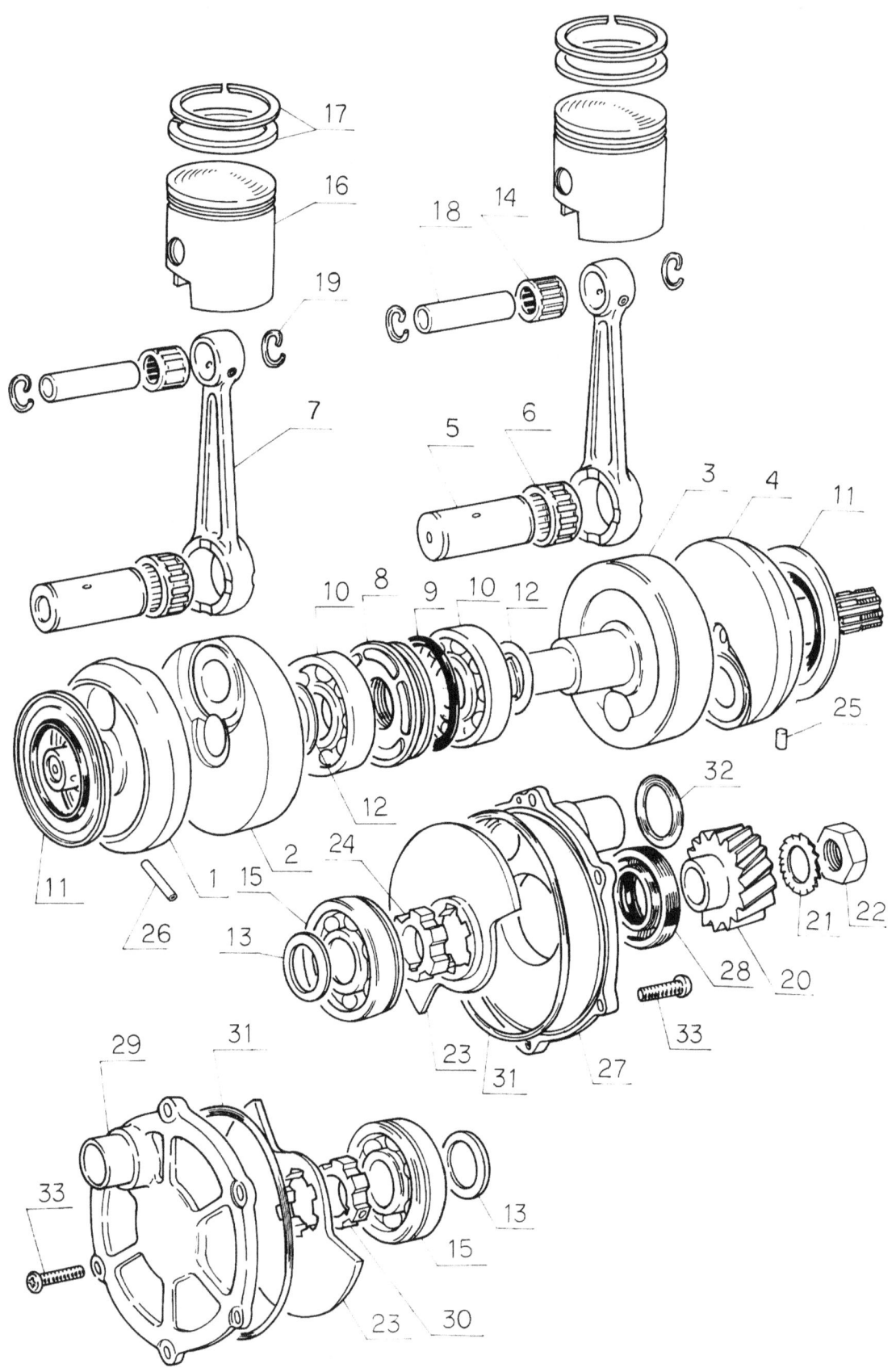

2) CRANK SHAFT · PISTON · ROTARY VALVE

Index No.	Part No.	Part Name	No. Req'd	Unit Price	Min. Lot	Remarks
2–	1301–9000	Crank shaft comp	1			
2– 1	1313–9000	Left crank shaft A	1			
2– 2	1314–9000	Left crank shaft B	1			
2– 3	1315–9000	Right crank shaft A	1			
2– 4	1316–9000	Right crank shaft B	1			
2– 5	1321–9000	Crank pin	2			
2– 6	1325–9000	Needle bearing	2			
2– 7	1331–9000	Connecting rod	2			
2– 8	1337–9000	Labyrinth packing	1		10	
2– 9	09066–120	59 O ring	1		10	
2–10	09075–104	Ball bearing	2		10	
2–11	09090–117	57 Oil seal	2		10	
2–12	09049–108	30×0.3 shim	2		10	
2–13	09049–109	25×0.3 shim	2		10	
2–14	1333–9000	Needle bearing	2		10	
2–15	09075–106	Ball bearing	2		10	
2–16	1341–9000	Piston	2			
2–17	1305–9000	Piston ring set	2			
2–18	1381–9000	Piston pin	2			
2–19	1382–9000	Piston pin circlip	4		10	
2–20	1385–9000	Drive pinion	1			
2–21	09045–103	20 external toothed washer	1		50	
2–22	09029–104	20 left thread nut	1		10	
2–23	1412–9000	Rotary valve	2			
2–24	1413–9000	Valve guide	1			
2–25	09056–102	4×8 A dowel	1		50	
2–26	09059–101	4×18 spring pin	1		50	
2–27	1430–9000	Valve cover comp	1			
2–28	09090–118	32 oil seal	1		10	
2–29	1441–9000	Left valve cover	1			
2–30	1423–9000	Left valve guide	1			
2–31	09066–121	125 O ring	2		10	
2–32	09066–122	33 O ring	1		10	
2–33	0311–0616	Cross recd pan head screw	12		50	

3) OIL PUMP · PUMP GEAR · AIR CLEANER

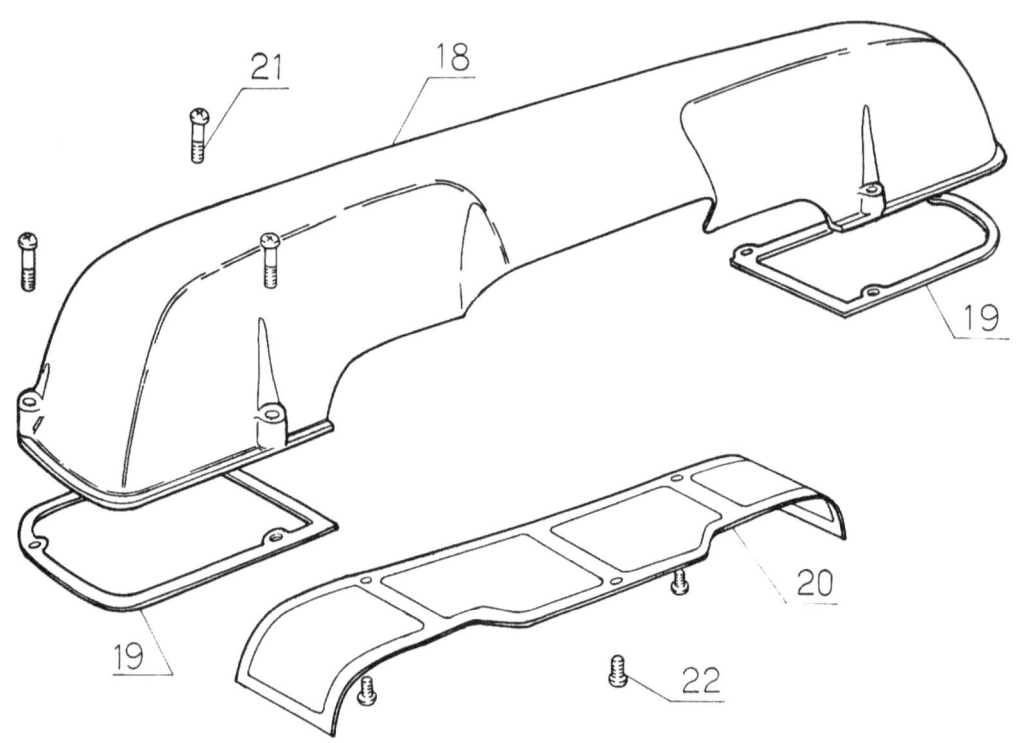
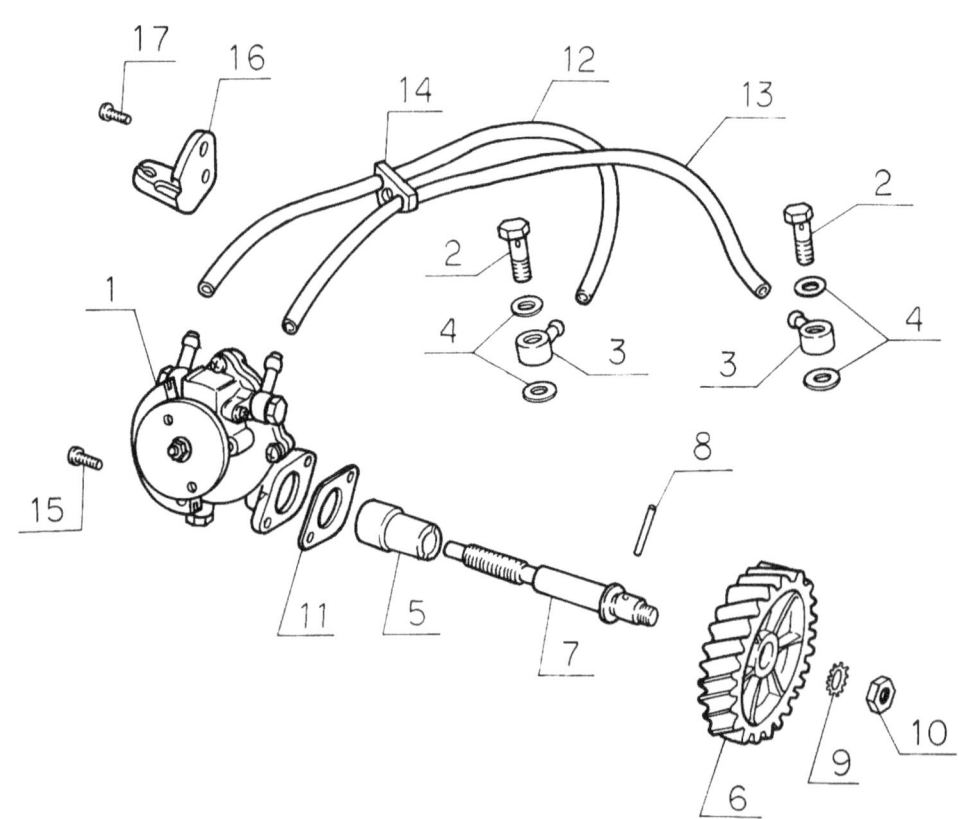

3) OIL PUMP · PUMP GEAR · AIR CLEANER

Index No.	Part No.	Part Name	No. Req'd	Unit Price	Min. Lot	Remarks
3- 1	1501-9000	Oil pump assy	1			
3- 2	1502-9000	Check valve assy	2			
3- 3	1575-9000	Union connection C	2			
3- 4	09065-104	8 Aluminium gasket	4		10	
3- 5	1513-9000	Worm shaft bush B	1			
3- 6	1552-9000	Pump gear B	1			
3- 7	1555-9000	Worm shaft	1			
3- 8	09056-109	3 × 24 A dowel	1		10	
3- 9	0451-0815	External toothed washer	1		50	
3-10	0231-0800	Hexagon nut C	1		50	
3-11	1563-5010	Pump gasket	1		10	
3-12	1566-9000	Oil tube A	1		10	
3-13	1567-9000	Oil tube B	1		10	
3-14	1573-9000	Oil tube grommet	1			
3-15	0311-0516	Cross recd pan head screw	2		50	
3-16	1582-9000	Wire bracket	1			
3-17	0311-0510	Coss recd pan head screw	2		50	
3-18	6221-9000	Air cleaner case	1			
3-19	6225-9000	Cleaner case gasket	2			
3-20	6214-9000	Air cleaner element	1			
3-21	0311-0525	Cross rec'd pan head screw	6		50	
3-22	0311-0510	Cross rec'd pan head screw	3		50	
Old Air Cleaner						
3-	6221-9000	Air cleaner case	1			
3-	6225-9000	Cleaner case gasket	2			
3-	6212-9000	Left air cleaner element	1			
3-	6213-9000	Right air cleaner element	1			
3-	0311-0625	Ceoss recd pan head screw	6		50	

MEMO

4) CARBURETOR

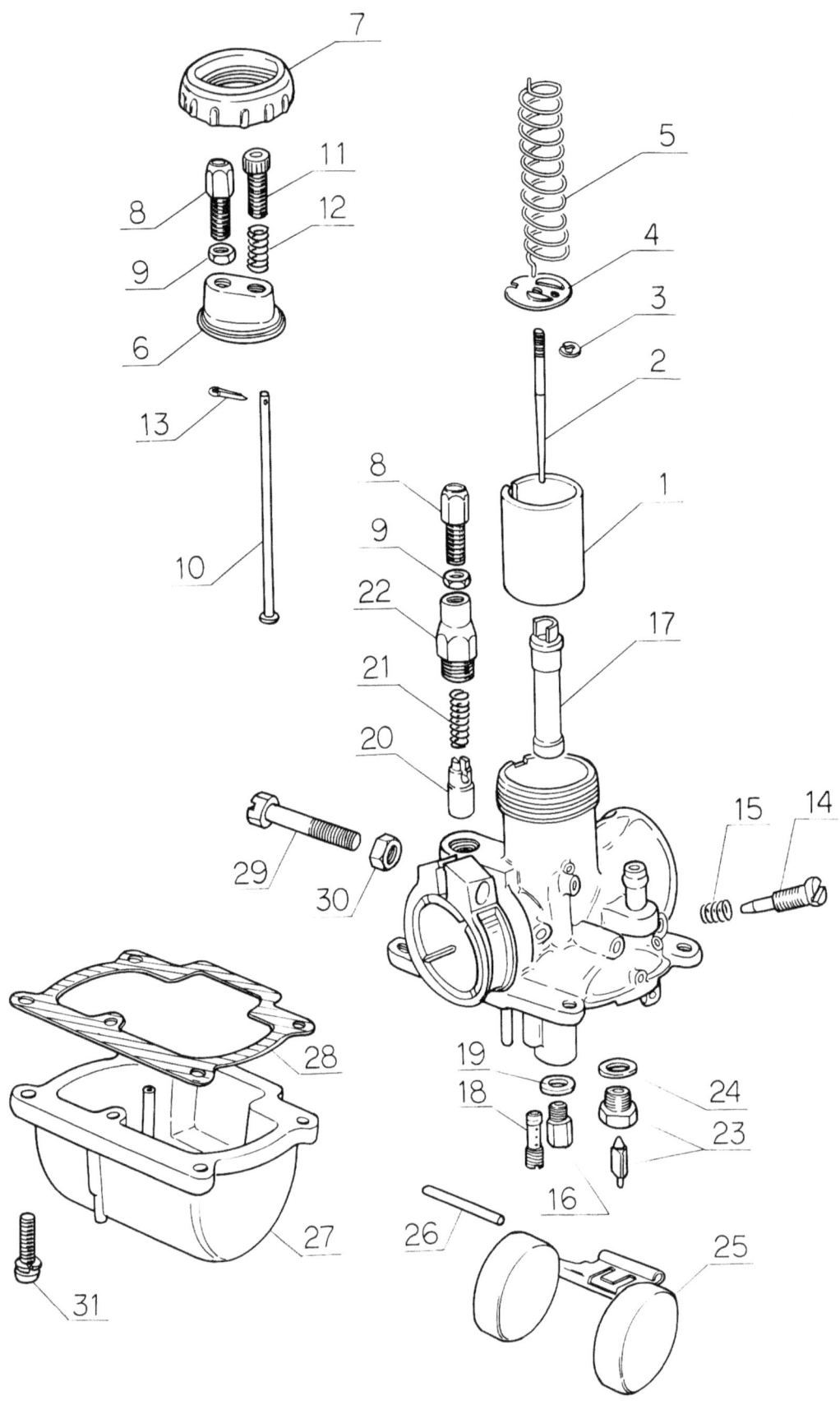

4) CARBURETOR

Index No.	Part No.	Part Name	No. Req'd	Unit Price	Min. Lot	Remarks
4–	1600-9000	Carburetor assy	2			
4- 1	1614-9000	Throttle valve	2			
4- 2	1615-9000	Jet needle	2			
4- 3	1616-9000	Needle clip	2			
4- 4	1617-9000	Spring seat	2			
4- 5	1618-9000	Throttle valve spring	2			
4- 6	1619-9000	Mixing chamber top	2			
4- 7	1621-9000	Mixing chamber cap	2			
4- 8	1622-5000	Cable adjuster	4			
4- 9	1623-5000	Adjuster lock nut	4			
4-10	1626-9000	Throttle stop rod	2			
4-11	1627-5000	Throttle stop screw	2			
4-12	1628-5010	Stop screw spring	2			
4-13	0551-1010	Split pin	2			
4-14	1631-9000	Pilot air screw	2			
4-15	1632-9000	Air screw spring	2			
4-16	1635-5010-140	140 main jet	2			
4-17	1633-9000	Needle jet	2			
4-18	1634-9000	Pilot jet	2			
4-19	1636-9000	Washer	2			
4-20	1645-5000	Starter plunger	2			
4-21	1646-5000	Plunger spring	2			
4-22	1647-5000	Plunger cap	2			
4-23	1660-9000	Float valve assy	2			
4-24	1665-9000	Valve seat gasket	2			
4-25	1666-9000	Float	2			
4-26	1667-9000	Float pin	2			
4-27	1656-9000	Float chamber body	2			
4-28	1657-9000	Float chamber gasket	2			
4-29	1613-5010	Clamp screw	2			
4-30	0211-0600	Hexagon nut A	2		50	
4-31	1659-9000	Set screw	8			

MEMO

5) DYNAMO · NEUTRAL SWITCH

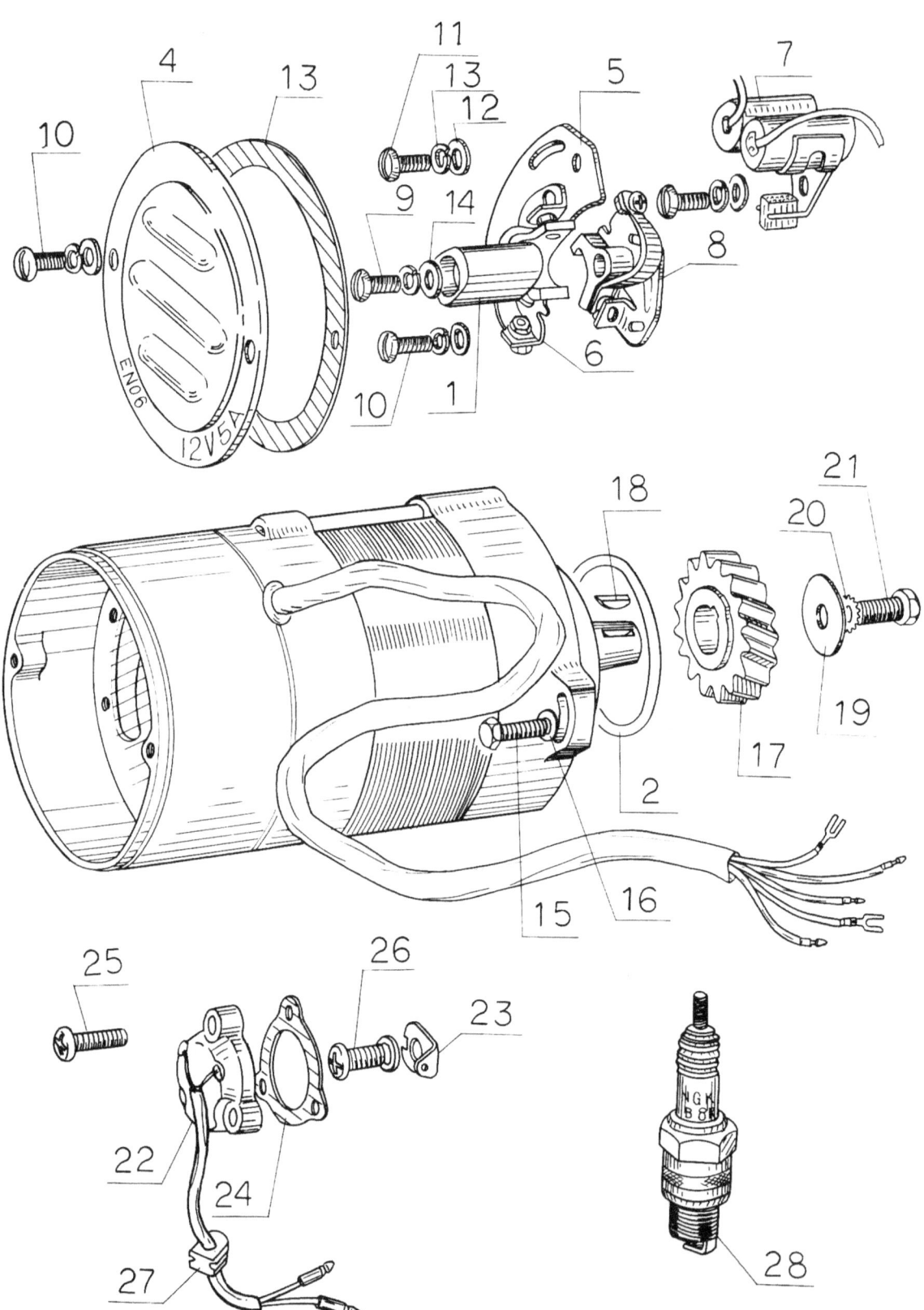

5) DYNAMO·NEUTRAL SWITCH

Index No.	Part No.	Part Name	No. Req'd	Unit Price	Min. Lot	Remarks
5-	1703-9000	A. C dynamo assy	1			
5- 1	1736-9000	Contact breaker cam	1			
5- 2	1737-8000	O ring	1			
5- 3	1738-8000	Contact breaker cover gasket	1			
5- 4	1739-8000	Contact breaker cover	1			
5- 5	1751-8001	Contact breaker base	1			
5- 6	1752-8001	Left contact breaker assy	1			
5- 7	1753-8000	Condenser	1			
5- 8	1757-8001	Right contact breaker assy	1			
5- 9	0361-0412	Pan head screw	1		50	
5-10	0361-0410	Pan head screw	5		50	
5-11	0361-0407	Pan head screw	4		50	
5-12	0421-0408	Plane washer B	6		50	
5-13	0431-0410	Spring washer	10		50	
5-14	09041-114	4 plane washer	1		50	
5-15	0111-0530	Hexagon bolt A	1		50	
5-16	0411-0512	Plane washer A	1		50	
5-17	1741-9000	Timing gear	1			
5-18	09067-102	3×13 woodruff key	1		50	
5-19	09041-112	6 plane washer	1		50	
5-20	0451-0611	External toothed washer	1		50	
5-21	0113-0616	Hexagon bolt A	1		50	
5-22	1761-9000	Neutral switch case	1			
5-23	1762-8001	Neutral switch contact plete	1			
5-24	1763-8000	Neutral switch gasket	1			
5-25	0311-0518	Cross recd pan head screw	3		50	
5-26	0311-0612	Cross recd pan head screw	1		50	
5-27	1764-9000	Neutral switch wire grommet	1			
5-28	1781-8000	Spark plug	2			NGK B-8H

MEMO

6) CRANK CASE

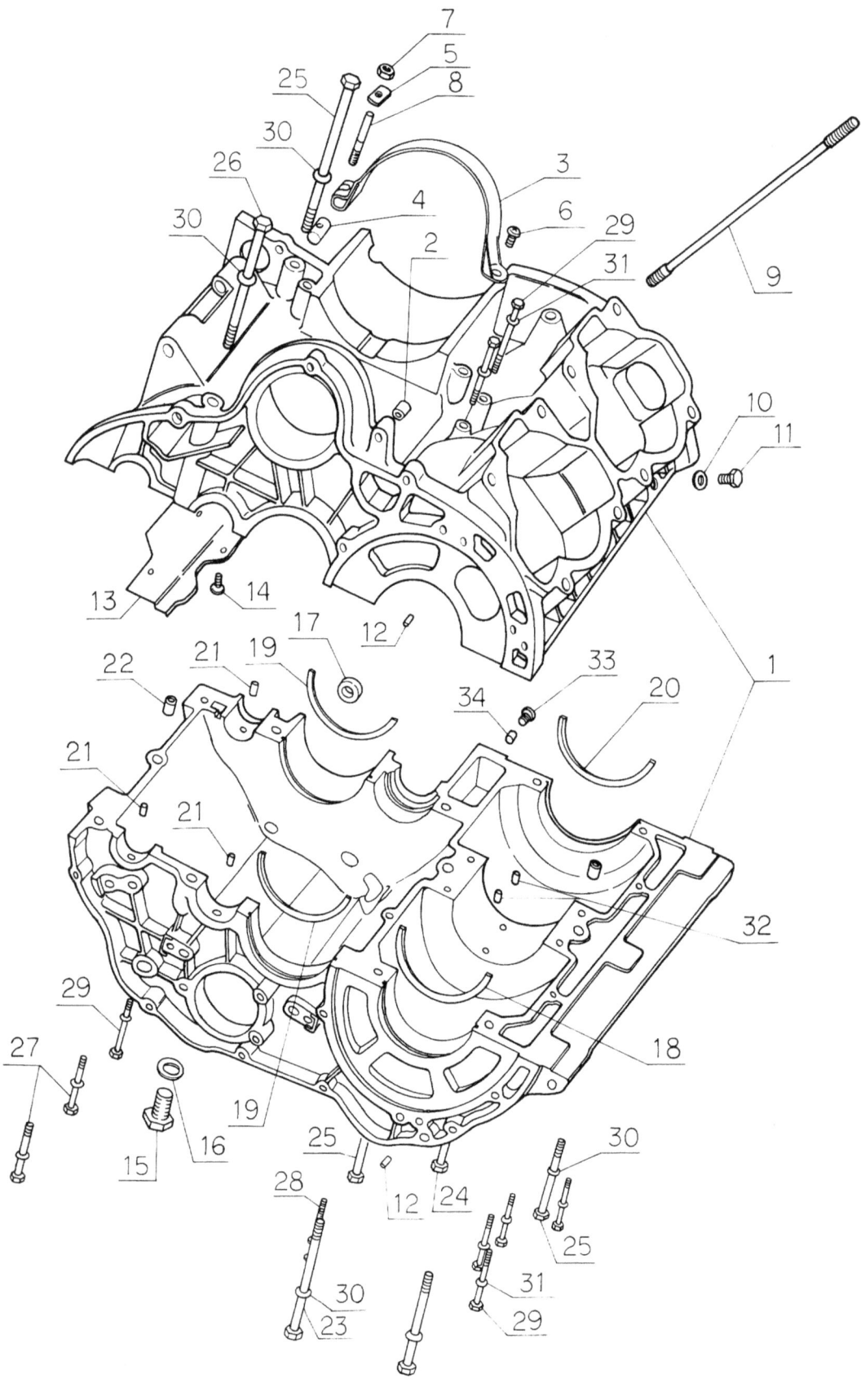

6) CRANK CASE

Index No.	Part No.	Part Name	No. Req'd	Unit Price	Min. Lot	Remarks
6- 1	2101-9000	Crank case assy	1			
6- 2	2116-9000	Dynamo spacer	1			
6- 3	2117-9000	Dynamo set band	1			
6- 4	2118-8000	Dynamo set pin	1			
6- 5	2149-8000	Set band washer	1			
6- 6	0311-0610	Cross recd pan head screw	1		50	
6- 7	09021-104	6 hexagon nut	1		10	
6- 8	09016-101	6×40 stud	1			
6- 9	09016-114	8×156 stud	8			
6-10	09064-103	8 fiber gasket	1		50	
9-11	0111-0812	Hexagon bolt A	1		50	
6-12	09056-102	4×8 A dowel	1		50	
6-13	2128-9000	Oil baffle plate	1			
6-14	0311-0510	Cross recd pan head screw	3		50	
9-15	09058-103	16 drain plug	1			
6-16	09065-102	16 aluminum gasket	1		10	
6-17	09090-101	12 oil seal	1		10	
6-18	2122-9000	Bearing retainer A	1			
6-19	2123-9000	Bearing retainer B	2			
6-20	2125-9000	Bearing retainer C	1			
6-21	09056-103	6×10 A dowel	3		10	
6-22	09057-102	8×12×14 B dowel	2		10	
6-23	09511-113	8×114 hexagon bolt	1			
6-24	09011-102	8×100 hexagon bolt	1			
6-25	0113-0890	Hexagon bolt A	4			
6-26	0113-0880	Hexagon bolt A	1			
6-27	0113-0862	Hexagon bolt A	2			
6-28	09011-106	6×70 hexagon bolt	1		10	
6-29	0113-0662	Hexagon bolt A	7		10	
6-30	0411-0818	Plane washer A	9		50	
6-31	0411-0613	Plane washer A	8		50	
6-32	09056-111	5×10 A dowel	2		10	
6-33	2137-9000	8 rubber plug	1			
6-34	2139-9000	8 plug	2			

MEMO

7) LEFT CRANK CASE COVER

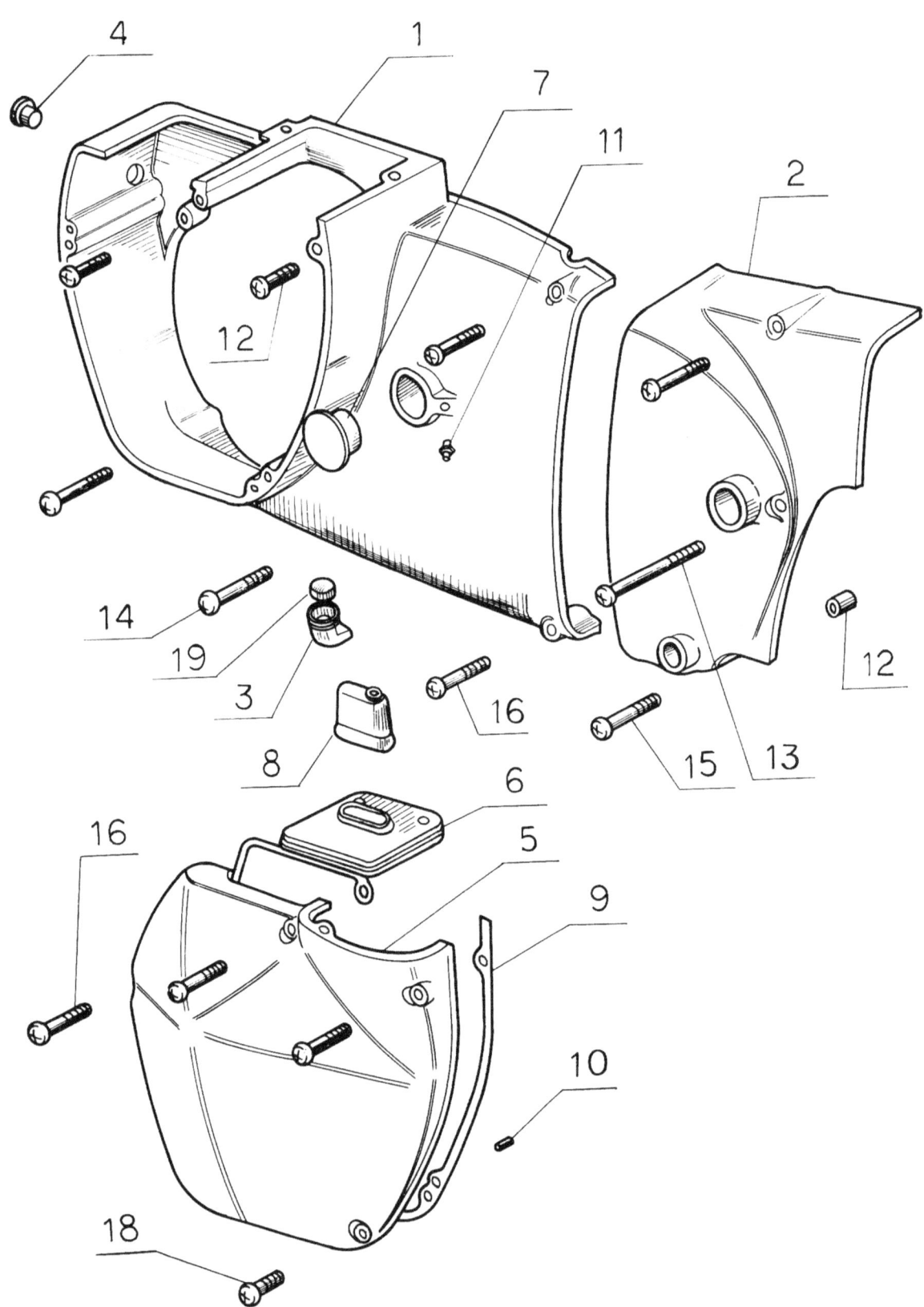

7) LEFT CRANK CASE COVER

Index No.	Part No.	Part Name	No. Req'd	Unit Price	Min. Lot	Remarks
7- 1	2151-9000	Left crank case cover	1			
7- 2	2153-9000	Dust cover A	1			
7- 3	2162-9000	Drain pipe	1			
7- 4	2168-5000	12 rubber plug	1			
7- 5	2171-9000	Left carburetor cover	1			
7- 6	2172-9000	Left carburetor cap	1			
7- 7	2179-9000	Release screw cap	1			
7- 8	2175-9000	Carburetor adjuster cap	1			
7- 9	2186-9000	Left cover gasket	1		10	
7-10	09056-102	4×8 A dowel	2		10	
7-11	7134-3002	Grease nipple	1			
7-12	09057-101	6×10×10 B dowel	1		10	
7-13	0313-0655	Cross recd pan head screw	1		50	
7-14	0313-0640	Cross recd pan head screw	2		50	
7-15	0313-0635	Cross recd pan head screw	2		50	
7-16	0311-0630	Cross recd pan head screw	5		50	
7-17	0311-0625	Cross recd pan head screw	2		50	
7-18	0311-0620	Cross recd pan head screw	1		50	
7-19	2163-9000	Drain filter	1			

MEMO

8) RIGHT CRANK CASE COVER

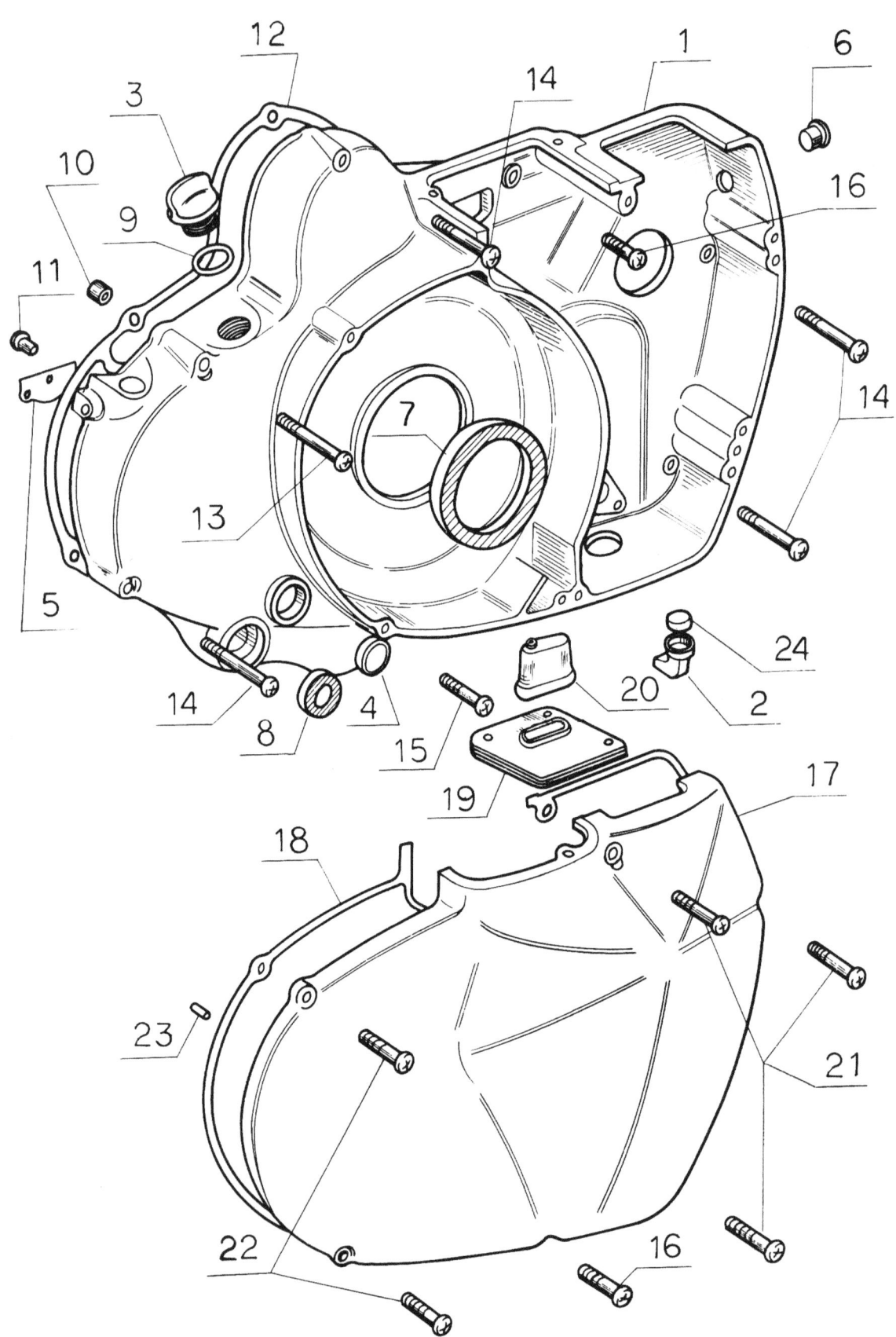

8) RIGHT CRANK CASE COVER

Index No.	Part No.	Part Name	No. Req'd	Unit Price	Min. Lot	Remarks
8-1	2161-9000	Right crank case cover	1			
8-2	2162-9000	Drain pipe	1			
8-3	2165-8000	Oil filler plug	1			
8-4	2166-9000	Oil gauge	1			
8-5	2167-9000	Oil baffle plate B	1			
8-6	2168-5000	12 rubber plug	1			
8-7	09090-119	47 oil seal	1		10	
8-8	09090-101	12 oil seal	1		10	
8-9	09066-107	21 O ring	1		10	
8-10	09057-101	6×10×10 B dowel	2		10	
8-11	0311-0510	Cross recd pan head screw	2		50	
8-12	2183-9000	Crank case cover gasket	1		10	
8-13	0313-0650	Cross recd pan head screw	1		50	
8-14	0313-0645	Cross recd pan head screw	4		50	
8-15	0313-0630	Cross recd pan head screw	3		50	
8-16	0311-0620	Cross recd pan head screw	2		50	
8-17	2176-9000	Carburetor cover	1			
8-18	2185-9000	Carburetor cover gasket	1		10	
8-19	2177-9000	Carburetor cap	1			
8-20	2175-9000	Carburetor adjusting cap	1			
8-21	0313-0635	Cross recd pan head screw	3		50	
8-22	0311-0625	Cross recd pan head screw	2		50	
8-23	09056-102	4×8 A dowel	2		10	
8-24	2163-9000	Drain filter	1			

MEMO

9) CLUTCH

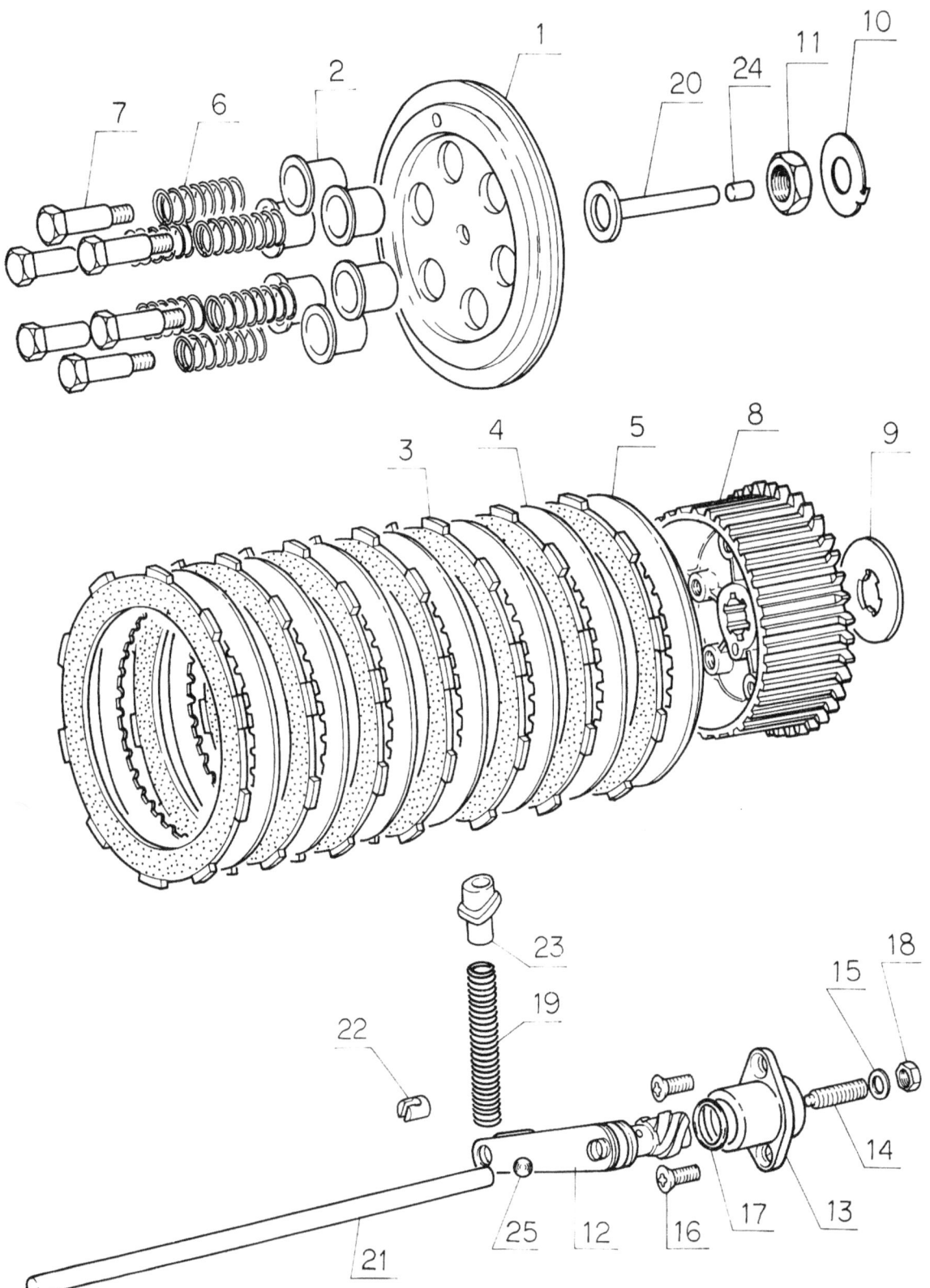

9) CLUTCH

Index No.	Part No.	Part Name	No. Req'd	Unit Price	Min. Lot	Remarks
9- 1	2211-9000	Pressure plate	1			
9- 2	2213-9000	Clutch spring holder	6			
9- 3	2214-9000	Friction plate	7			
9- 4	2215-9000	Inner plate	6			
9- 5	2216-9000	Outer plate	1			
9- 6	2218-9000	Clutch spring	6			
9- 7	2219-9000	Clutch set bolt	6			
9- 8	2221-9000	Clutch hub	1			
9- 9	09048-112	22 thrust washer	1		10	
9-10	09047-104	16 lock washer	1		10	
9-11	09021-102	16 hexagon nut	1		10	
9-12	2260-9000	Release arm	1			
9-13	2264-9000	Release screw	1			
9-14	2267-5000	Release adjust screw	1			
9-15	0411-0613	6 plane washer	1		50	
9-16	0331-0614	Cross rec'd round head screw	2		50	
9-17	09066-123	18 O ring	1		10	
9-18	0211-0600	Hexagon nut A	1		10	
9-19	2271-5010	Release arm return spring	1			
9-20	2273-9000	Release push rod A	1			
9-21	2274-9000	Release push rod B	1			
9-22	2275-5010	Release arm pin	1			
9-23	2276-9000	Clutch wire holder	1			
9-24	09056-105	6×10 A dowel	1		10	
9-25	0611-0104	Ball	1		50	

MEMO

10) TRANSMISSION

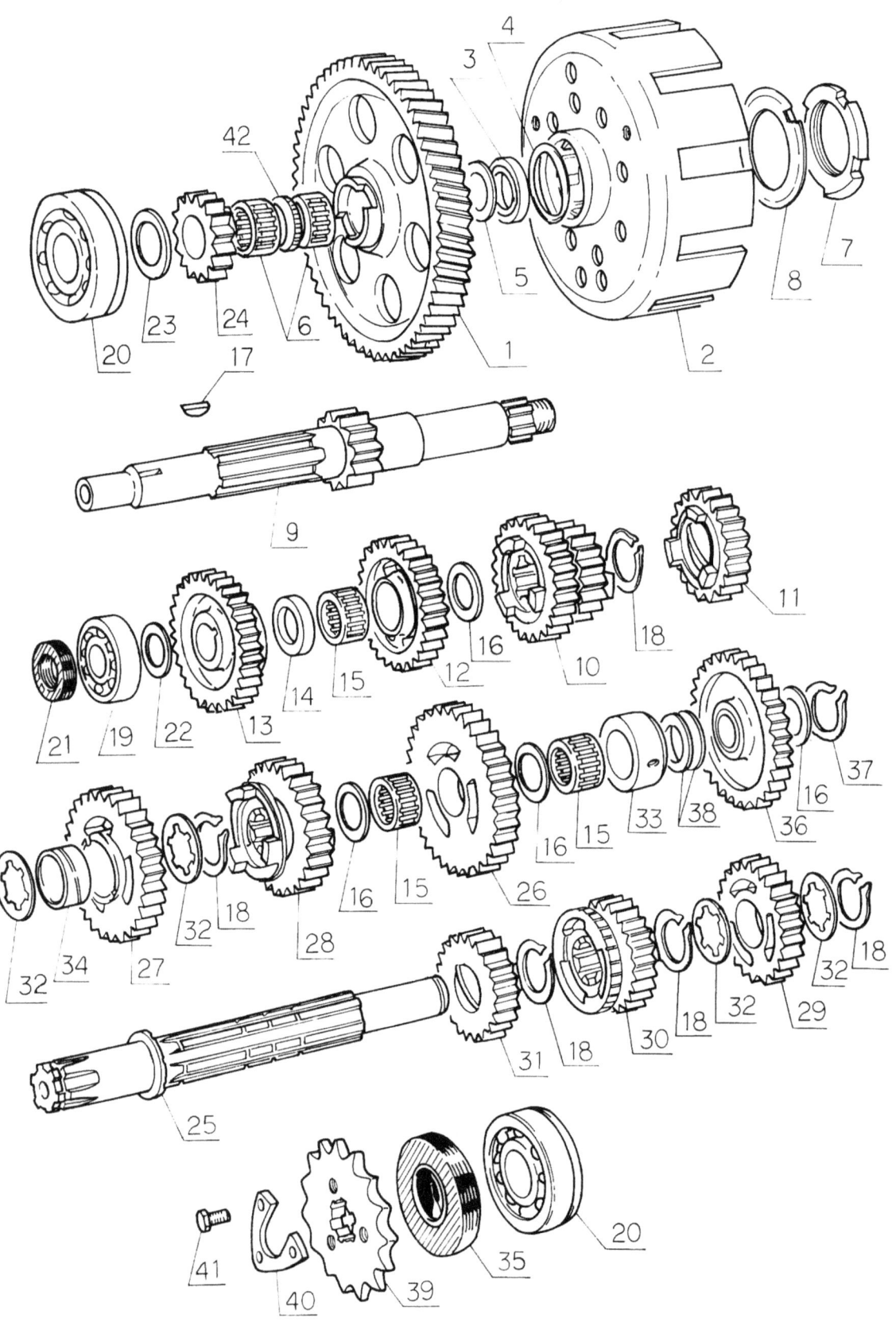

10) TRANSMISSION

Index No.	Part No.	Part Name	No. Req'd	Unit Price	Min. Lot	Remarks
10-1	2411-9000	Driven gear	1			
10-2	2412-9000	Clutch housing	1			
10-3	09090-124	22 oil seal	1		10	
10-4	09066-124	35 O ring	1		10	
10-5	09048-112	22 thrust washer	1		10	
10-6	09070-113	Needle bearing	2		10	
10-7	09028-101	40 ring nut	1		10	
10-8	09047-106	40 lock washer	1		10	
10-9	2421-9000	Counter shaft	1			
10-10	2426-9000	2nd gear A	1			
10-11	2431-9000	3rd gear A	1			
10-12	2441-9000	5th gear A	1			
10-13	2443-9000	6th gear A	1			
10-14	2423-9000	Counter shaft spacer	1			
10-15	09070-112	Needle bearing	3		10	
10-16	09048-114	20 thrust washer	4		10	
10-17	09067-101	3×15 woodruff key	1			
10-18	09002-107	25 B snap ring	5		10	
10-19	07-6203-03	Ball bearing	1		10	
10-20	07-6305-63	Ball bearing	2		10	
10-21	09090-104	17 oil seal	1		10	
10-22	09048-115	17 thrust washer	1		10	
10-23	09048-116	22 thrust washer	1		10	
10-24	2611-9000	Kick starter gear A	1			
10-25	2446-9000	Drive shaft	1			
10-26	2451-9000	1st gear B	1			
10-27	2456-9000	2nd gear B	1			
10-28	2461-9000	3nd gear B	1			
10-29	2466-9000	4th gear B	1			
10-30	2471-9000	5th gear B	1			
10-31	2473-9000	6th gear B	1			
10-32	09048-117	25 thrust washer	4		10	
10-33	2133-9000	Drive shaft bushing	1			
10-34	2457-9000	2nd gear B bushing	1			
10-35	09090-126	25 oil seal	1		10	
10-36	2616-9000	Kick starter gear B	1			
10-37	09002-105	20 B snap ring	1		10	
10-38	09049-106	20×0.3 shim	2~3		10	
10-39	2484-9000	Drive sprocket	1			
10-40	2485-9000	Sprocket set plate	1			
10-41	0111-0610	Hexagoh bolt A	3		50	
10-42	2494-9000	Needle bearing spacer	1			

11) GEAR CHANGE PEDAL · SHIFT DRUM

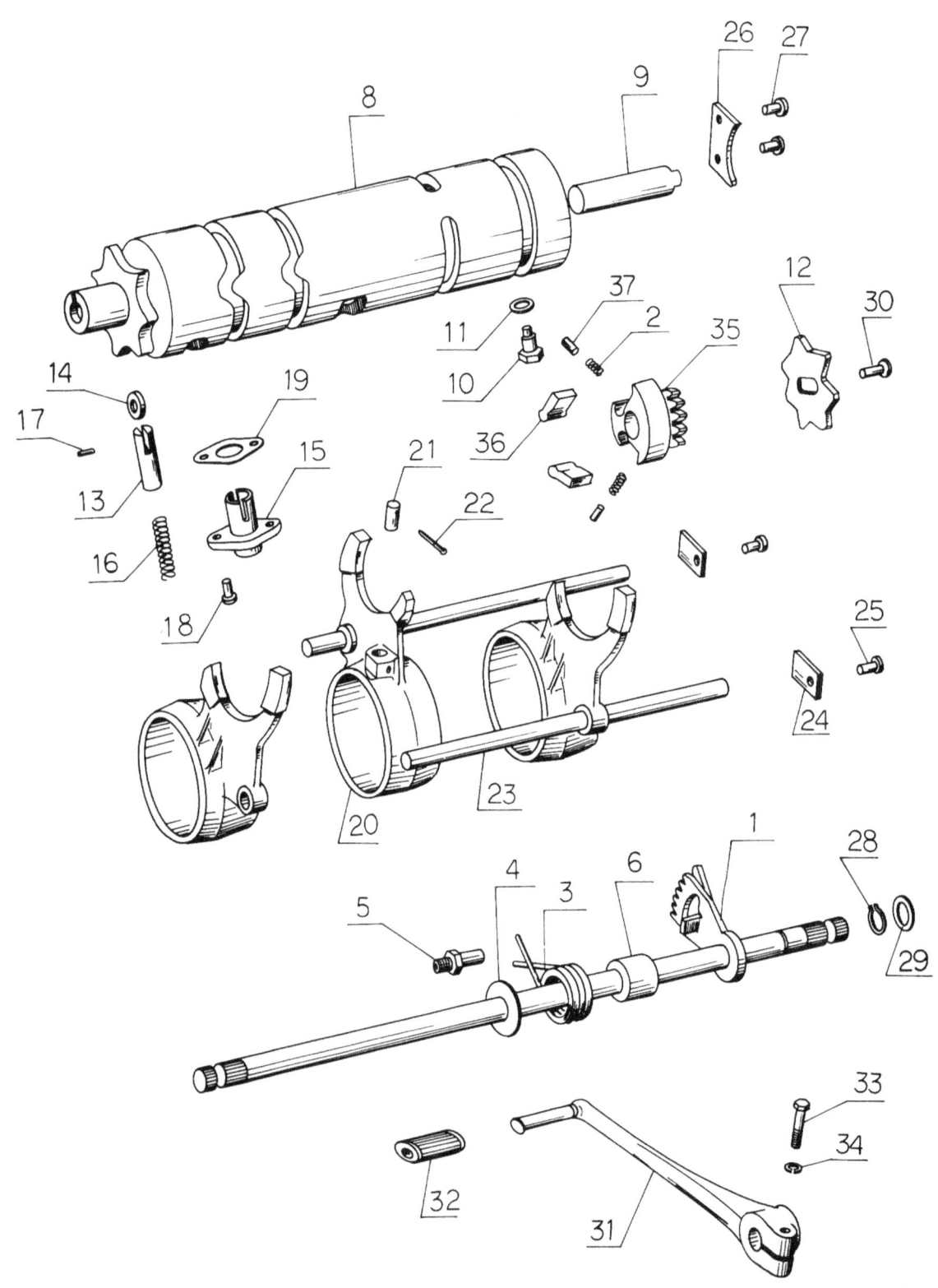

11) GEAR CHANGE PEDAL · SHIFT DRUM

Index No.	Part No.	Part Name	No. Req'd	Unit Price	Min. Lot	Remarks
11- 1	2510-9000	Change arm comp	1			
11- 2	2634-8000	Ratchet spring	2			
11- 3	2551-5000	Change shaft return spring	1			
11- 4	2552-3001	Change shaft spring seat	1			
11- 5	2553-5000	Change arm stopper pin	1			
11- 6	2557-8000	Change shaft spacer	1			
11- 7	2520-9000	Shift drum comp	1			
11- 8	2521-9000	Gear shifter drum	1			
11- 9	2527-9000	Drum shifter shaft	1			
11-10	2528-9000	Drum guide bolt	1			
11-11	09065-104	8 aluminium gasket	1		10	
11-12	2535-9000	Stopper plate	1			
11-13	2531-9000	Drum stopper arm	1			
11-14	2532-9000	Drum stopper roller	1			
11-15	2534-9000	Drum stopper boss	1			
11-16	2538-9000	Drum stopper spring	1		10	
11-17	09056-102	4×8 A dowel	1		10	
11-18	0311-0616	Cross recd pan head screw	2		50	
11-19	2561-9000	Drum stopper gasket	1		10	
11-20	2541-9000	Shift fork	3			
11-21	2544-9000	Fork guide	3			
11-22	0551-2520	Split pin	3		50	
11-23	2113-9000	Fork guide pin	2			
11-24	2558-9000	Fork guide stopper	2			
11-25	0311-0610	Cross recd pan head screw	2		50	
11-26	2549-9000	Drum guide plate	1			
11-27	0311-0614	Cross recd pan head screw	2		50	
11-28	09002-101	12 B snap ring	1		10	
11-29	09048-101	12 thrust washer	1		10	
11-30	0331-0512	Cross flat head screw	1		50	
11-31	2581-9000	Gear change pedal	1		50	
11-32	2582-9000	Change pedal rubber	1		50	
11-33	0113-0625	Hexagon bolt A	1		50	
11-34	0432-0615	Spring washer	1		50	
11-35	2513-9000	Drum shifter	1			
11-36	2633-8000	Ratchet	2			
11-37	2642-8000	Ratchet pole	2			

12) KICK STARTER

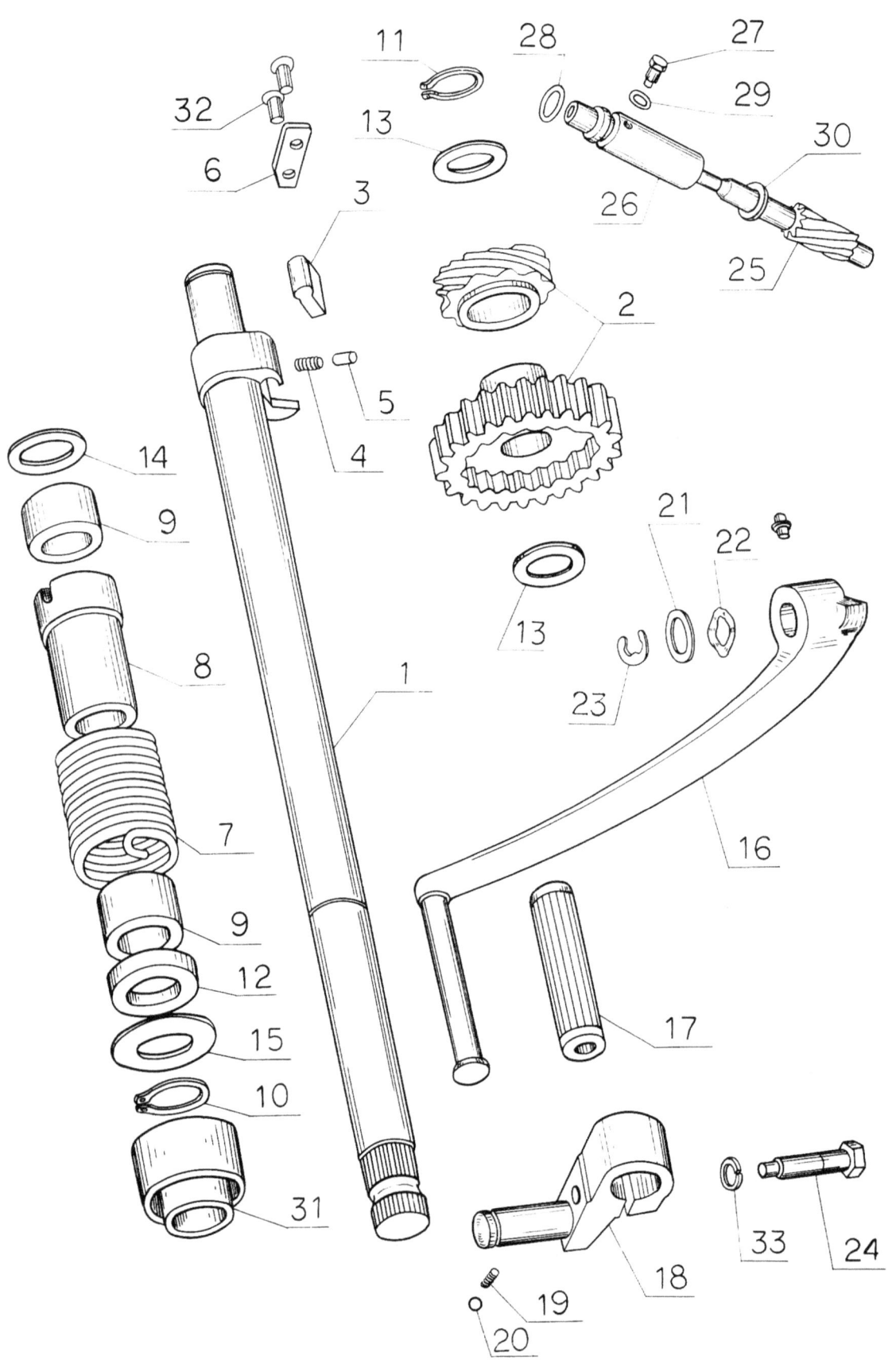

12) KICK STARTER

Index No.	Part No.	Part Name	No. Req'd	Unit Price	Min. Lot	Remarks
12-1	2621-9000	Kick starter shaft	1			
12-2	2630-9000	Kick gear C comp.	1			
12-3	2633-8000	Ratchet	1			
12-4	2634-8000	Ratchet spring	1			
12-5	2642-8000	Ratchet pole	1			
12-6	2635-9000	Kick starter ratchet stopper	1			
12-7	2636-9000	Kick starter return spring	1			
12-8	2638-9000	Return spring spacer	1			
12-9	2115-9000	Kick starter shaft bush	2			
12-10	09002-108	18 B snap ring	1			
12-11	09006-101	15 F snap ring	1			
12-12	09090-112	18 oil seal	1		10	
12-13	09048-104	15 thrust washer	2		10	
12-14	09048-118	18 thrust washer	1		10	
12-15	0411-1836	Plane washer A	1		50	
12-	2680-9000	Kick starter arm assy	1			
12-16	2681-9000	Kick starter arm	1			Not for sale
12-17	2683-9000	Kick starter pedal rubber	1			
12-18	2685-9000	Kick starter arm boss	1			
12-19	2686-9000	Kick starter set spring	1			
12-20	0611-0732	Ball	2		50	
12-21	09041-115	15 plane washer	1		50	
12-22	09046-105	15 wave washer	1		50	
12-23	09004-102	10 D snap ring	1		10	
12-24	2687-9000	Kick starter shaft bolt	1			
12-25	2812-9000	Tachometer gear B	1			
12-26	2813-9000	Tachometer gear bush	1			
12-27	2815-9000	Tachometer bush bolt	1			
12-28	09066-125	12 O ring	1		10	
12-29	09064-102	6 fiber gasket	1		10	
12-30	09048-119	8 thrust washer	1		10	
12-31	2688-9000	Chain guide	1			
12-32	0331-0614	Cross rec'd round head screw	2		50	
12-33	0431-1025	Spring washer	2		50	

13) FRAME · REAR FENDER

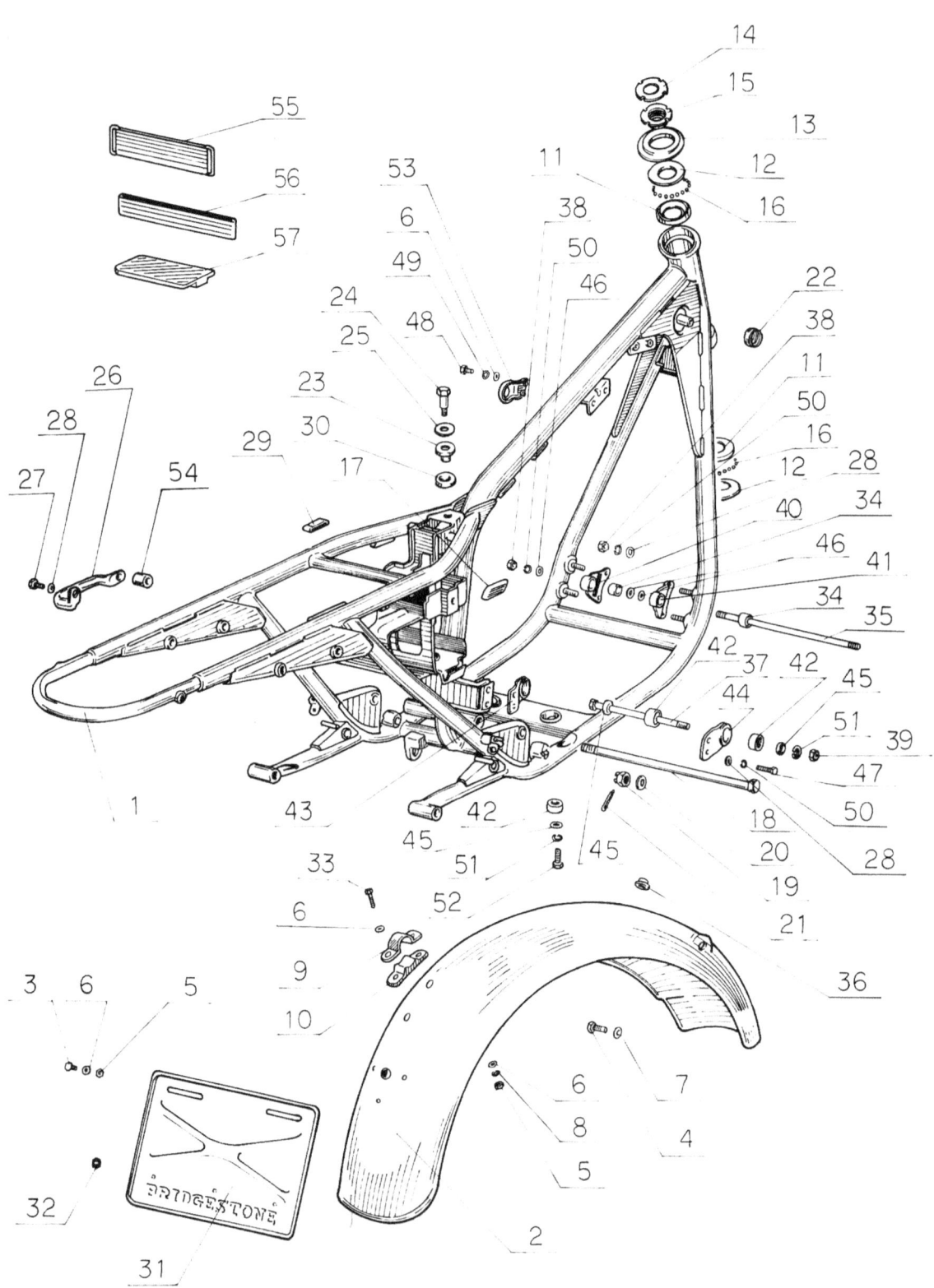

13) FRAME · REAR FENDER

Index No.	Part No.	Part Name	No. Req'd	Unit Price	Min. Lot	Remarks
13- 1	3110-9010-CBK	Frame comp	1			
13- 1	3110-9000-CBK	Frame comp	1			For U.S.A.
13- 2	3260-9000	Rear fender comp	1			
13- 3	0111-0614	Hexagon bolt A	4		50	
13- 4	0111-0812	Hexagon bolt A	3		50	
13- 5	0211-0600	Hexagon nut A	4		50	
13- 6	0411-0613	Plane washer A	6		50	
13- 7	0411-0818	Plane washer A	3		50	
13- 8	0432-0615	Spring washer	2		50	
13- 9	3388-9000	Rear fender clamp	1			
13-10	3442-9000	Fender mounting rubber	1			
13-11	3311-8000	Outer race	2			
13-12	3313-8000	Inner race	2			
13-13	3319-8000	Race cap	1			
13-14	3321-5000	Race lock nut	1			
13-15	3322-5000	Race adjuster	1			
13-16	0511-0104	Ball	38		50	
13-17	3339-9000	Oil tank pad	1			
13-18	3414-9000	Pivot shaft	1			
13-19	09522-102	14 hexagon sloted nut	1		10	
13-20	09541-119	15 Plane washer	1		50	
13-21	0551-3025	Split pin	1		50	
13-22	3416-8000	Front tank cushion rubber	2			
13-23	3417-9000	Rear tank cushion rubber	1			
13-24	3419-9000	Tank mounting bolt	1			
13-25	09541-118	18 Plane washer	4		50	
13-26	3428-9000	Frame handle	1			
13-27	0112-0812	Hexagon bolt A	1		50	
13-28	0411-0818	Plane washer A	1		50	
13-29	3447-9000	Cover pad	1			
13-30	5149-9000	Tank cushion rubber	1			
13-31	3443-3210	Number plate supporter	1			
13-32	3452-3210	Supporter pad	3			
13-33	0113-0620	Hexagon bolt	2			
13-34	3358-9000	Engine cushion rubber A	2			
13-35	3373-9000	Engine mounting bolt	1			
13-36	3412-8000	Rear fender grommet	1			
13-37	09511-145	10×145 hexagon bolt	1		10	
13-38	0211-0800	Hexagon nut A	6		10	
13-39	0241-1000	Hexagon nut D	1		10	

13) FRAME · REAR FENDER

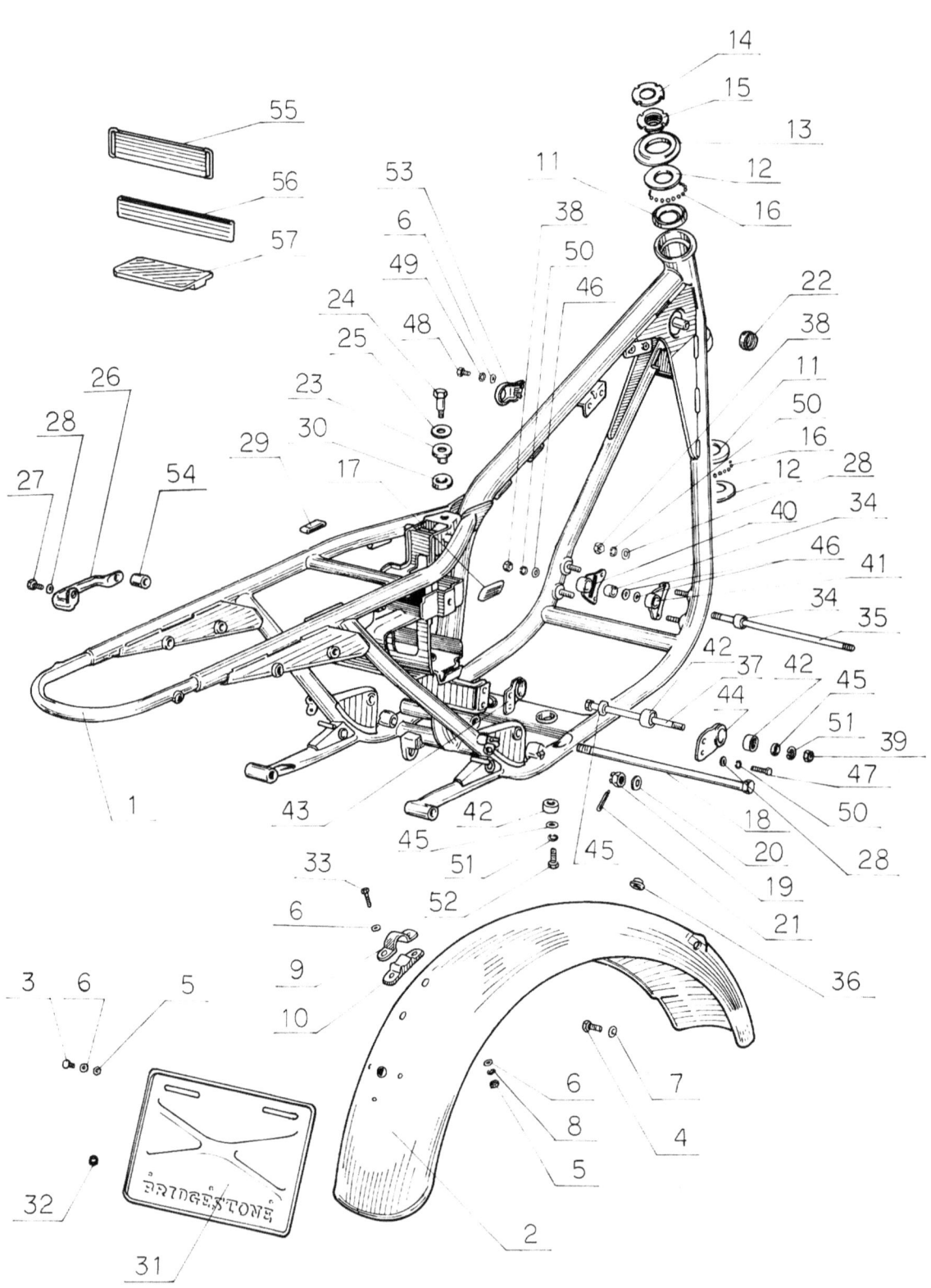

13) FRAME · REAR FENDER

Index No.	Part No.	Part Name	No. Req'd	Unit Price	Min. Lot	Remarks
13-40	3365-9000-CBK	Left engine bracket	1			
13-41	3366-9000-CBK	Right engine bracket	1			
13-42	3367-9000	Engine cushion rubber B	4			
13-43	3371-9000-CBK	Left engine hanger	1			
13-44	3372-9000-CBK	Right engine hanger	1			
13-45	09541-120	10 plane washer	4		50	
13-46	09541-121	8 plane washer	4		50	
13-47	0111-0818	Hexagon bolt A	4		50	
13-48	0111-0612	Hexagon bolt A	2		50	
13-49	0431-0615	Spring washer	2		50	
13-50	0431-0820	Spring washer	10		50	
13-51	0431-1025	Spring washer	3		50	
13-52	09511-150	10 × 38 hexagon bolt	2		10	
13-53	3166-9000	Main switch bracket	1			
13-54	3386-9000	Spacer A	1			
13-55	3353-3001	Battery band	1			
13-56	3345-9000	Battery pad	1			
13-57	3346-9000	Battery seat	1			

MEMO

14) MAIN STAND · BRAKE PEDAL

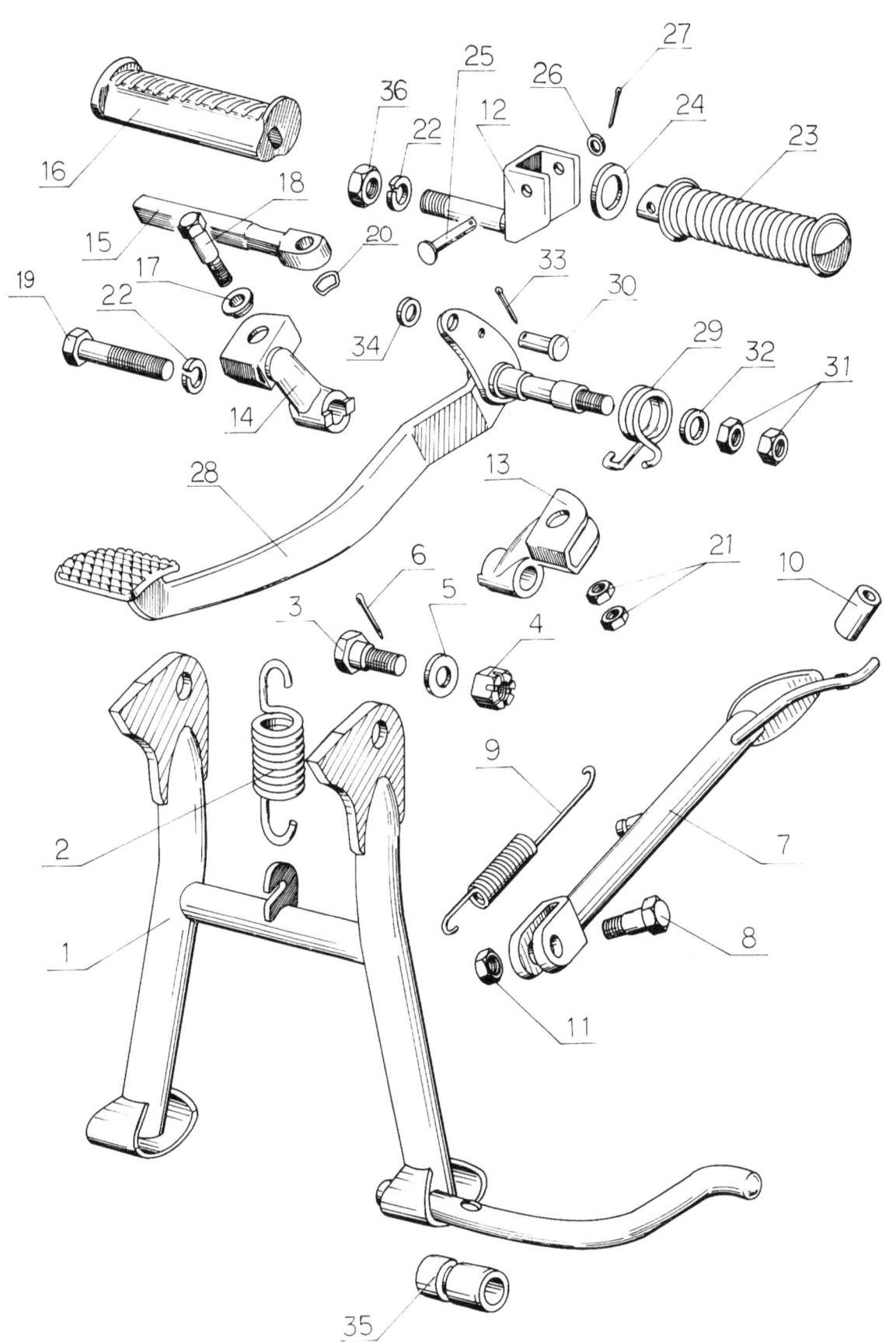

14) MAIN STAND · BRAKE PEDAL

Index No.	Part No.	Part Name	No. Req'd	Unit Price	Min. Lot	Remarks
14- 1	3610-9000-CBK	Main stand comp	1			
14- 2	3624-9000	Main stand spring	1			
14- 3	3625-9000	Left stand bolt	2			
14- 4	09522-105	12 sloted hexagon nut	2		10	
14- 5	09541-117	12 plane washer	2		50	
14- 6	0551-3025	Split pin	2		50	
14- 7	3650-9000	Side stand comp	1			
14- 8	3662-8000	Side stand bolt	1			
14- 9	3663-9000	Side stand spring	1			
14-10	3664-9000	Side stand rubber	1			
14-11	09521-106	10 hexagon nut	1		10	
14-12	3259-9000-CBK	Footrest bracket	2			
14-13	3715-9000	Left footrest	1			
14-14	3716-9000	Right footrest	1			
14-15	3711-5010	Footrest bar	2			
14-16	3721-3002	Footrest rubber	2			
14-17	3722-5010	Footrest mounting spacer	2			
14-18	3723-5010	Footrest mounting bolt	2			
14-19	09511-127	12×50 hexagon bolt	2		10	
14-20	09546-104	10 wave washer	2		50	
14-21	0231-0800	Hexagon nut C	4		50	
14-22	0431-1230	Spring washer	2		50	
14-23	3702-5000	Rear foot rest assy	2			
14-24	3762-5000	Rear footrest washer	2			
14-25	3763-5000	Rear footrest pin	2			
14-26	0411-0613	Plane washer A	2		50	
14-27	0552-1612	Split pin	2		50	
14-28	3810-9000	Brake pedal comp	1			
14-29	3821-9000	Brake pedal spring	1			
14-30	3822-9000	Brake pedal pin	1			
14-31	0231-0800	Hexagon nut C	2		50	
14-32	0411-1022	Plane washer A	1		50	
14-33	0551-2018	Split pin	1		50	
14-34	09546-104	10 wave washer	2		50	
14-35	3335-9000	Stand rubber stopper	1			
14-36	0241-1200	Hexagon nut A	2		10	

15) FRONT FORK

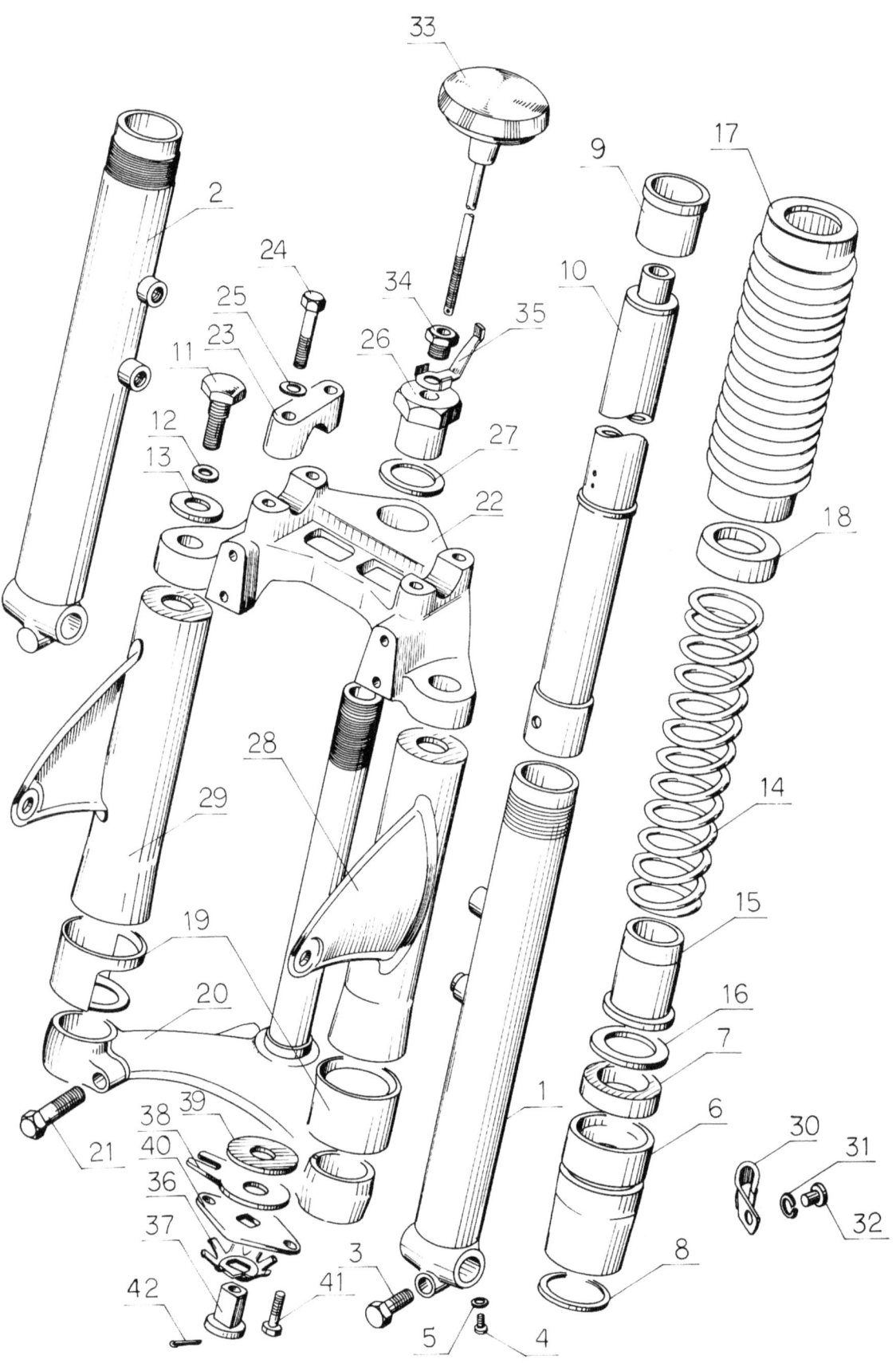

15) FRONT FORK

Index No.	Part No.	Part Name	No. Req'd	Unit Price	Min. Lot	Remarks
15–	4100-9000-FAR	Front fork assy	1			
15- 1	4131-9000-MS	Outer tube B	1			
15- 2	4111-9000-MS	Outer tube A	1			
15- 3	09511-147	8×26 hexagon bolt	1		10	
15- 4	09531-101	4×7 cross pan head screw	2		50	
15- 5	4118-5000	Drain plug gasket	2			
15- 6	4114-9000	Outer tube nut	2			
15- 7	09590-122	34 oil seal	2		10	
15- 8	09566-107	40 O ring	2		10	
15- 9	4116-9000	Cushion slide metal	2			
15-10	4113-9000	Inner tube A	2			
15-11	4124-9000	Upper bridge bolt	2			
15-12	09566-112	9 O ring	2		10	
15-13	4125-9000	Upper bridge washer	2			
15-14	4121-9000	Front main cushion spring	2			
15-15	4127-9000	Dust seal	2			
15-16	4115-9000	Main spring seat	2			
15-17	4177-9000	Front fork boot	2			
15-18	4178-9000	Upper boot holder	2			
15-19	4174-9000	Fork cover guide	2			
15-20	4151-9000-CBK	Lower bridge	1			
15-21	09511-121	10×32 hexagon bolt	2		10	
15-22	4161-9000	Upper bridge	1			
15-23	4162-8000	Handle holder	2			
15-24	0134-0836	Hexagon bolt C	4		10	
15-25	0421-0816	Plane washer B	4		50	
15-26	4164-9000	Steering head nut	1			
15-27	4165-5000	Steering head washer	1			
15-28	4171-9000-FAR	Left fork cover	1			
15-29	4181-9000-FAR	Right fork cover	1			
15-30	4182-9000	Cable clip	1			
15-31	0431-0615	Sping washer	1			
15-32	0311-0608	Cross recd pan head screw	1			
15-33	4311-9000	Steering damper knob	1			

15) FRONT FORK

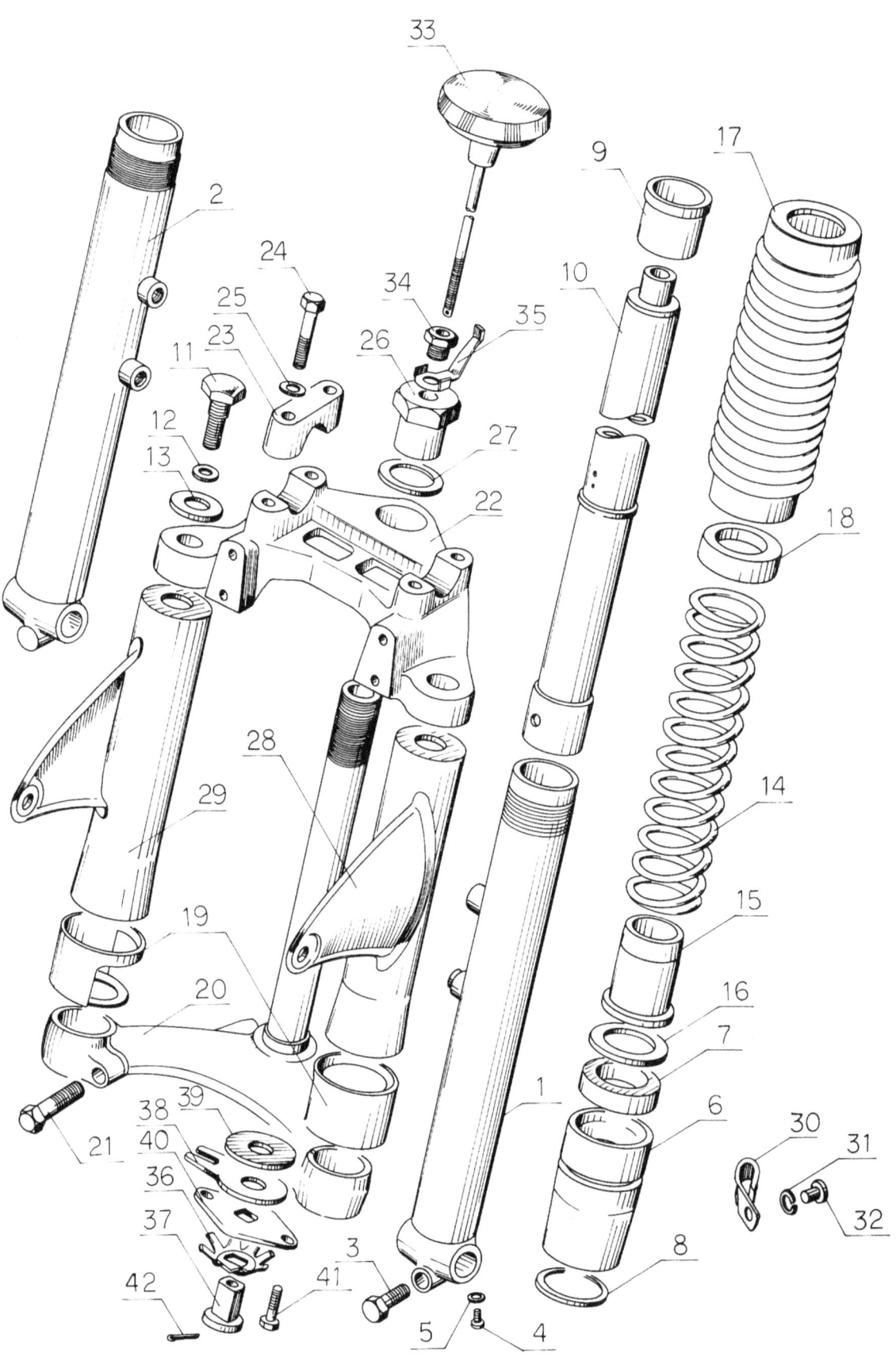

15) FRONT FORK

Index No.	Part No.	Part Name	No. Req'd	Unit Price	Min. Lot	Remarks
15-34	4312-8000	Damper knob guide	1			
15-35	4313-8000	Damper lock spring	1			
15-36	4319-8000	Steering damper spring	1			
15-37	4321-8000	Damper spring guide	1			
15-38	4315-9000	Friction plate	1			
15-39	4314-9000	Damper facing	1			
15-40	4322-9000	Damper guide plate	1			
15-41	09511-148	6×18 hexagon bolt	2			
15-42	0552-1612	Split pin	1		50	

MEMO

16) FRONT FENDER · HANDLE BAR

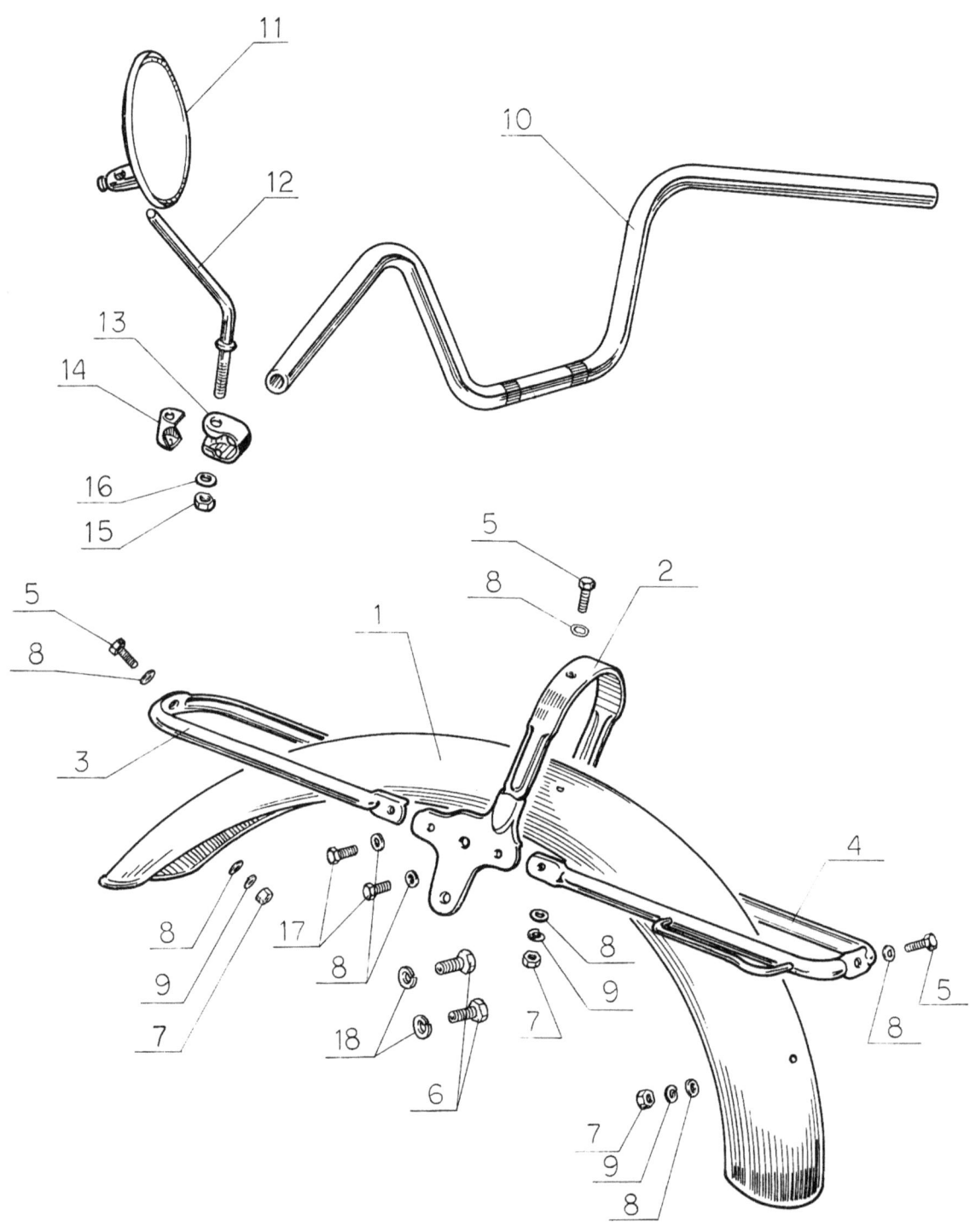

16) FRONT FENDER · HANDLE BAR

Index No.	Part No.	Part Name	No. Req'd	Unit Price	Min. Lot	Remarks
16- 1	4411-9000-XCl	Front fender	1			
16- 2	4412-9000	Fender bracket A	1			
16- 3	4423-9000-XCl	Fender stay A	1			
16- 4	4424-9000-XCl	Fender stay B	1			
16- 5	0112-0614	Hexagon bolt A	4		50	
16- 6	0111-0812	Hexagon bolt A	4		50	
16- 7	0211-0600	Hexagon nut A	4		50	
16- 8	0411-0613	Plane washer A	12		50	
16- 9	0432-0615	Spring washer	4		50	
16-10	4511-9000	Up handle bar	1			
16-	4601-8000	Back mirror assy	1			
16-11	4610-8000	Back mirror comp	1			
16-12	4621-8000	Back mirror stay	1			
16-13	4622-8000	Back mirror clamp	1			
16-14	4624-8000	Clamp spacer	1			Not for sale
16-15	0211-0800	Hexagon nut A	1		50	
16-16	0421-0816	Plane washer B	1		50	
16-17	0112-0614	Hexagon bolt A	4		50	
16-18	0431-0820	Spring washer	4		50	

MEMO

17) REAR FORK · REAR CUSHION

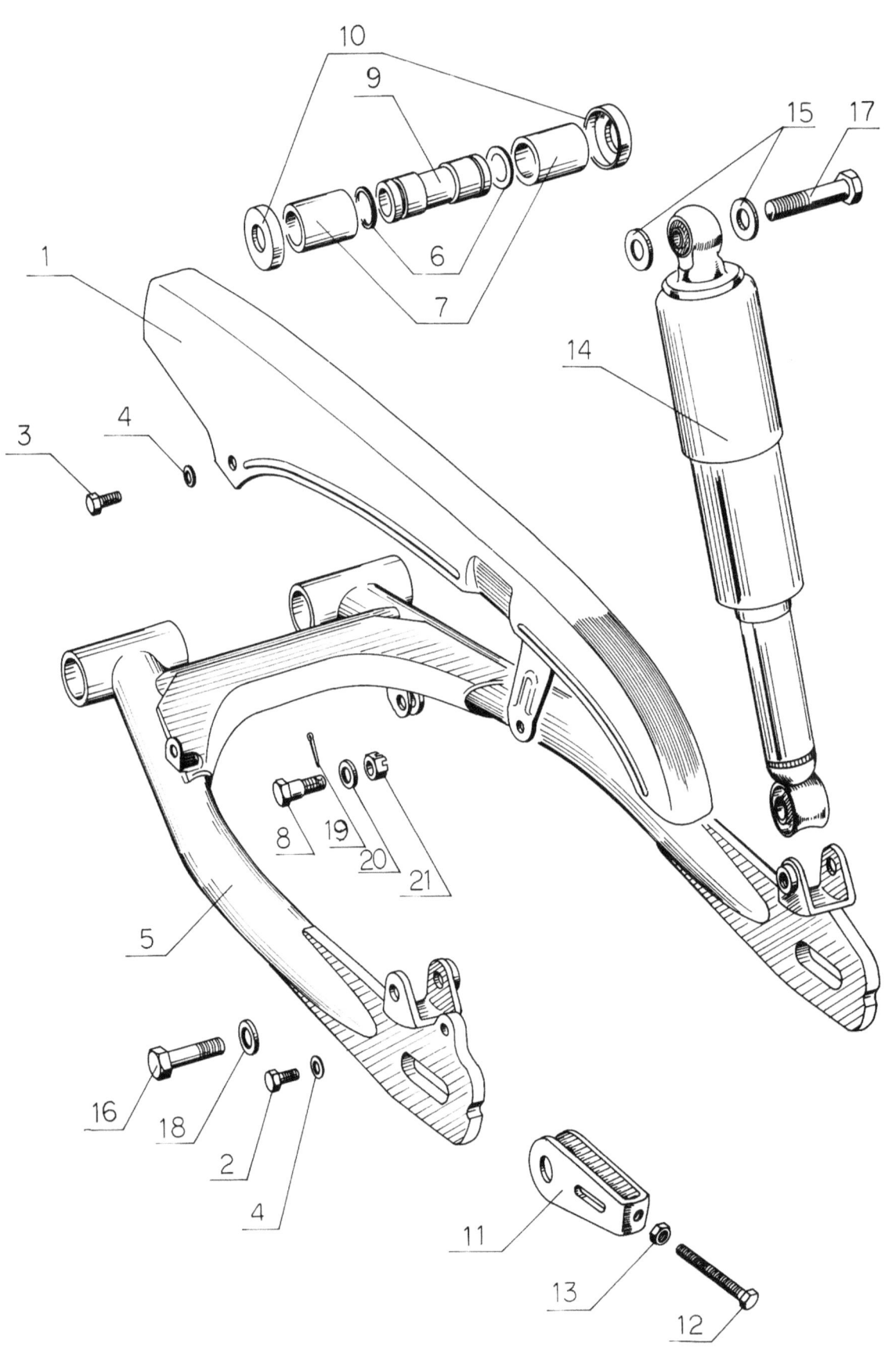

17) REAR FORK · REAR CUSHION

Index No.	Part No.	Part Name	No. Req'd	Unit Price	Min. Lot	Remarks
17- 1	4751-9000-XCI	Half chain case	1			
17- 2	0112-0614	Hexagon bolt B	1		50	
17- 3	0112-0608	Hexagon bolt A	1		50	
17- 4	0411-0613	Plane washer A	2		50	
17- 5	4810-9000-CBK	Rear fork comp	1			
17- 6	09566-106	18 O ring	4		10	
17- 7	4851-9000	Rear fork bush	4			
17- 8	4855-9000	Torque rod bolt	1			
17- 9	4856-9000	Rear fork collar	2			
17-10	4858-9000	Fork pivot cap	4			
17-11	4861-9000	Chain adjuster	2			
17-12	4864-8000	Chain adjuster bolt	2			
17-13	0231-0600	Hexagon nut C	2		50	
17-14	4901-9000-XCI	Rear cushion assy	2			
17-15	09541-117	12 plane washer	4		50	
17-16	0124-1032	Hexagon bolt B	2		50	
17-17	09511-149	12×45 hexagon bolt	2		10	
17-18	0411-1022	Plane washer A	2		10	
17-19	0551-2018	Split pin	1		50	
17-20	0411-0818	Plane washer A	1		50	
17-21	09522-101	8 Hexagon sloted nut	1		10	

MEMO

18) FUEL TANK · OIL TANK

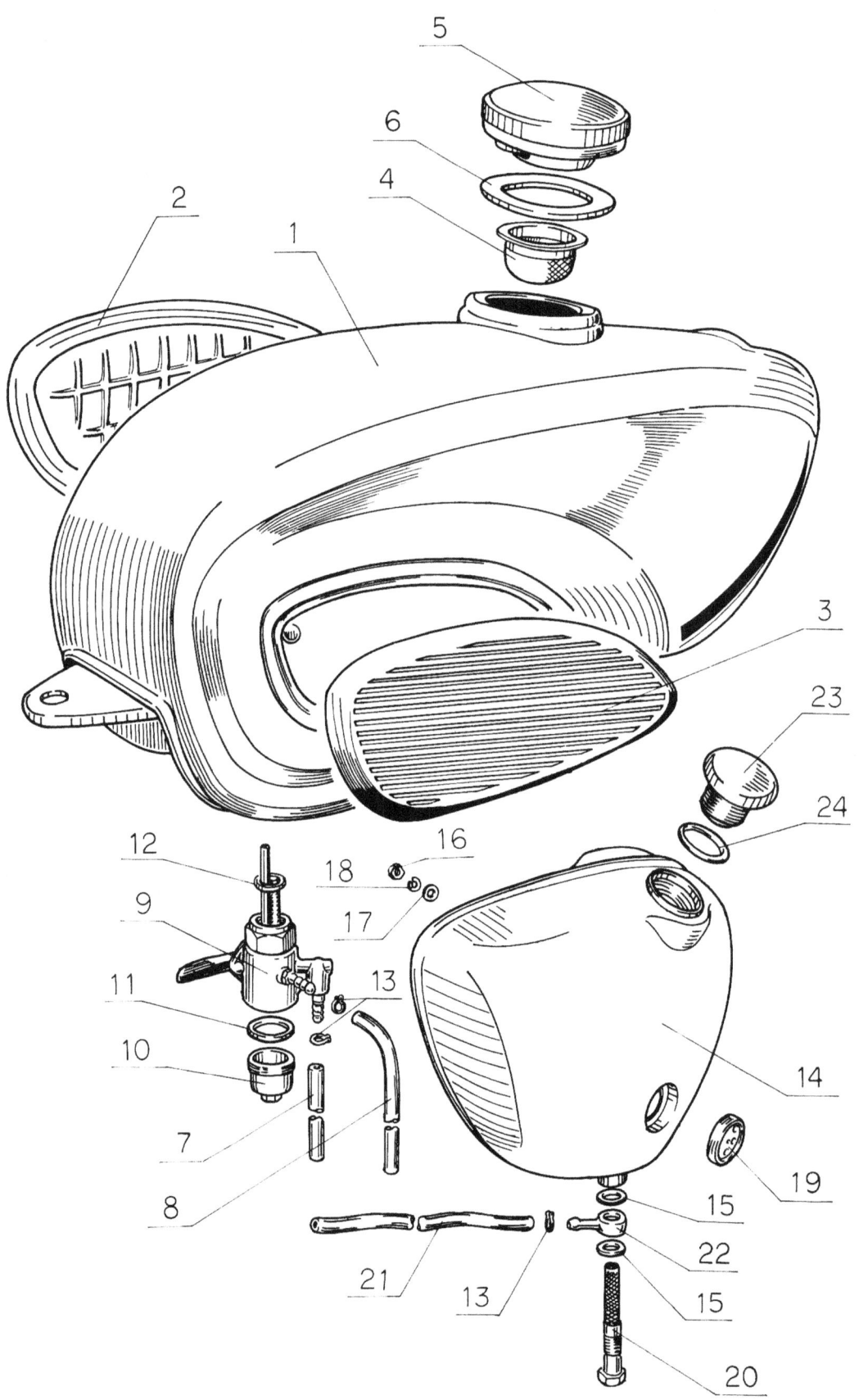

18) FUEL TANK · OIL TANK

Index No.	Part No.	Part Name	No. Req'd	Unit Price	Min. Lot	Remarks
18- 1	5110-9000-FAR	Fuel tank comp	1			
18- 2	5141-9000	Left knee grip	1			
18- 3	5142-9000	Right knee grip	1			
18- 4	5145-8000	Fuel tank filter	1			
18- 5	5102-8000	Tank cap assy	1			
18- 6	5171-8000	Tank cap gasket	1			
18- 7	5172-3100	Fuel tube	1			
18- 8	5174-9000	Right fuel tube	1			
18- 9	5103-9000	Fuel cock assy	1			
18-10	5182-8000	Fuel strainer cup	1			
18-11	5183-8000	Strainer cup gasket	1			
18-12	5184-8000	Fuel cock gasket	1			
18-13	5187-3004	Fuel tube clip	3			
18-14	5510-9000-FAR	Oil tank comp	1			
18-15	09564-101	10 fiber gasket	2		50	
18-16	0211-0800	Hexagon nut A	1		50	
18-17	0411-0818	Plane washer A	1		50	
18-18	0431-0820	Spring washer	1		50	
18-19	5531-5010	Oil gauge	1			
18-20	5532-5010	Oil tank filter	1			
18-21	5533-9000	Oil tube C	1			
18-22	5534-5010	Union connector	1			
18-23	5560-5010-CBK	Oil tank cap comp	1			
18-24	09566-108	27 O ring	1			

MEMO

19) CLUTCH GRIP

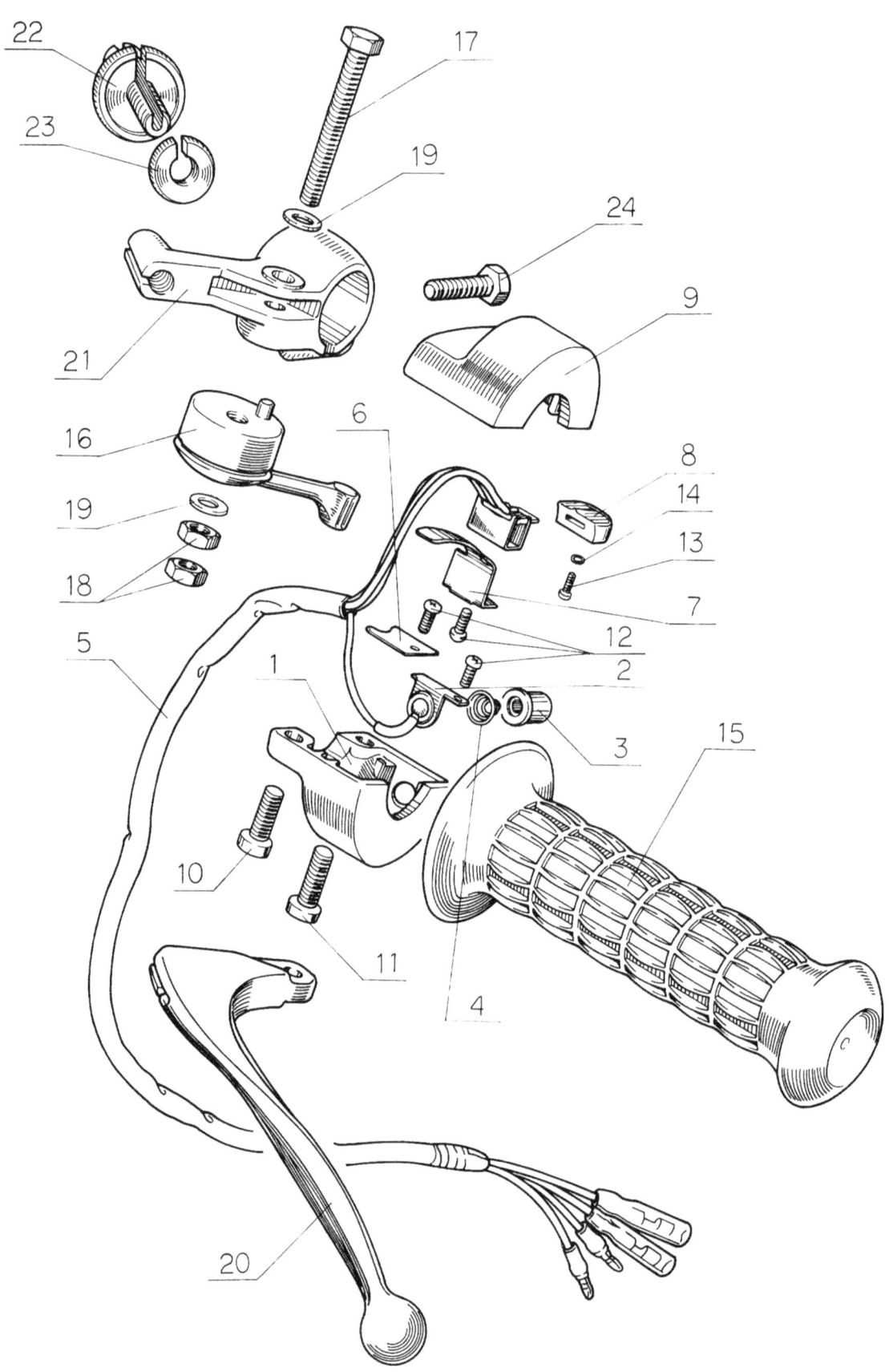

136

19) CLUTCH GRIP

Index No.	Part No.	Part Name	No. Req'd	Unit Price	Min. Lot	Remarks
19-	6101-9000	Clutch grip assy	1			
19- 1	6111-8000	Left switch case	1			
19- 2	6112-3100	Horn switch contact plate	1			
19- 3	6113-3100	Horn switch button	1			
19- 4	6114-3100	Horn switch spring	1			
19- 5	6115-8000	Left handle wire	1			
19- 6	6116-8000	Left wire clamp	1			
19- 7	6117-8000	Dipper switch clamp	1			
19- 8	6119-8000	Dipper switch knob	1			
19- 9	6121-8000	Left switch case cover	1			
19-10	0311-0614	Cross recd pan head screw	1		50	
19-11	0311-0616	Cross recd pan head screw	1		50	
19-12	0311-0306	Cross recd pan head screw	3		50	
19-13	0361-0206	Pan head screw	2		50	
19-14	0431-0205	Spring washer	2		50	
19-15	6123-5010	Left handle grip	1			
19-16	6103-8000	Starter lever assy	1			
19-17	09511-131	6×45 hexagon bolt	1		10	
10-18	0231-0600	Hexagon nut C	2		50	
19-19	0421-0612	Plane washer B	2		50	
19-20	6122-8000	Clutch lever	1			
19-21	6125-8000	Left lever holder	1			
19-22	6126-8000	Wire adjuster	1			
19-23	6127-8000	Wire adjuster lock nut	1			
19-24	0111-0625	Hexagon bolt A	1		50	

MEMO

20) THROTTLE GRIP

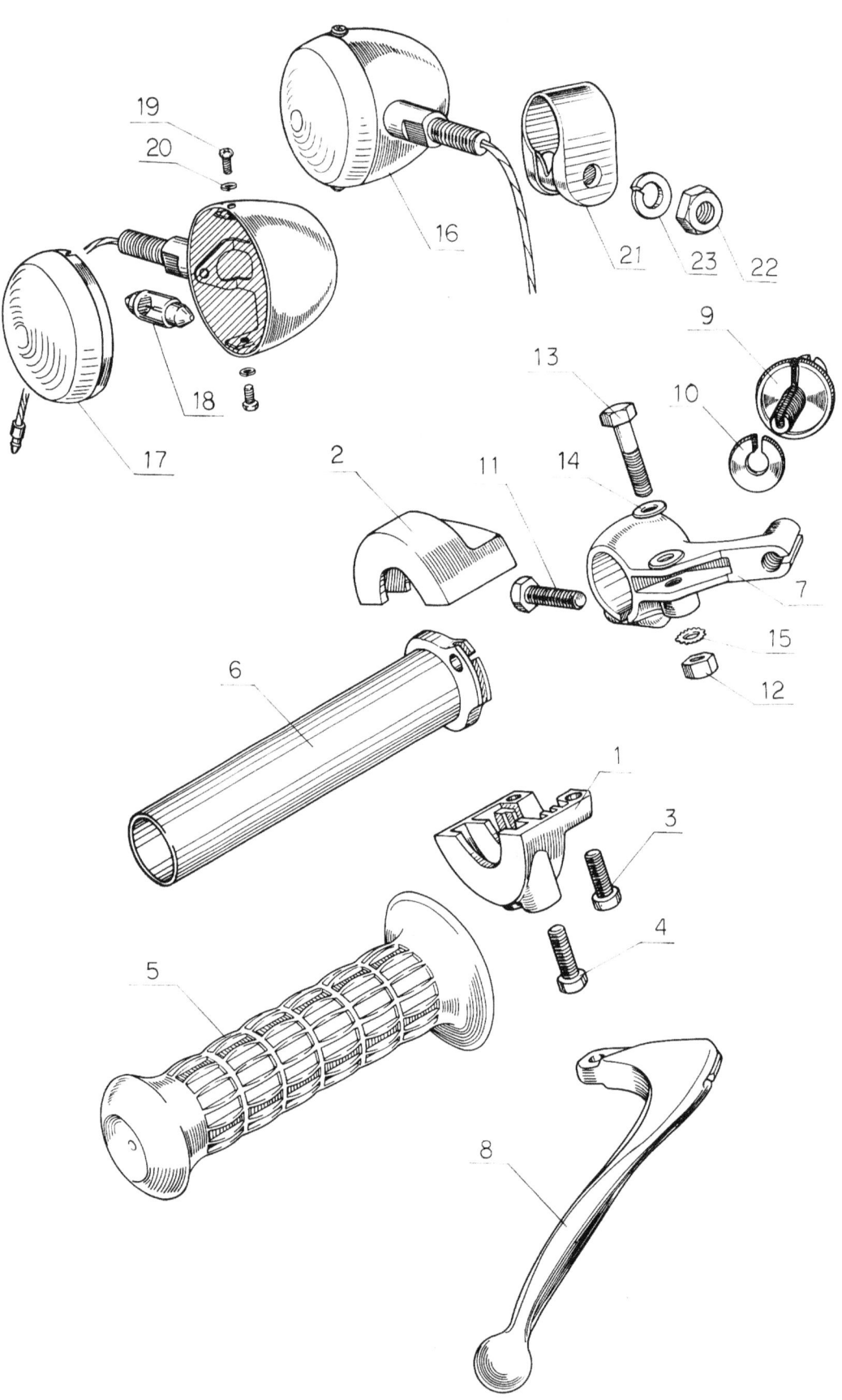

20) THROTTLE GRIP

Index No.	Part No.	Part Name	No. Req'd	Unit Price	Min. Lot	Remarks
20-	6104-9010	Throttle grip assy	1			
20-	6104-9000	Throttle grip assy	1			For U.S.A.
20- 1	6141-8010	Right switch case	1			*
20- 2	6151-8010	Right switch case cover	1			*
20- 2	6151-8000	Right switch case cover	1			For U.S.A.
20- 3	0311-0614	Cross recd pan head screw	1			*
20- 4	0311-0616	Cross recd pan head screw	1		50	*
20- 5	6153-5010	Right handle grip	1			*
20- 6	6154-8000	Throttle grip pipe	1			*
20- 7	6149-8000	Right lever holder	1			*
20- 8	6152-8000	Front brake lever	1			*
20- 9	6126-8000	Wire adjuster	1			*
20-10	6127-8000	Wire adjuster lock nut	1			*
20-11	09511-132	6×25 hexagon bolt	1		50	*
20-12	0211-0600	Hexagon nut A	1		50	*
20-13	0111-0625	Hexagon bolt A	1		50	*
20-14	0421-0612	Plane washer B	1		50	*
20-15	0451-0611	External toothed washer	1		50	*
20-	6146-8010	Right wire clamp	1			
20-	6145-8010	Right handle wire	1			
20-	6147-8010	Turn signal switch clamp	1			Exclusive parts for the model with winker lamp.
20-	6119-8000	Dipper switch knob	1			
20-	0311-0306	Cross recd pan head screw	2		50	
20-	0361-0206	Pan head screw	2		50	
20-	0431-0205	Spring washer	2		50	
20-16	8301-8010	Left front winker assy	1			
20-16	8302-8010	Right front winker assy	1			
20-16	8303-9010	Left rear winker assy	1			
20-16	8304-9010	Right rear winker assy	1			
20-17	8331-3210	Winker lens	4			
20-18	8332-3000	Winker bulb	4			
20-19	0322-0306	Cross recd round head screw	8			
20-20	0433-0307	Spring washer	8			
20-21	4622-8000	Back mirror clamp	2			For rear winker
20-22	0231-0800	Hexagon nut C	4			
20-23	0431-0820	Spring washer	2			For rear winker

MEMO: Parts with mark "*" in the Remarks Column are common between models with winker and without winker lamp.

21) SPEEDOMETER CABLE · WIRES

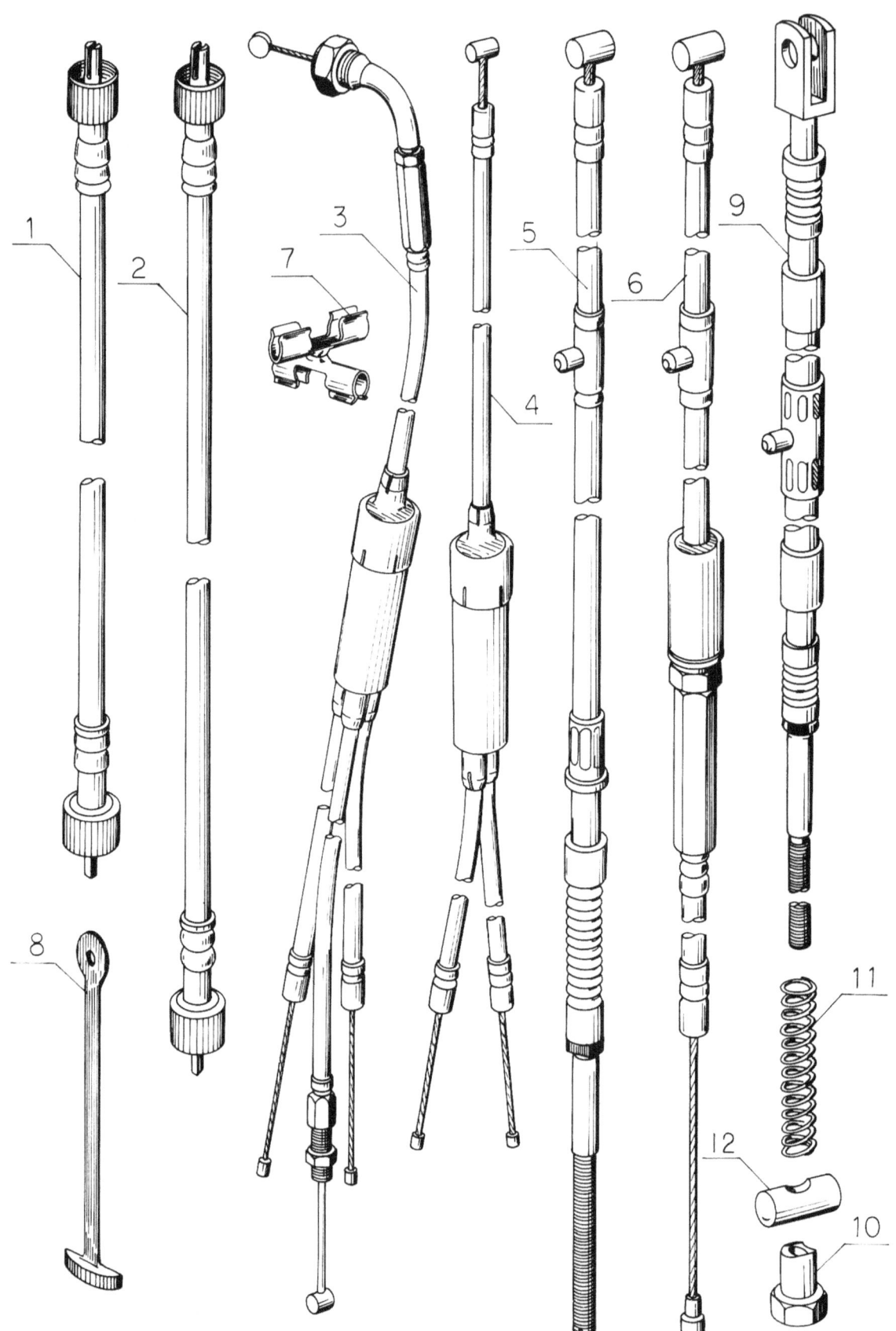

21) SPEEDOMETER CABLE · WIRES

Index No.	Part No.	Part Name	No. Req'd	Unit Price	Min. Lot	Remarks
21- 1	6171-9000	Speedometer cable	2			
21- 2	6172-9000	Tachometer cable	1			
21- 3	6176-9000	Throttle wire	1			
21- 4	6178-9000	Carburetor starter wire	1			
21- 5	6181-9000	Front brake wire	1			
21- 6	6186-9000	Clutch wire	1			
21- 7	6187-9000	Wire clamp C	1			
21- 8	3424-3010	Wire harness strap	3			
21- 9	3841-9000	Rear brake wire	1			
21-10	3832-3000	Brake rod adjuster	2			
21-11	3833-8000	Brake rod spring	2			
21-12	7361-3003	Brake arm pin	2			

MEMO

22) MUFFLER · EXHAUST PIPE

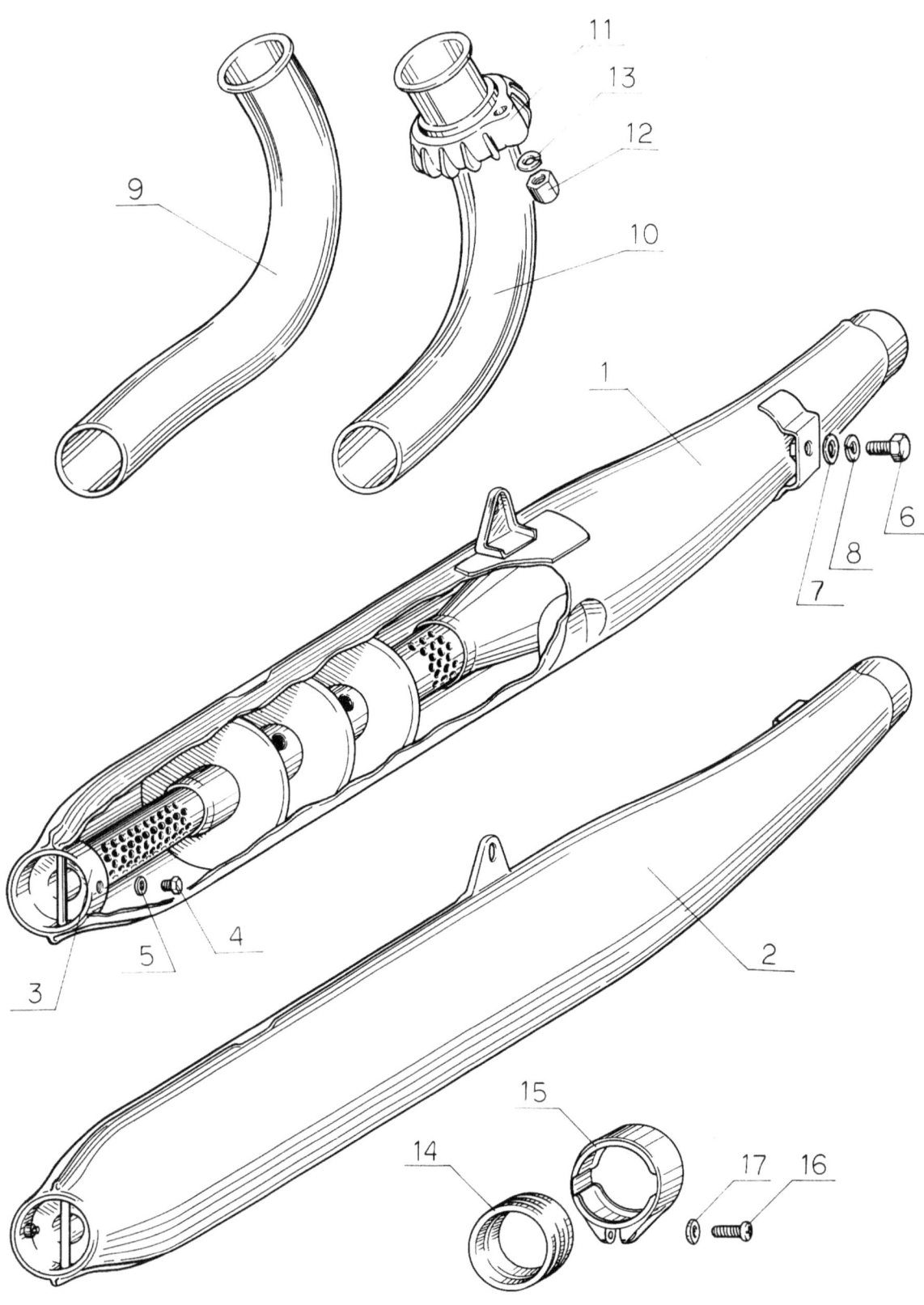

22) MUFFLER · EXHAUST PIPE

Index No.	Part No.	Part Name	No. Req'd	Unit Price	Min. Lot	Remarks
22- 1	6302-9000	Left muffler assy	1			
22- 2	6303-9000	Right muffler assy	1			
22- 3	6320-9000	Diffuser pipe	2			
22- 4	0121-0506	Hexagon bolt B	2		50	
22- 5	0411-0512	Plane washer A	2		50	
22- 6	0111-0816	Hexagon bolt A	2		50	
22- 7	0411-0818	Plane washer A	2		50	
22- 8	0431-0820	Spring washer	2		50	
22- 9	6352-9000	Left exhaust pipe	1			
22-10	6353-9000	Right exhaust pipe	1			
22-11	6361-9000	Exhaust pipe clamp	2			
22-12	09521-107	8 hexagon nut	2		50	
22-13	0431-0820	Spring washer	2		50	
22-14	6362-9000	Muffler joint rubber	2			
22-15	6363-9000	Muffler joint stopper	2			
22-16	0311-0620	Cross recd pan head screw	2		50	
22-17	0411-0613	Plane washer A	2		50	

MEMO

23) DUAL SEAT · WINKER RELAY

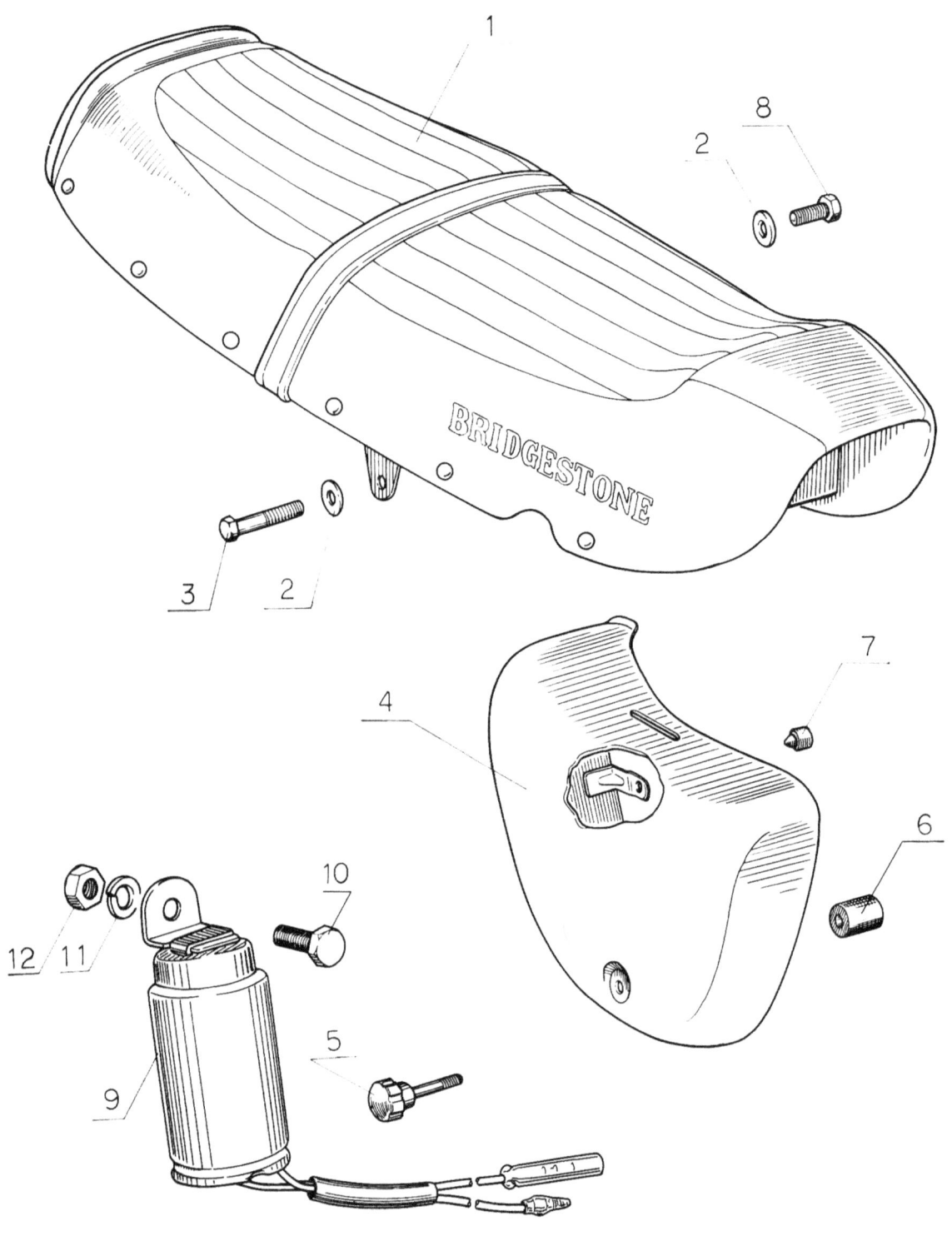

23) DUAL SEAT · WINKER RELAY

Index No.	Part No.	Part Name	No. Req'd	Unit Price	Min. Lot	Remarks
23- 1	6460-9000	Dual seat comp	1			
23- 2	09541-117	12 plane washer	2		50	
23- 3	09511-149	12×45 hexagon bolt	1		10	
23- 4	6811-9000-FAR	Left cover	1			
23- 5	6831-9000	Cover knob	1			
23- 6	6833-9000	Cover stopper	1			
23- 7	3452-3210	Supporter pad	1			
23- 8	0142-1220	Hexagon bolt D	1		50	
23- 9	8305-9010	Winker relay	1			
23-10	0111-0614	Hexagon bolt	1		50	
23-11	0431-0615	Spring washer	1		50	
23-12	0211-0600	Hexagon nut	1		50	
23-	3424-3010	Wire harness strap	2			For winker wire

MEMO

24) FRONT WHEEL

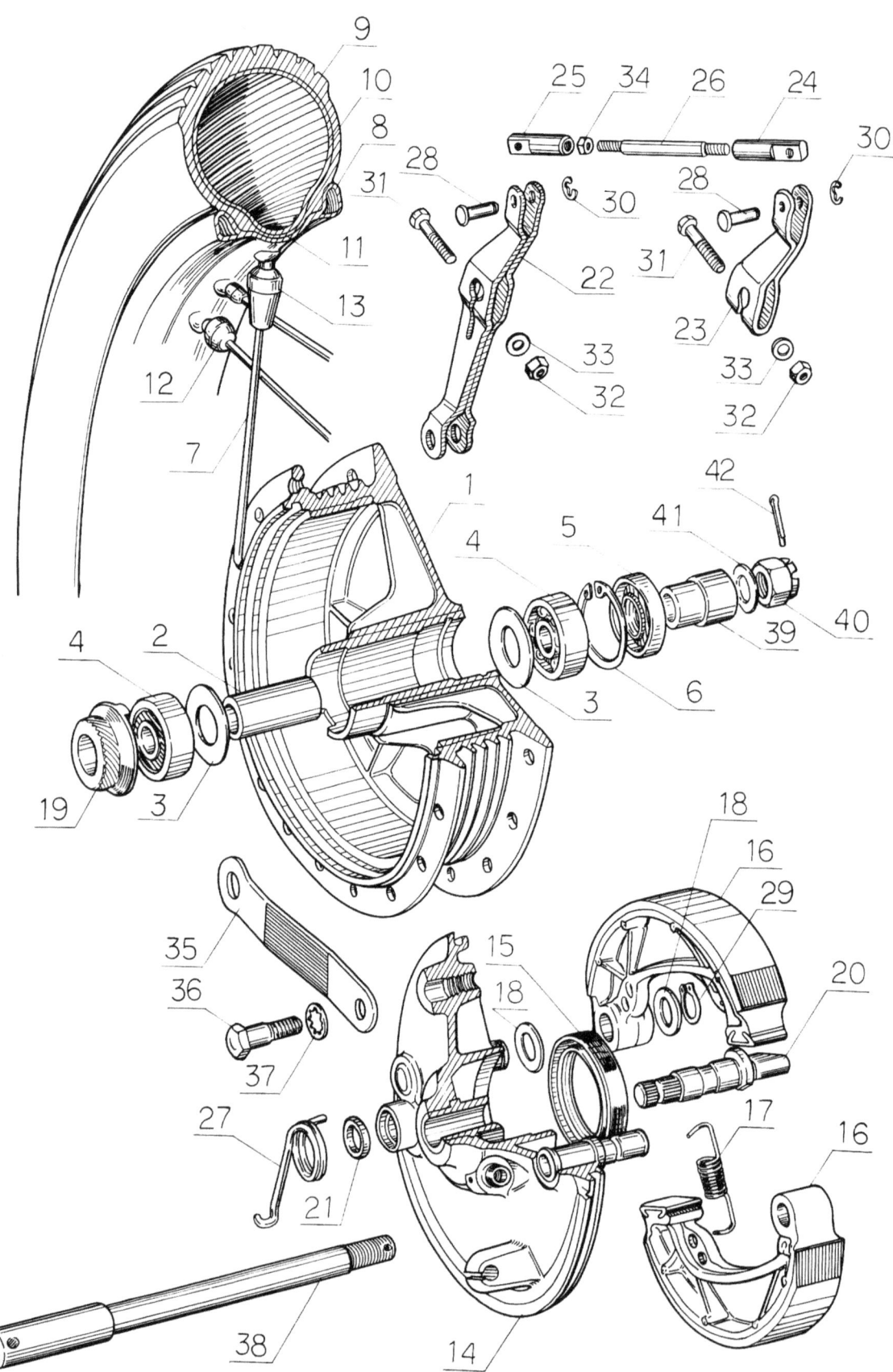

24) FRONT WHEEL

Index No.	Part No.	Part Name	No. Req'd	Unit Price	Min. Lot	Remarks
24- 1	7111-8000	Front brake drum	1			
24- 2	7114-8000	Front drum collar	1			
24- 3	7115-8000	Collar supporter	2			
24- 4	07-6302-43	Ball bearing	2		10	
24- 5	09590-110	22 oil seal	1		10	
24- 6	09501-101	42 A snap ring	1		10	
24- 7	7108-9000	Front spoke assy	1			
24- 8	7241-9000	Front wheel rim	1			
24- 9	7251-9000	Front wheel tire	1			3.25-19
24-10	7252-9000	Wheel tube	1			
24-11	7253-9000	Tire flap	1			
24-12	7245-9000	Wheel balancing weight A	1			
24-13	7246-9000	Wheel balancing weight B	1			
24-14	7130-9000	Front panel comp	1			
24-15	09590-111	48 oil seal	1		10	
24-16	7140-9000	Brake shoe comp	2			
24-17	7145-8000	Brake shoe spring	2			
24-18	09548-101	14 thrust washer	4		10	
24-19	7148-9000	Speedometer gear	1			
24-20	7151-9000	Front brake cam	2			
24-21	7152-8000	Cam dust seal	2			
24-22	7153-9000	Brake arm A	1			
24-23	7154-9000	Brake arm B	1			
24-24	7156-9000	Rod end A	1			
24-25	7157-9000	Rod end B	1			
24-26	7158-9000	Brake arm rod	1			
24-27	7159-9000	Front arm return spring	1			
24-28	7161-9000	Brake arm pin	2			
24-29	09502-101	14 A snap ring	2		10	
24-30	09504-101	5 D snap ring	2		10	
24-31	0111-0632	Hexagon bolt A	2		10	
24-32	0211-0600	Hexagon nut A	2		50	
24-33	0411-0613	Plane washer A	2		50	
24-34	0232-0500	Hexagon nut C	1		50	
24-35	7166-9000	Front torque link	1			
24-36	7167-8000	Front link bolt	1			
24-37	0441-1018	Internal toothed washer	1		50	
24-38	7221-9000	Front wheel axle	1			
24-39	7226-8000	Front axle collar	1			
24-40	09522-102	14 sloted hexagon nut	1		10	

24) FRONT WHEEL

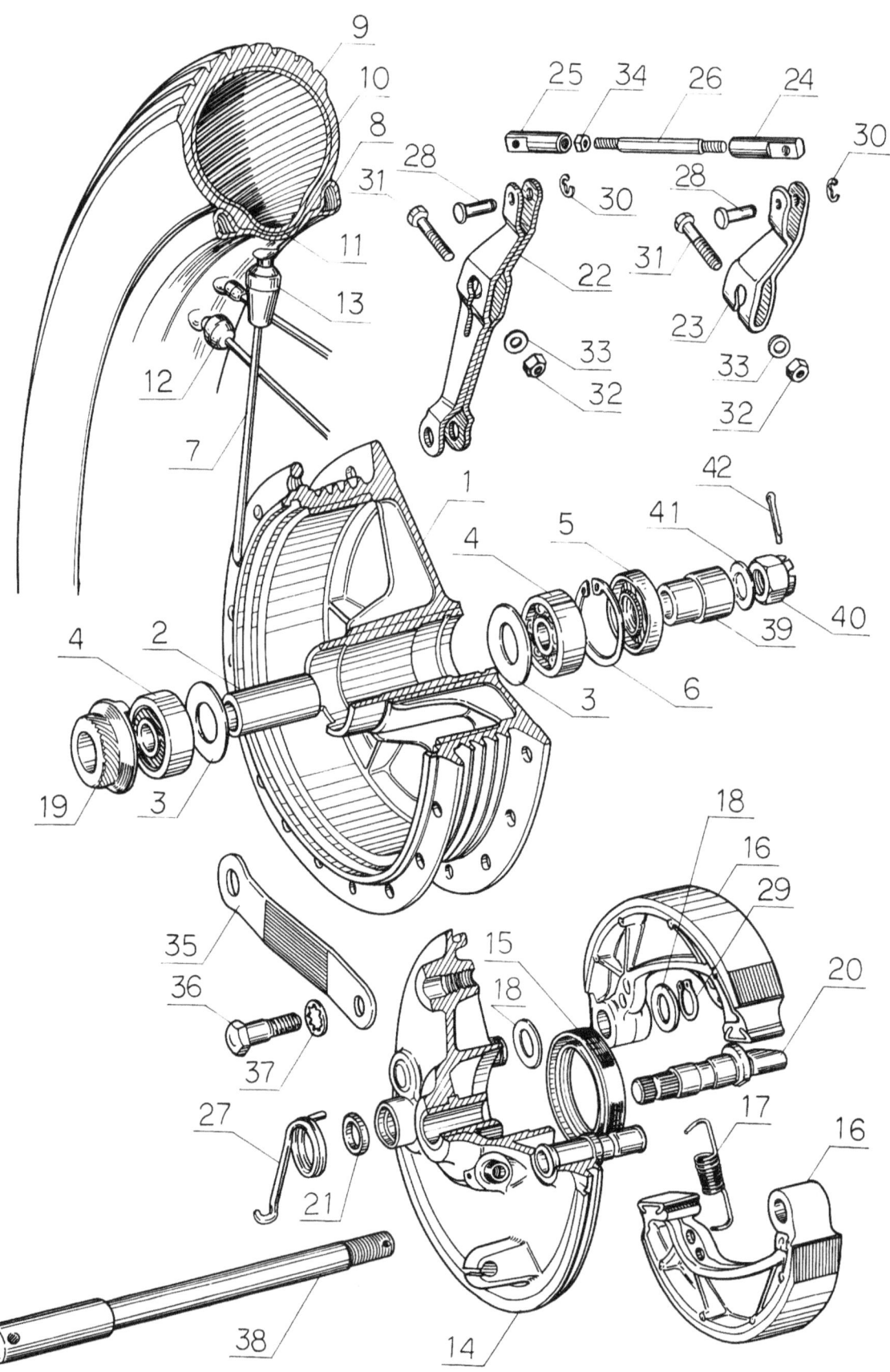

24) FRONT WHEEL

Index No.	Part No.	Part Name	No. Req'd	Unit Price	Min. Lot	Remarks
24-41	09541-109	14 plane washer	1		10	
24-42	0551-3025	Split pin	1		50	

MEMO

When placing order of " * " items, please order by separate cover.

25) REAR WHEEL

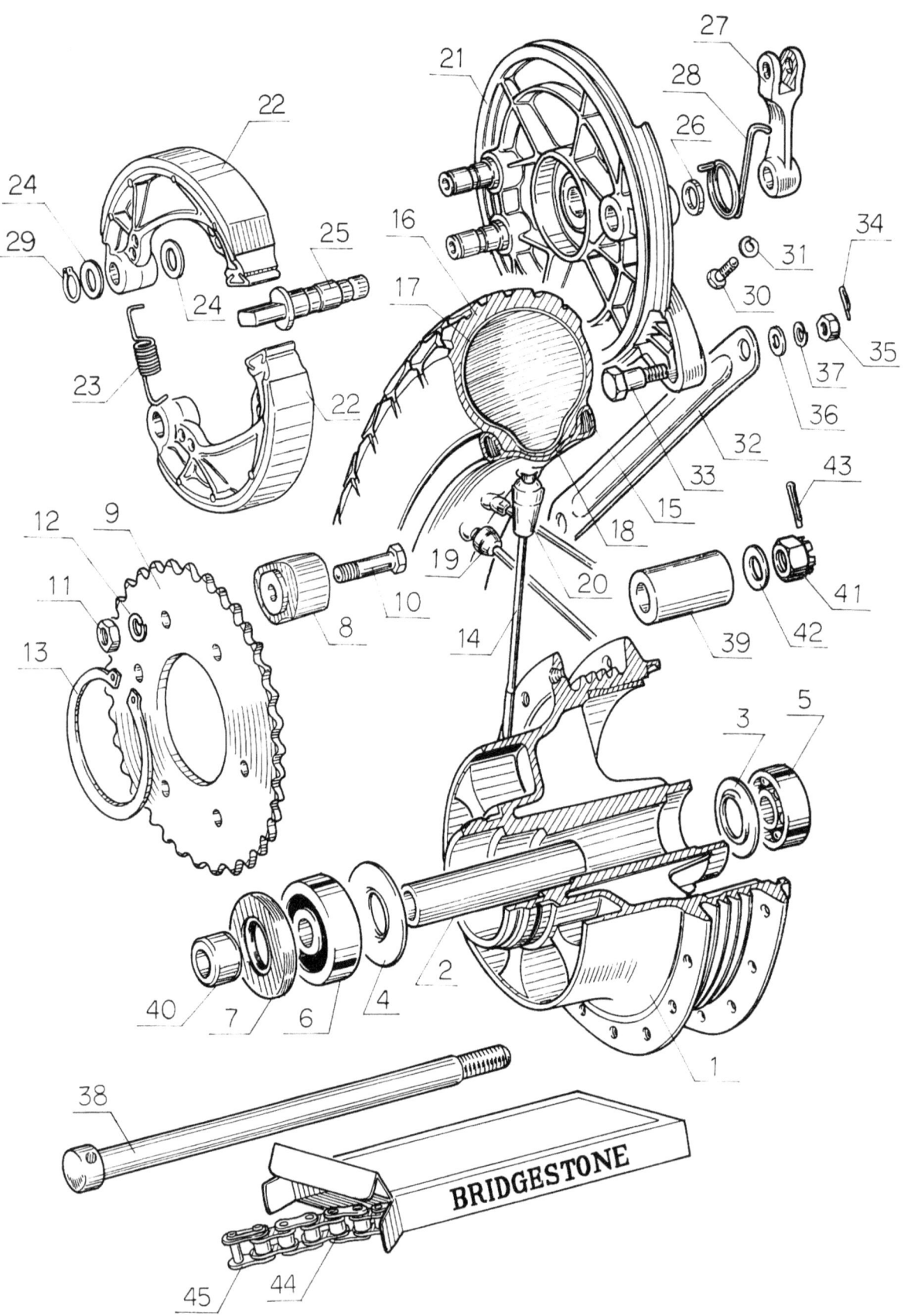

25) REAR WHEEL

Index No.	Part No.	Part Name	No. Req'd	Unit Price	Min. Lot	Remarks
25- 1	7311-9000	Rear brake drum	1			
25- 2	7314-9000	Rear drum collar	1			
25- 3	7315-8010	Collar supportor B	1			
25- 4	7315-9000	Collar supportor B	1			
25- 5	07-6303-43	Ball bearing	1		10	
25- 6	07-6403-43	Ball bearing	1		10	
25- 7	09590-123	28 oil seal	1		10	
25- 8	7319-9000	Rear wheel damper	6			
25- 9	7381-9000	Driven sprocket	1			
25-10	09511-146	10×35 hexagon bolt	6		10	
25-11	0231-1000	Hexagon nut C	6		10	
25-12	0431-1025	Spring washer	6		50	
25-13	09502-103	78 B snap ring	1		10	
25-14	7108-9000	Front spoke assy	1			
25-15	7241-9000	Front wheel rim	1			
25-16	7451-9000	Rear wheel tire	1			3.25-19
25-17	7252-9000	Wheel tube	1			
25-18	7253-9000	Tire flap	1			
25-19	7245-9000	Wheel balancing weight A	1			
25-20	7246-9000	Wheel balancing weight B	1			
25-21	7330-9000	Rear panel comp	1			
25-22	7140-9000	Brake shoe comp	2			
25-23	7145-8000	Brake shoe spring	2			
25-24	09548-101	14 thrust washer	4		10	
25-25	7351-9000	Rear brake cam	1			
25-26	7152-8000	Cam dust seal	1			
25-27	7353-8000	Brake arm C	1			
25-28	7359-8000	Rear arm return spring	1			
25-29	09502-101	14 A snap ring	2		50	
25-30	0112-0620	Hexagon bolt A	1		50	
25-31	0431-0615	Spring washer	1		50	
25-32	7366-9000	Rear torque link	1			
25-33	7367-9000	Rear link bolt	1			
25-34	7369-8000	Latch clip	1			
25-35	0211-0800	Hexagon nut A	1		50	
25-36	0411-0818	Plane washer A	1		50	
25-37	0431-0820	Spring washer	1		50	
25-38	7421-9000	Rear wheel axle	1			
25-39	7426-9000	Rear axle collar	1			
25-40	7377-9000	Oil seal collar	1			

25) REAR WHEEL

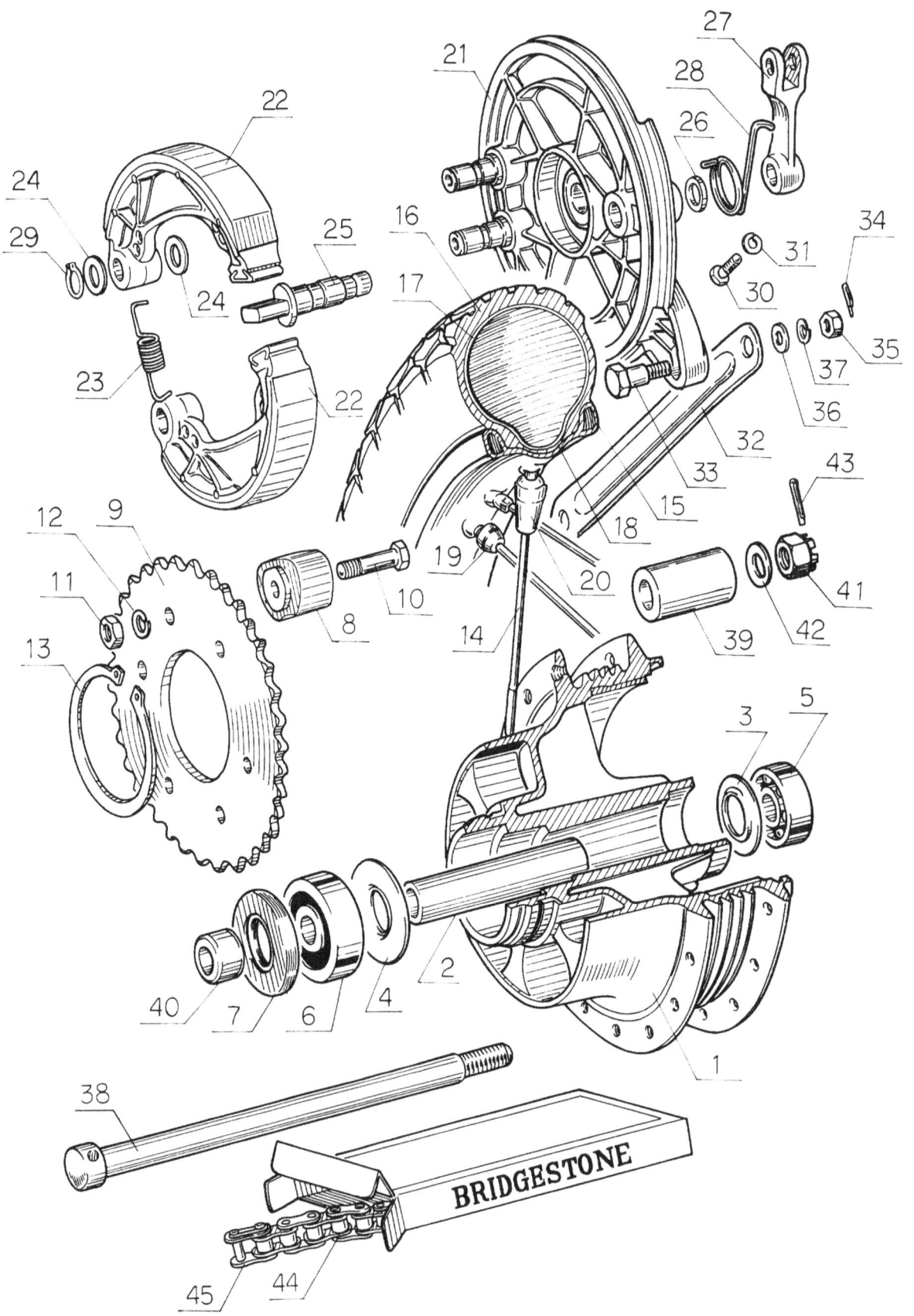

25) REAR WHEEL

Index No.	Part No.	Part Name	No. Req'd	Unit Price	Min. Lot	Remarks
25-41	09522-102	14 sloted hexagon nut	1		10	
25-42	09541-109	14 Plane washer	1		10	
25-43	0551-3025	Split pin	1		50	
25-44	7501-9000	Roller chain assy	1			
25-45	7520-9000	Chain joint comp	1			

MEMO

When placing order of "*" items, please order by separate cover.

26) HEAD LAMP · TAIL LAMP

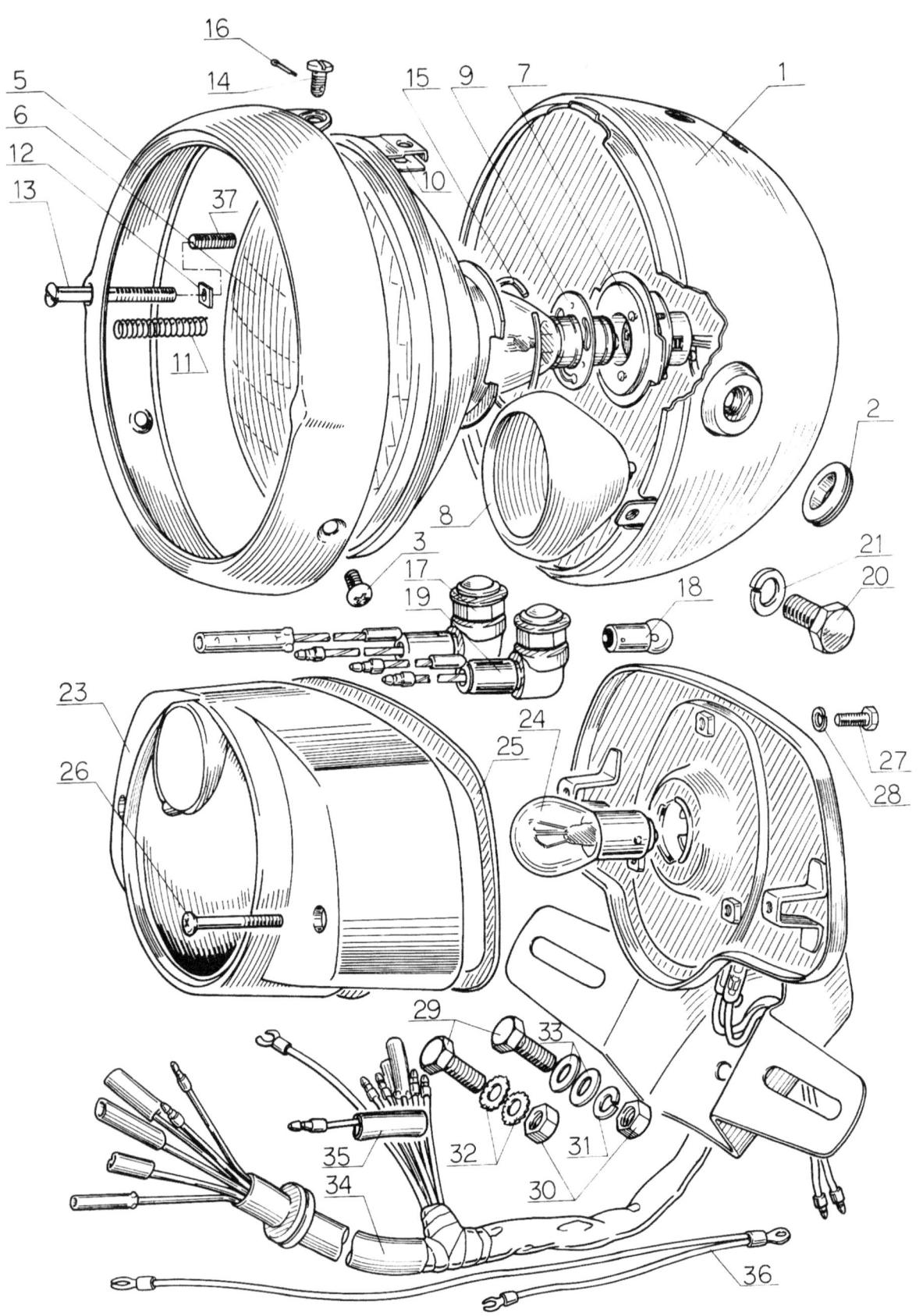

26) HEAD LAMP · TAIL LAMP

Index No.	Part No.	Part Name	No. Req'd	Unit Price	Min. Lot	Remarks
26- 1	8111-9000-XCl	Head lamp body	1			
26- 2	8125-5020	Head lamp grommet	1			
26- 3	0342-0510	Cross oval head screw	2		50	
26- 4	8102-9000	Head lamp assy	1			
26- 5	8140-9000	Head lamp rim comp	1			
26- 6	8150-9000	Head lamp lens comp	1			
26- 7	8160-9000	Socket comp	1			
26- 8	8178-8010	Shield rubber	1			
26- 9	8171-8010	Head lamp bulb	1			
26-10	8173-9000	Quick acting nut	2			
26-11	8174-9000	Adjuster spring	1			
26-12	8175-9000	Square nut	1			
26-13	8176-9000	Adjuster screw	1			
26-14	8177-9000	Holder screw	2			
26-15	8179-9000	Socket set ring	1			
26-16	09555-101	Split pin	2		50	
26-17	8404-9000	Neutral lamp assy	1			
26-18	8424-8000	Speedometer bulb	2			
26-19	8405-9000	High beam lamp assy	1			
26-20	0112-0812	Hexagon bolt A	2		10	
26-21	0431-0820	Spring washer	2		50	
26-22	8205-9000	Tail lamp assy	1			
26-23	8251-9000	Tail lamp lens	1			
26-24	8252-3040	Tail lamp bulb	1			
26-25	8253-9000	Tail lamp gasket	1			
26-26	0342-0436	Cross oval head screw	2		50	
26-27	0111-0410	Hexagon bolt A	3		50	
26-28	0431-0410	Spring washer	3		50	
26-29	0111-0614	Hexagon bolt A	3		50	
26-30	0211-0600	Hexagon nut A	3		50	
26-31	0432-0615	Spring washer	2		50	
26-32	0451-0611	External toothed washer	2		50	
26-33	0411-0613	Plane washer A	8		50	
26-34	8811-9010	Wire harness	1			
26-34	8811-9000	Wire harness	1			For U.S.A.
26-35	8824-5010	High beam wire	1			
26-36	8831-9000	Body earth wire	1			
26-37	8181-9010	Cover tube	1			For the model with winker relay

27) SPEEDOMETER · IGNITION COIL · MAIN SWITCH

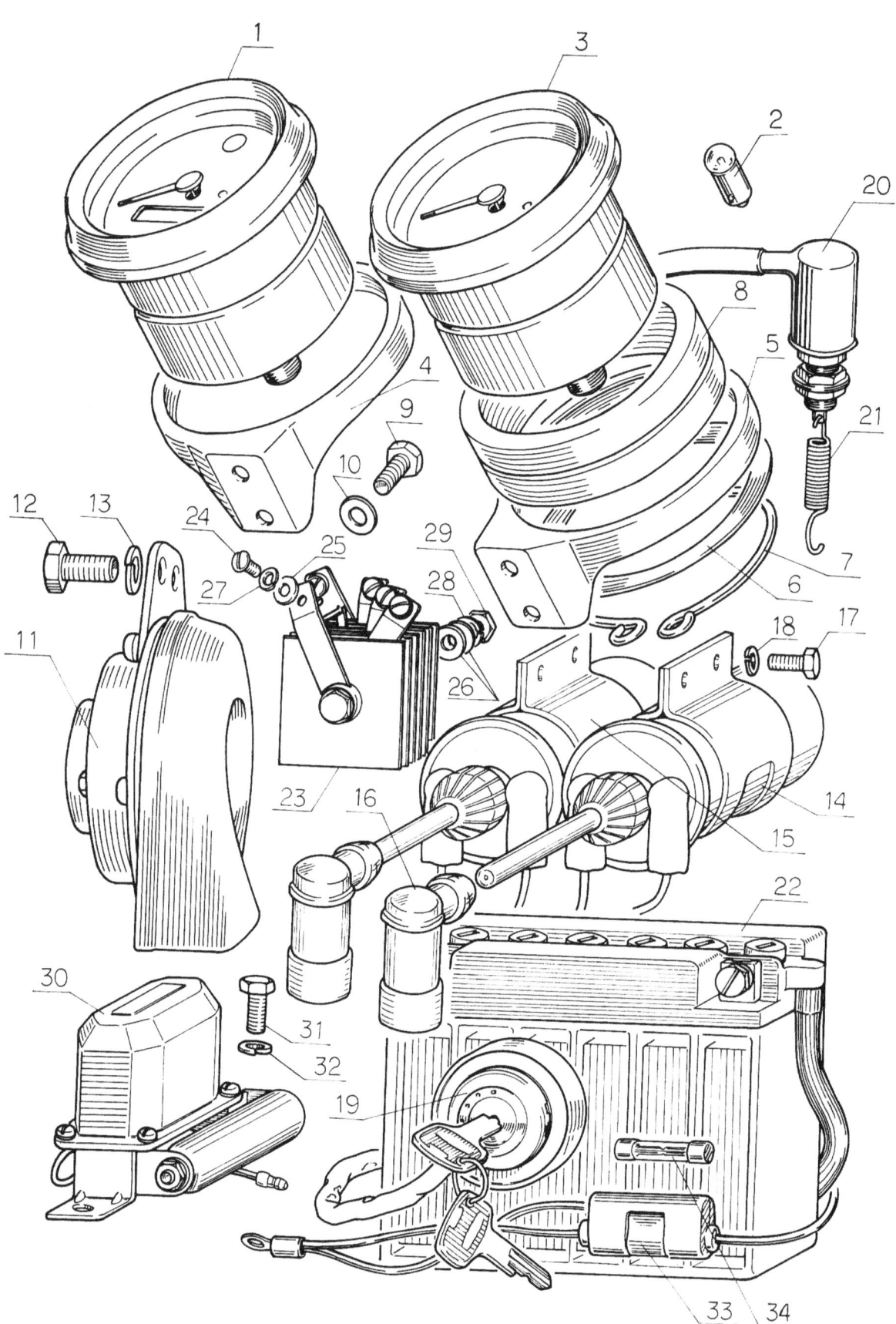

27) SPEEDOMETER · IGNITION COIL · MAIN SWITCH

Index No.	Part No.	Part Name	No. Req'd	Unit Price	Min. Lot	Remarks
27- 1	8401-9000	Speedometer assy	1			MILE/H
27- 1	8401-9010	Speedometer assy	1			KM/H
27- 2	8424-8000	Speedometer bulb	3		10	
27- 3	8403-9000	Tachometer assy	1			
27- 4	3471-9000	Left meter holder	1			
27- 5	3472-9000	Right meter holder	1			
27- 6	8428-9000	Speedometer washer	2			
27- 7	8429-9000	Speedometer set spring	2			
27- 8	8435-9000	Meter cushion rubber	2			
27- 9	0111-0612	Hexagon bolt A	4		50	
27-10	0411-0613	Plane washer A	4		50	
27-11	8402-9000	Horn assy	1			
27-12	0111-0816	Hexagon bolt A	2		50	
27-13	0431-0820	Spring washer	2		50	
27-14	8502-9000	Left ignition coil assy	1			
27-15	8503-9000	Right ignition coil assy	1			
27-16	8520-5000	Plug cap comp	2			
27-17	0111-0512	Hexagon bolt A	4		50	
27-18	0431-0513	Spring washer	4		50	
27-19	8601-9000	Main switch assy	1			
27-20	8650-5000	Stop switch comp	1			
27-21	8661-9000	Stop switch spring	1			
27-22	8701-3032	Battery	1			
27-23	8702-8000	Rectifier assy	1			
27-24	0361-0406	Pan head screw	5		50	
27-25	0411-0410	Plane washer A	5		50	
27-26	0411-0512	Plane washer A	2		50	
27-27	0431-0410	Spring washer	5		50	
27-28	0431-0513	Spring washer	1		50	
27-29	0231-0500	Hexagon nut C	1		50	
27-30	8703-9000	Regulator assy	1			
27-31	0111-0612	Hexagon bolt A	2		50	
27-32	0431-0615	Spring washer	2		50	
27-33	8802-9000	Fuse assy	1			
27-34	8861-3000	Fuse	2		10	

MEMO

28) SERVICE TOOL SET · SPECIAL TOOL SET

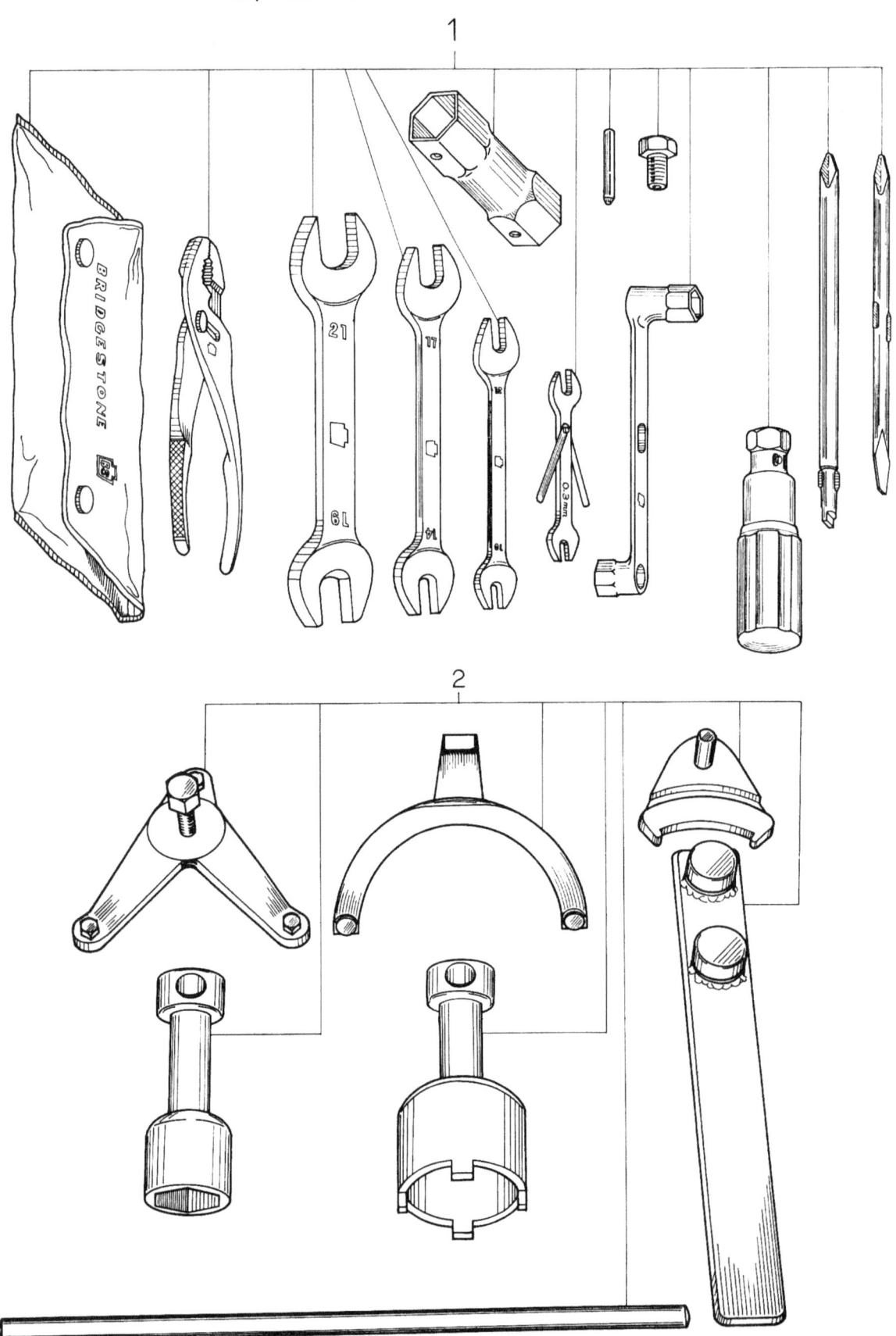

28) SERVICE TOOL SET · SPECIAL TOOL SET

Index No.	Part No.	Part Name	No. Req'd	Unit Price	Min. Lot	Remarks
28- 1	9201-9000	Service tool set	1			
28- 2	9300-9010	Special tool set	1			

MEMO

SERVICE MEMO

P9 350GTO WO

EXCLUSIVE

PARTS CATALOG

BRIDGESTONE 350 *GTO*

CONTENTS

INDEX NO.	DESCRIPTION	PAGE
29)	TOOL BOX · MAIN STAND · KICK STARTER	66~67
30)	FRONT FENDER	68~69
31)	HANDLE BAR · FUEL COCK · ENGINE PROTECTOR	70~71
32)	OIL TANK	72~73
33)	MUFFLER	74~75
34)	COVER	76~77
35)	REFLEX REFLECTOR	78~79
36)	RIGHT HANDLE GRIP · FRONT STOP SWITCH	80~81

INSTRUCTIONS FOR USING THE PARTS CATALOG

1. The parts listed in this catalog are exclusive for model 350GTO.

2. The other parts are identical with those of 350GTR.

3. Please file this catalog with the 350 GTR parts catalog by following index No. 28–page 65.

Printed in Japan. Dec., '69

BRIDGESTONE 350 *GTO*

29) TOOL BOX · MAIN STAND

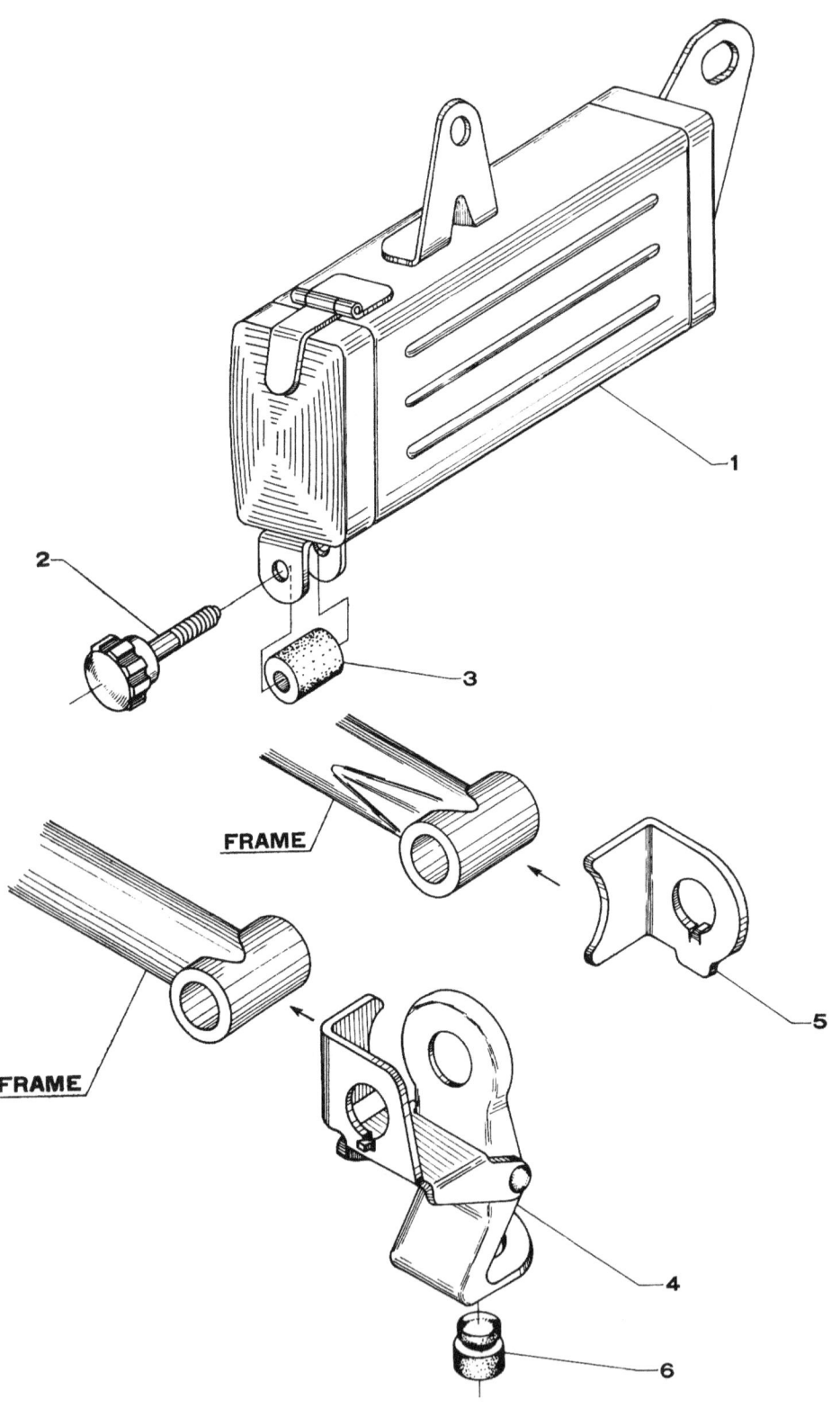

29) TOOL BOX · MAIN STAND · KICK STARTER

Index No.	Part No.	Part Name	No. Req'd	Unit Price US $ (F.O.B.)	Interchangeability			Remarks
					GTR	MIIRS	MIISS	
1	3301-9010	Tool box ass'y	1					
2	6831-9000	Cover knob	1		○			
3	6833-9000	Cover stopper	1		○			
4	3336-9010	Stand stopper braket	1					
5	3765-9010	Tandem footrest stopper	1					
6	3335-3000	Stand rubber stopper	1					Interchangeable with 50~90 models
	2680-9020	Kick starter arm	1		○			Kick starter arm without nipple of GTR is applicable to GTO

30) FRONT FENDER

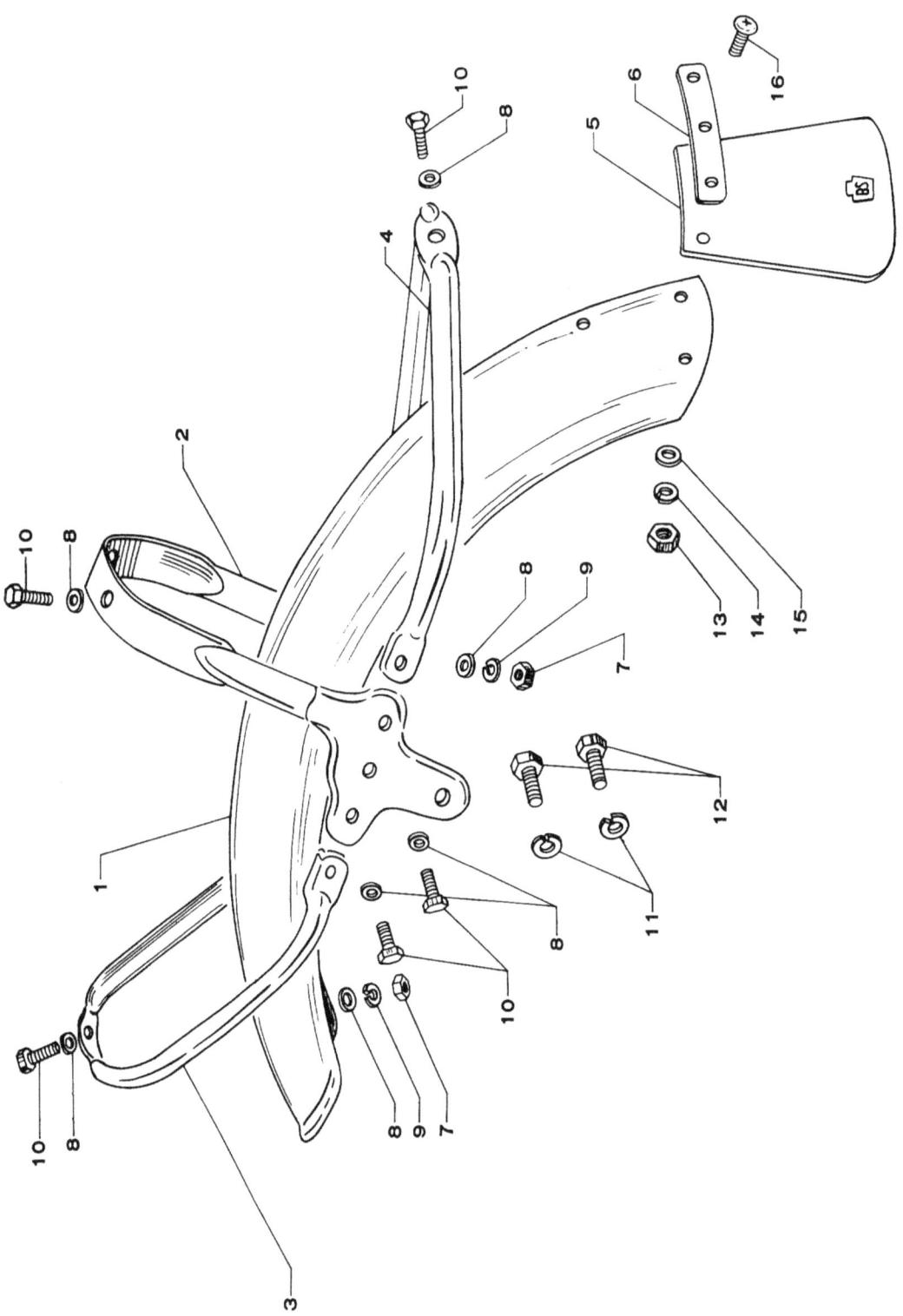

30) FRONT FENDER

Index No.	Part No.	Part Name	No. Req'd	Unit Price US $ (F.O.B.)	Interchangeability			Remarks
					GTR	MIIRS	MIISS	
1	4411-9010	Front fender	1					
2	4412-9010	Front fender braket A	1					
3	4423-9010	Fender stay A	1					
4	4424-9010	Fender stay B	1					
5	4451-5010	Front mudguard	1				○	
6	4452-5010	Front mudguard band	1				○	
7	0211-0600	Hexagon nut A	4					
8	0411-0613	Plain washer A	12					
9	0431-0615	Spring washer	4					
10	0112-0612	Hexagon bolt A	8					
11	0431-0820	Spring washer	4					
12	0111-0812	Hexagon bolt A	4					
13	0211-0500	Hexagon nut A	3					
14	0431-0513	Spring washer	3					
15	0411-0512	Plain washer A	3					
16	0311-0510	Cross rec'd pan head screw	3					

31) HANDLE BAR · FUEL COCK · ENGINE PROTECTOR

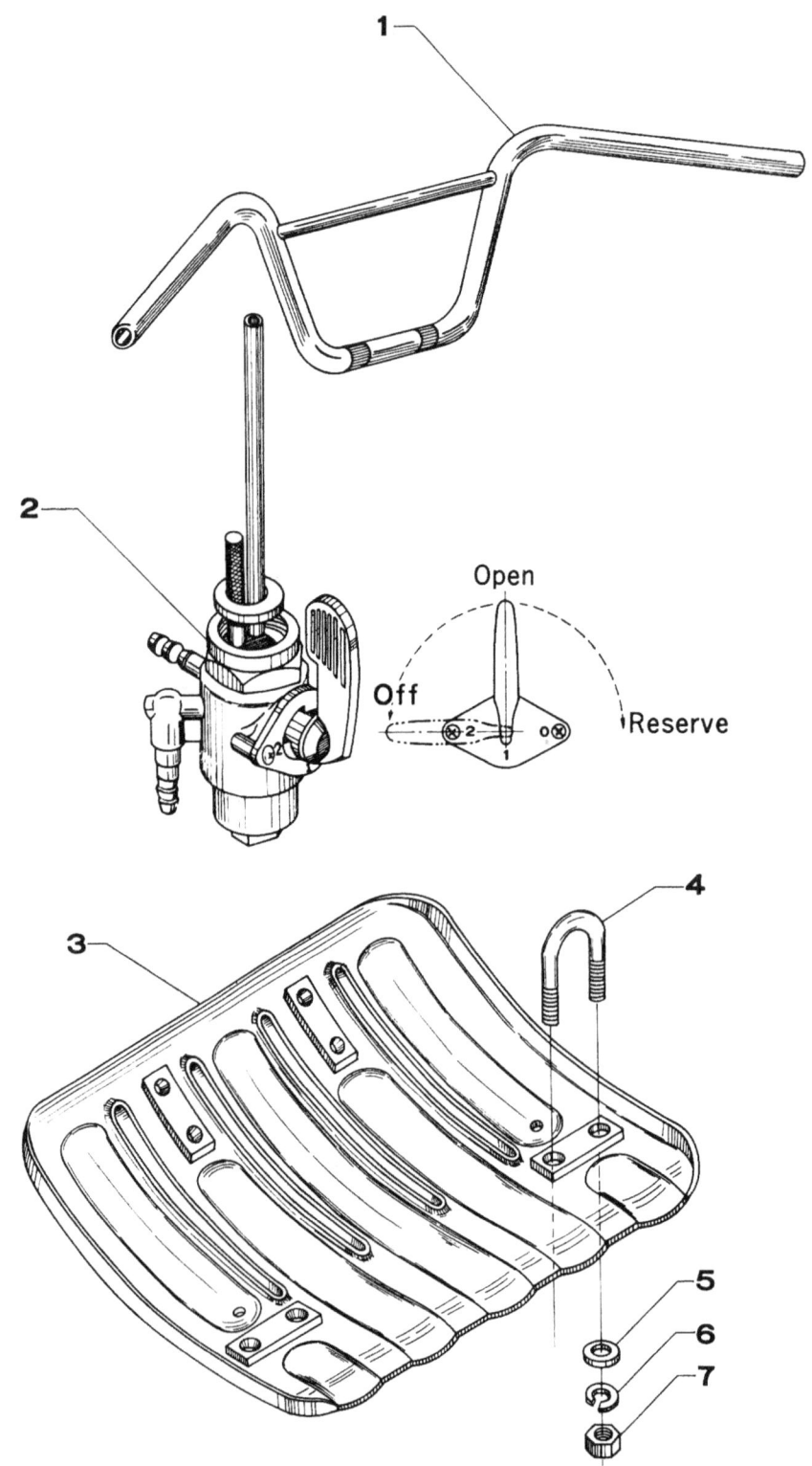

31) HANDLE BAR · FUEL COCK · ENGINE PROTECTOR

Index No.	Part No.	Part Name	No. Req'd	Unit Price US $ (F.O.B.)	Interchangeability GTR	MIIRS	MIISS	Remarks
1	4511-9010	Up handle bar	1					
2	5103-9010	Fuel cock ass'y	1					
3	6761-9010	Engine protector	1					
4	6762-9010	Engine protector U bolt	4					
5	0411-0818	Plain washer A	8					
6	0431-0820	Spring washer	8					
7	0211-0800	Hexagon nut A	8					
	5189-9000	Wire guard spring	5		○			Cable-and-tube protector against heat
	5110-9000-FBG	Fuel tank comp	1		○			Flamboyant Bead-Gold

32) OIL TANK

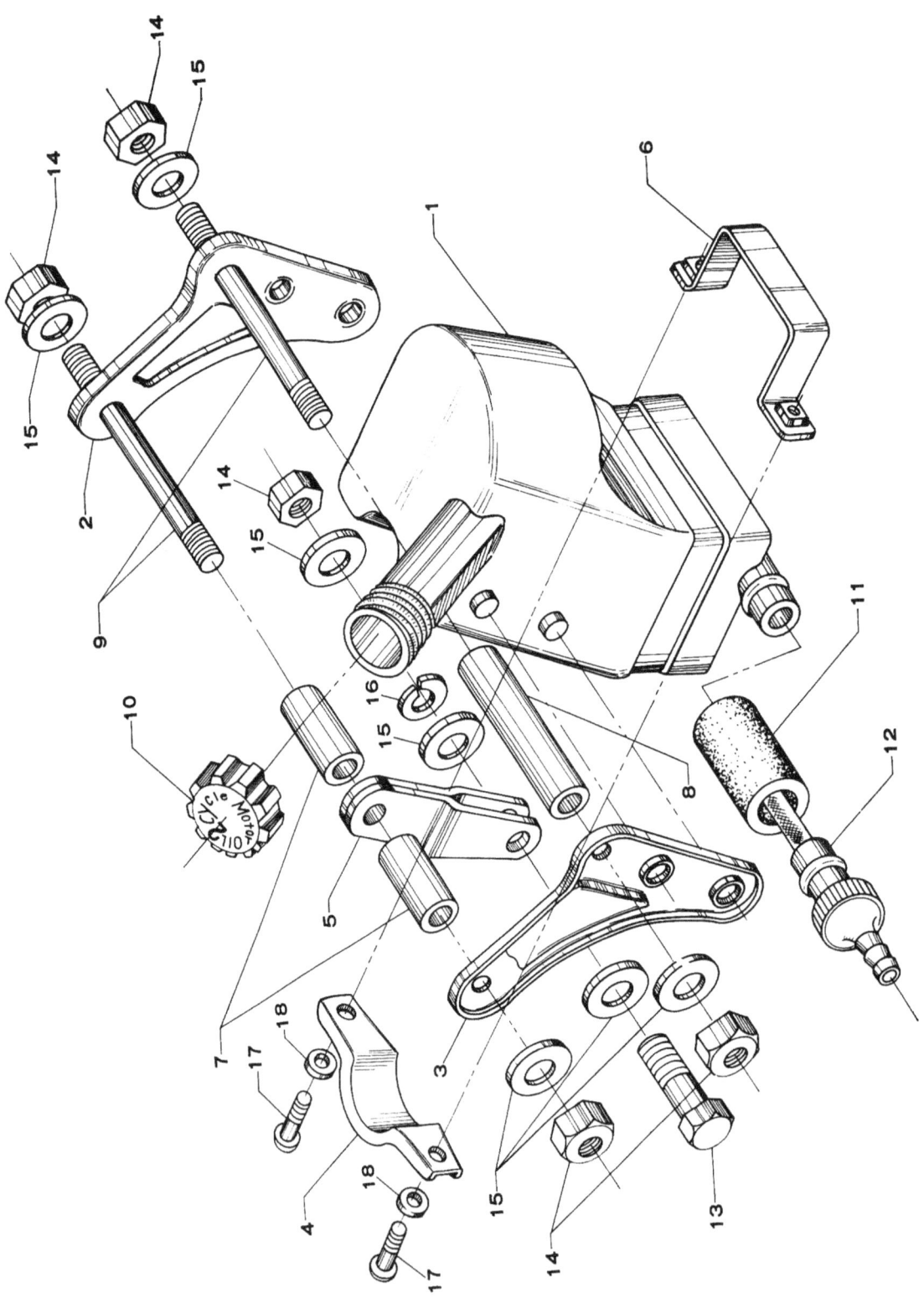

32) OIL TANK

Index No.	Part No.	Part Name	No. Req'd	Unit Price US $ (F.O.B.)	Interchangeability GTR	MIIRS	MIISS	Remarks
1	5510-9010	Oil tank comp	1					
2	5540-9010	Left oil tank upper bracket	1					
3	5541-9010	Right oil tank upper bracket	1					
4	5543-9010	Oil tank lower bracket	1					
5	5542-9010	Oil tank upper bracket	1					
6	5544-9010	Oil tank setband	1					
7	5545-9010	Oil tank spacer A	2					
8	5546-9010	Oil tank spacer B	1					
9	5547-9010	Oil tank set-bolt	2					
10	5560-9010	Oil tank cap comp	1					
11	5512-9010	Oil tank connecting tube	1					
12	5532-9010	Oil tank filter	1					
13	0121-0822	Hexagon bolt B	1					
14	0211-0800	Hexagon nut A	5					
15	0411-0818	Plain washer A	7					
16	0431-0820	Spring washer	1					
17	0311-0614	Cross rec'd pan head screw	2					
18	0411-0613	Plain washer A	2					

33) MUFFLER

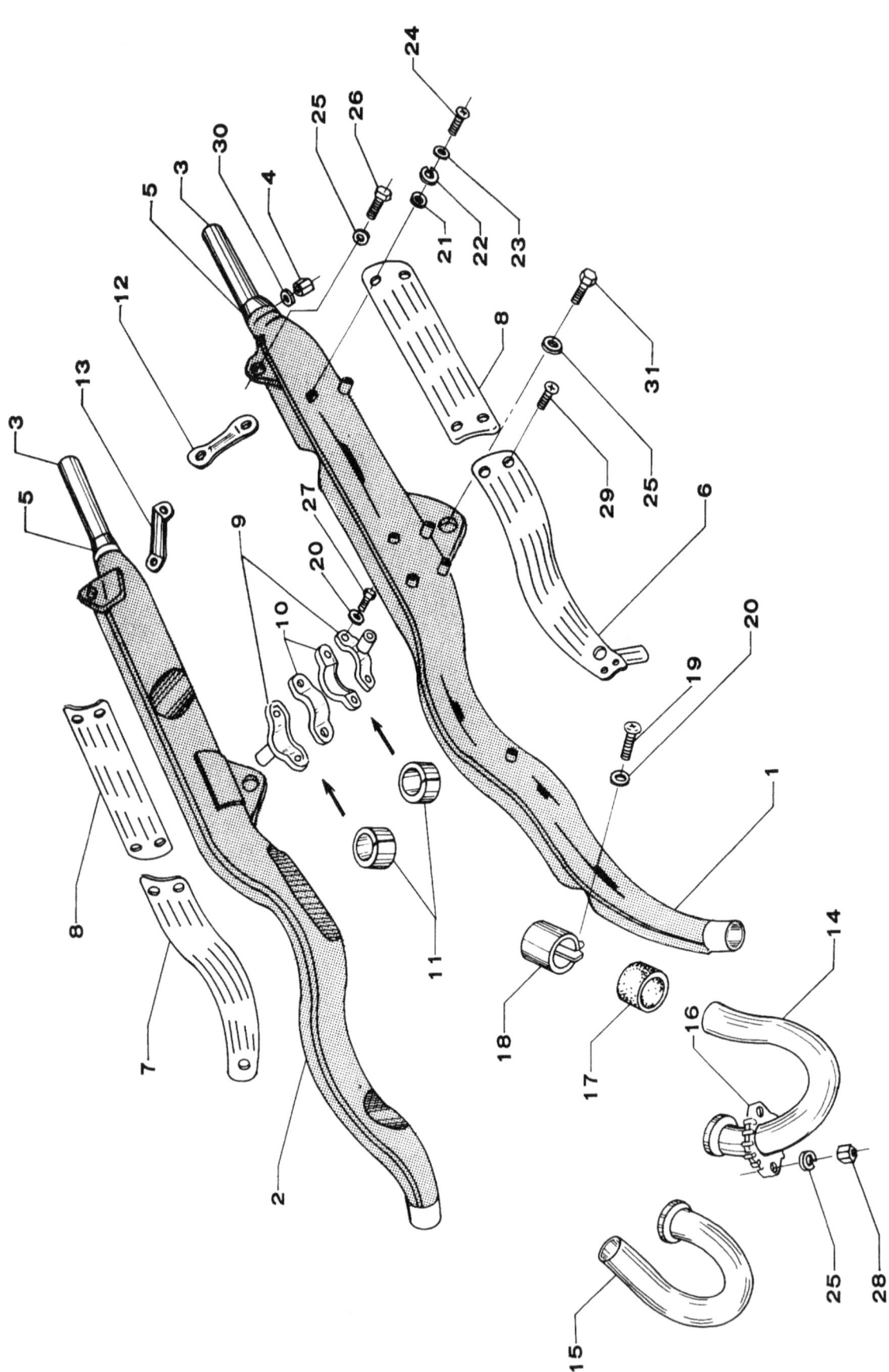

33) MUFFLER

Index No.	Part No.	Part Name	No. Req'd	Unit Price US $ (F.O.B.)	GTR	MIIRS	MIISS	Remarks
1	6302-9010-GBK	Left muffler ass'y	1					Black
2	6303-9010-GBK	Right muffler ass'y	1					Black
3	6320-9010	Diffuser pipe	2					
4	6321-9010	Diffuser pipe nut	2					
5	6322-9010	Diffuser pipe seal	2					
6	6343-9010	Left front muffler protector	1					
7	6344-9010	Right front muffler protector	1					
8	6333-5010	Rear muffler protector	2			○	○	
9	6369-9010	Band B	2					
10	6367-9010	Band A	2					
11	6368-9010	Band cushion rubber	2					
12	6341-9010	Left muffler stay	1					
13	6342-9010	Right muffler stay	1					
14	6352-9010	Left exhaust pipe	1					
15	6353-9010	Right exhaust pipe	1					
16	6361-9000	Exhaust pipe clamp	2		○			
17	6362-9000	Muffler joint rubber	2		○			
18	6363-9000	Muffler joint stopper	2		○			
19	0311-0620	Cross rec'd oval head screw	2					
20	0411-0613	Plain washer A	6					
21	6323-8010	Screw cover packing A	8			○	○	
22	6338-8010	Screw cover	8			○	○	
23	6324-8010	Screw cover packing B	8			○	○	
24	09531-102	Cross rec'd pan head screw	8					
25	0431-0820	Spring washer	8					
26	0111-0816	Hexagon bolt A	2					
27	0111-0614	Hexagon bolt A	4					
28	09521-107	Hexagon nut	4					
29	0341-0608	Cross rec'd oval head screw	6					
30	0411-0512	Plain washer A	2					
31	0111-0812	Hexagon bolt	2					

34) COVER

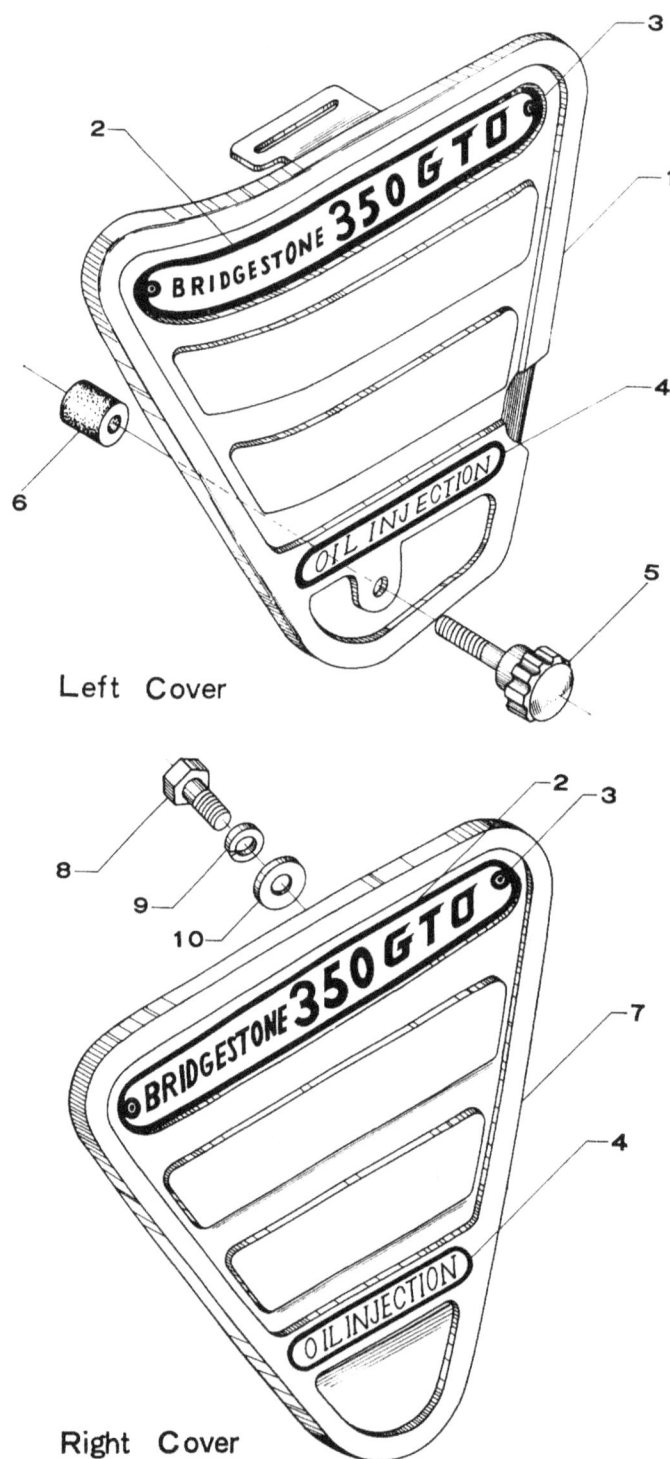

Left Cover

Right Cover

34) COVER

Index No.	Part No.	Part Name	No. Req'd	Unit Price US $ (F.O.B.)	Interchangeability			Remarks
					GTR	MIIRS	MIISS	
1	6811-9010-FBG	Left cover	1					Flamboyant Bead-Gold
2	6815-9010	Cover ornament	2					
3	6823-8000	Eyelet	4		○	○	○	
4	9116-5010	Oil injection label	2			○	○	
5	6831-9000	Cover knob	1		○			
6	6833-9000	Cover stopper	1		○			
7	6821-9010-FBG	Right cover	1					Flamboyant Bead-Gold
8	0121-0822	Hexagon bolt B	1					
9	0431-0820	Spring washer	1					
10	0411-0818	Plain washer A	1					

35) REFLEX REFLECTOR

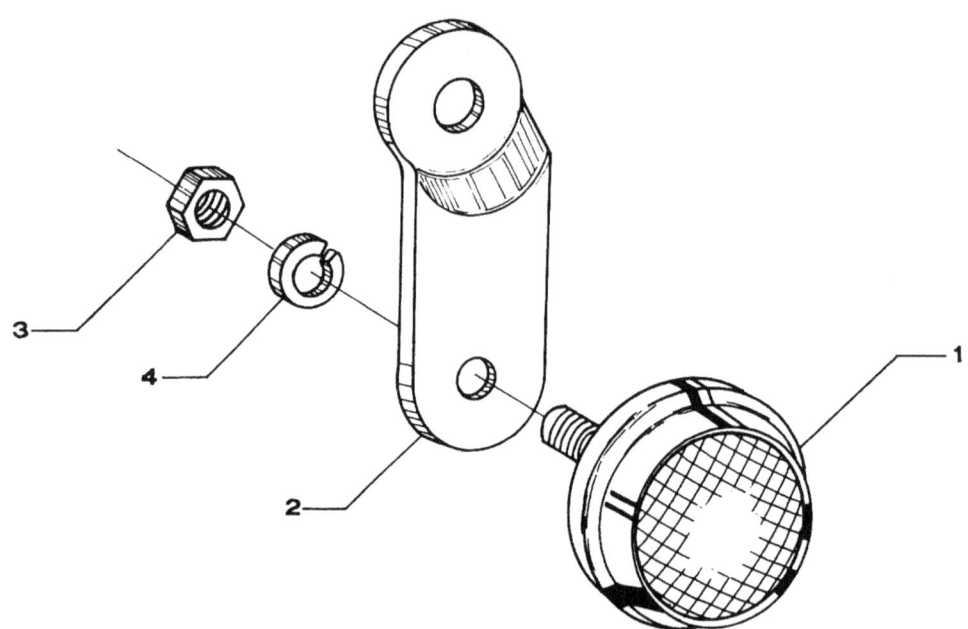

Front Reflex Reflector

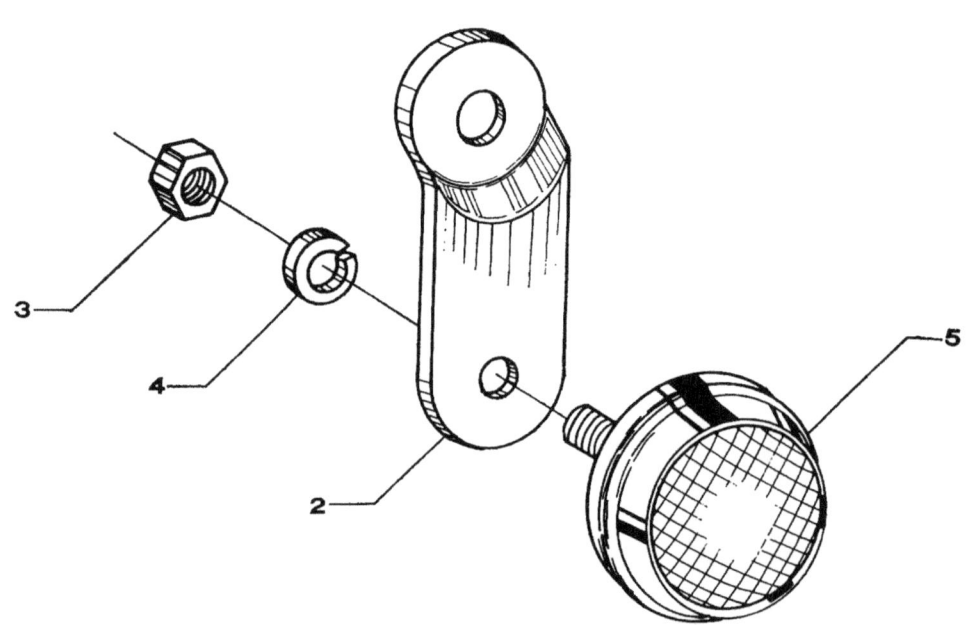

Rear Reflex Reflector

35) REFLEX REFLECTOR

Index No.	Part No.	Part Name	No. Req'd	Unit Price US $ (F.O.B.)	Interchangeability GTR	Interchangeability MIIRS	Interchangeability MIISS	Remarks
	8206-5610	Front reflector ass'y	2		○	○	○	
1	8271-5610	Front reflector	2		○	○	○	Amber
2	8272-5610	Front reflector bracket	4		○	○	○	
3	0211-0600	Hexagon nut A	4		○	○	○	
4	0433-0615	Spring washer	4		○	○	○	
	8207-9010	Rear reflector ass'y	2		○			
5	8281-9010	Rear reflector	2		○			Red

36) RIGHT HANDLE GRIP · FRONT STOP SWITCH

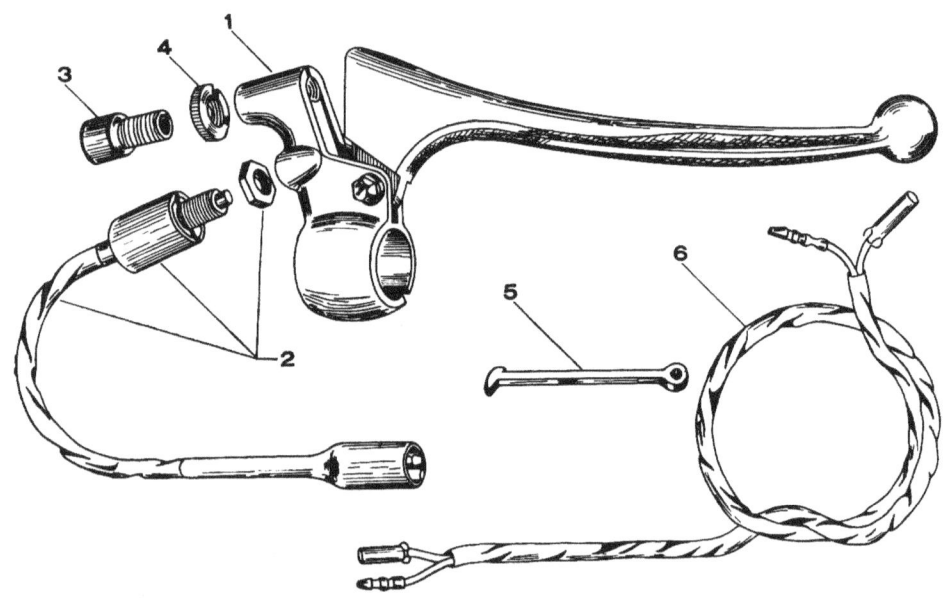

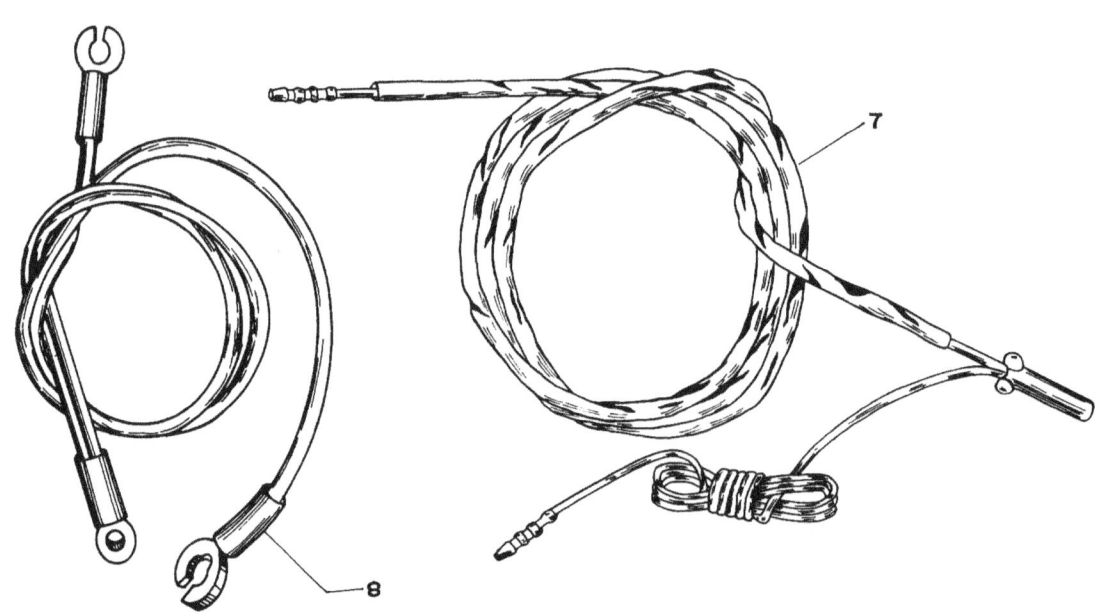

36) RIGHT HANDLE GRIP · FRONT STOP SWITCH

Index No.	Part No.	Part Name	No. Req'd	Unit Price US $ (F.O.B.)	GTR	MIIRS	MIISS	Remarks
	6104-8200	Throttle grip ass'y	1			○	○	
1	6149-8200	Right lever holder	1			○	○	
2	6134-8200	Front stop switch	1			○	○	
3	6126-8200	Wire adjuster	1			○	○	
4	6127-9000	Wire adjuster lock nut	2			○	○	
	6141-8010	Right switch case	1		○	○	○	
	6151-8010	Right switch case cover	1		○	○	○	
	6153-5010	Right handle grip	1		○	○	○	
	6154-8000	Throttle grip pipe	1		○	○	○	
	0311-0614	Cross rec'd pan head screw	1		○	○	○	
	0311-0616	Cross rec'd pan head screw	1		○	○	○	
5	3424-3010	Wire harness strap	1			○	○	
6	8836-8200	Front stop switch connecter	1			○	○	
7	8813-9010	Sub wire harness	1					
8	8831-9010	Body earth wire	1					

VELOCEPRESS MANUALS - MOTORCYCLE

1930'S BRITISH MOTORCYCLE CARBS & ELEC COMPONENTS (BOOK OF)
1930'S BRITISH MOTORCYCLE ENGINES (OVERHAUL & MAINTENANCE)
1930'S BRITISH MOTORCYCLE GEARBOXES & CLUTCHES (BOOK OF)
AJS 1932-1948 SINGLES & TWINS 250cc THRU 1000cc (BOOK OF)
AJS 1945-1960 SINGLES 350cc & 500cc MODELS 16 & 18 (BOOK OF)
AJS 1955-1965 SINGLES 350cc & 500cc (BOOK OF)
ARIEL UP TO 1932 (BOOK OF)
ARIEL 1932-1939 PREWAR MODELS (BOOK OF)
ARIEL 1933-1951 (WORKSHOP MANUAL)
ARIEL 1939-1960 4 STROKE SINGLES (BOOK OF)
ARIEL 1958-1964 LEADER & ARROW (BOOK OF)
BMW R26 R27 (1956-1967) FACTORY WORKSHOP MANUAL
BMW R50 R50S R60 R69S (1955-1969) FACTORY WORKSHOP MANUAL
BRIDGESTONE 90 SERIES FACTORY WSM & PARTS CATALOGUE
BRIDGESTONE 175 SERIES FACTORY WSM & PARTS CATALOGUE
BRIDGESTONE 350 SERIES FACTORY WSM & PARTS CATALOGUES
BSA BANTAM ALL MODELS FROM 1948 ONWARDS (BOOK OF)
BSA SINGLES & V-TWINS UP TO 1927 (BOOK OF)
BSA SINGLES & V-TWINS UP TO 1930 (BOOK OF)
BSA SINGLES & V-TWINS UP TO 1935 (BOOK OF)
BSA SINGLES & V-TWINS 1936-1939 (BOOK OF)
BSA OHV & SV SINGLES 250-600cc 1945-1959 (BOOK OF)
BSA OHV & SV SINGLES 250cc (ONLY) 1954-1970 (BOOK OF)
BSA OHV SINGLES 350 & 500cc 1955-1967 (BOOK OF)
BSA TWINS 1948-1962 (BOOK OF)
BSA TWINS 1962-1969 (SECOND BOOK OF)
CYCLEMOTOR (BOOK OF)
DOUGLAS 1929-1939 PREWAR ALL MODELS (BOOK OF)
DOUGLAS 1948-1957 POSTWAR ALL MODELS FACTORY SHOP MANUAL
DUCATI 160cc, 250cc & 350cc OHC MODELS FACTORY SHOP MANUAL
HONDA 50 ALL MODELS UP TO 1970 INC MONKEY & TRAIL (BOOK OF)
HONDA 90 ALL MODELS UP TO 1966 (BOOK OF)
HONDA 125-150cc TWINS C/CS/CB/CA FACTORY WORKSHOP MANUAL
HONDA 250-305 TWINS C/CS/CB FACTORY WORKSHOP MANUAL
HONDA 450 CB/CL 1965-1974 K0 TO K7 WORKSHOP MANUAL
HONDA C100 SUPER CUB FACTORY WORKSHOP MANUAL
HONDA C110 SPORT CUB 1962-1969 FACTORY WORKSHOP MANUAL
HONDA TWINS & SINGLES 50cc THRU 305cc 1960-1966 (BOOK OF)
HONDA TWINS ALL MODELS 125cc THRU 450cc UP TO 1968 (BOOK OF)
INDIAN PONYBIKE, BOY RACER & PAPOOSE ILL PARTS LIST & SALES LIT
J.A.P. ENGINES 1927-1952 & MOTORCYCLES 1934-1952 (BOOK OF)
LAMBRETTA 1947-1957 ALL 125 & 150cc MODELS (BOOK OF)
LAMBRETTA 1957-1970 LI & TV MODELS (SECOND BOOK OF)
MATCHLESS 1931-1939 ALL MODELS 250cc THRU 990cc (BOOK OF)
MATCHLESS 1945-1956 350 & 500cc SINGLES (BOOK OF)
MATCHLESS 1955-1966 350 & 500cc SINGLES (BOOK OF)
NEW IMPERIAL ALL SV & OHV FROM 1935 ONWARDS (BOOK OF)
NORTON 1932-1939 PREWAR MODELS (BOOK OF)
NORTON 1932-1947 (BOOK OF)
NORTON 1938-1956 (BOOK OF)
NORTON 1955-1963 MODELS 19, 50 & ES2 (BOOK OF)
NORTON 1955-1965 DOMINATOR TWINS (BOOK OF)
NORTON 1957-1970 TWINS FACTORY WORKSHOP MANUAL
NSU PRIMA 1956-1964 ALL MODELS (BOOK OF)
NSU QUICKLY 1953-1963 ALL MODELS (BOOK OF)
PANTHER 1932-1958 LIGHTWEIGHT MODELS 250 & 350cc (BOOK OF)
PANTHER 1938-1966 HEAVYWEIGHT MODELS 600 & 650cc (BOOK OF)
RALEIGH MOPEDS 1960-1969 (BOOK OF)
RALEIGH MOTORCYCLES 1919-1933 (BOOK OF)
ROYAL ENFIELD 1934-1946 SINGLES & V TWINS (BOOK OF)
ROYAL ENFIELD 1937-1953 SINGLES & V TWINS (BOOK OF)
ROYAL ENFIELD 1946-1962 SINGLES (BOOK OF)
ROYAL ENFIELD 1958-1966 250cc & 350cc SINGLES (SECOND BOOK OF)
ROYAL ENFIELD 736cc INTERCEPTOR FACTORY WORKSHOP MANUAL
RUDGE 1933-1939 (BOOK OF)
SUNBEAM 1928-1939 (BOOK OF)
SUNBEAM 1946-1957 S7 & S8 (BOOK OF)
SUZUKI 50cc & 80cc UP TO 1966 (BOOK OF)
SUZUKI T10 1963-1967 FACTORY WORKSHOP MANUAL
SUZUKI T20 & T200 1965-1969 FACTORY WORKSHOP MANUAL
SUZUKI TWINS 1962 ONWARDS 125-500cc WORKSHOP MANUAL
TRIUMPH 1935-1939 PREWAR MODELS (BOOK OF)
TRIUMPH 1935-1949 (BOOK OF)
TRIUMPH 1937-1951 (WORKSHOP MANUAL)
TRIUMPH 1945-1955 FACTORY WORKSHOP MANUAL
TRIUMPH 1945-1958 TWINS (BOOK OF)
TRIUMPH 1956-1969 TWINS (BOOK OF)
VELOCETTE 1925-1970 ALL SINGLES & TWINS (BOOK OF)
VESPA 1951-1961 (BOOK OF)
VESPA 1955-1963 125 & 150cc & GS MODELS (SECOND BOOK OF)
VESPA 1955-1968 GS & SS (BOOK OF)
VESPA 1963-1972 90, 125 & 150cc (THIRD BOOK OF)
VILLIERS ENGINE UP TO 1959 INC. 3 WHEELERS (BOOK OF)
VILLIERS ENGINE UP TO 1969 (BOOK OF)
VINCENT 1935-1955 (WORKSHOP MANUAL)
YAMAHA 1961-1967 YA5 & YA6 (WORKSHOP MANUAL & ILL PARTS LIST)
YAMAHA 1971-1972 JT1& JT2 (WORKSHOP MANUAL & ILL PARTS LIST)

VELOCEPRESS TECHNICAL BOOKS – MOTORCYCLE

CATALOG OF BRITISH MOTORCYCLES (1951 MODELS)
MOTORCYCLE ENGINEERING (P.E. Irving)
MOTORCYCLE ROAD TESTS 1949-1953 (Motor Cycle Magazine UK)
SPEED AND HOW TO OBTAIN IT (Motor Cycle Magazine UK)
TUNING FOR SPEED (P.E. Irving)

VELOCEPRESS MANUALS - THREE WHEELER'S

BSA THREE WHEELER (BOOK OF)
VINTAGE MORGAN THREE WHEELER (BOOK OF)

VELOCEPRESS MANUALS - AUTOMOBILE

ALFA ROMEO GIULIA WORKSHOP MANUAL 1300 TO 2000cc 1962-1975
ALFA ROMEO GIULIA TECH MANUAL CARBURETED CARS FROM 1962
ALFA ROMEO GIULIA TECH MANUAL FUEL INJECTED CARS FROM 1969
AUSTIN-HEALEY 6-CYLINDER WORKSHOP MANUAL
AUSTIN-HEALEY SPRITE & MG MIDGET WORKSHOP MANUAL 1958-1971
BMW 600 LIMOUSINE FACTORY WORKSHOP MANUAL
BMW 600 LIMOUSINE OWNERS HAND BOOK & SERVICE MANUAL
BMW 2000 & 2002 1966-1976 WORKSHOP MANUAL
BMW ISETTA FACTORY WORKSHOP MANUAL
CORVAIR 1960-1969 WORKSHOP MANUAL
CORVETTE V8 1955-1962 WORKSHOP MANUAL
FIAT 500 FACTORY WORKSHOP MANUAL 1957-1973
FIAT 600, 600D & MULTIPLA FACTORY WORKSHOP MANUAL 1955-1969
JAGUAR E-TYPE 3.8 & 4.2 SERIES 1 & 2 WORKSHOP MANUAL
JAGUAR MK 7, 8, 9 & XK120, 140, 150 WORKSHOP MANUAL 1948-1961
METROPOLITAN FACTORY WORKSHOP MANUAL
MGA & MGB OWNERS HANDBOOK & WORKSHOP MANUAL
MG MIDGET TC, TD, TF & TF1500 WORKSHOP MANUAL
PORSCHE 356 1948-1965 WORKSHOP MANUAL
PORSCHE 911 2.0, 2.2, 2.4 LITRE 1964-1973 WORKSHOP MANUAL
PORSCHE 911 2.7, 3.0, 3.2 LITRE 1973-1989 WORKSHOP MANUAL
PORSCHE 912 WORKSHOP MANUAL
TRIUMPH TR2, TR3, TR4 1953-1965 WORKSHOP MANUAL
VOLKSWAGEN TRANSPORTER, TRUCKS & WAGONS 1950-1979 WSM
VOLVO 1944-1968 ALL MODELS WORKSHOP MANUAL

VELOCEPRESS TECHNICAL BOOKS - AUTOMOBILE

FERRARI 250/GT SERVICE AND MAINTENANCE
FERRARI GUIDE TO PERFORMANCE
FERRARI OWNER'S HANDBOOK
FERRARI TUNING TIPS & MAINTENANCE TECHNIQUES
HOW TO BUILD A FIBERGLASS CAR
HOW TO BUILD A RACING CAR
HOW TO RESTORE THE MODEL 'A' FORD
MASERATI OWNER'S HANDBOOK
OBERT'S FIAT GUIDE
PERFORMANCE TUNING THE SUNBEAM TIGER
SOUPING THE VOLKSWAGEN
SOLEX CARBURETORS (EMPHASIS ON UK & EU AUTOMOBILES)
SU CARBURETORS (EMPHASIS ON UK AUTOMOBILES)
WEBER CARBURETORS (EMPHASIS ON ALFA & FIAT)

VELOCEPRESS BOOKS & GUIDES - AUTOMOBILE

ABARTH BUYERS GUIDE
COMPLETE CATALOG OF JAPANESE MOTOR VEHICLES
FERRARI 308 SERIES BUYER'S AND OWNER'S GUIDE
FERRARI BERLINETTA LUSSO
FERRARI BROCHURES AND SALES LITERATURE 1946-1967
FERRARI BROCHURES AND SALES LITERATURE 1968-1989
FERRARI OPP, MAINTENANCE & SERVICE H/BOOKS 1948-1963
FERRARI SERIAL NUMBERS PART I - ODD NUMBERS TO 21399
FERRARI SERIAL NUMBERS PART II - EVEN NUMBERS TO 1050
FERRARI SPYDER CALIFORNIA
HENRY'S FABULOUS MODEL "A" FORD
MASERATI BROCHURES AND SALES LITERATURE

VELOCEPRESS BOOKS – RACING

CARRERA PANAMERICANA - MEXICAN ROAD RACE (BOOK OF)
DIALED IN - THE JAN OPPERMAN STORY
IF HEMINGWAY HAD WRITTEN A RACING NOVEL
VEDA ORR'S NEW REVISED HOT ROD PICTORIAL

AUTOBOOKS WORKSHOP MANUALS & BROOKLANDS ROAD TEST PORTFOLIOS

FOR A COMPLETE LISTING OF THE AUTOBOOKS & BROOKLANDS TITLES THAT WE CURRENTLY HAVE AVAILABLE, PLEASE VISIT OUR WEBSITE.

www.VelocePress.com

www.ingramcontent.com/pod-product-compliance
Lightning Source LLC
Chambersburg PA
CBHW080434230426
43662CB00015B/2272